Snapshots of Reality:

A Practical Guide to Formative Assessment in Library Instruction

by

Mary Snyder Broussard
Rachel Hickoff-Cresko, and
Jessica Urick Oberlin

Association of College and Research Libraries
A division of the American Library Association
Chicago, Illinois 2014

The paper used in this publication meets the minimum requirements of American National Standard for Information Sciences–Permanence of Paper for Printed Library Materials, ANSI Z39.48-1992. ∞

Library of Congress Cataloging-in-Publication Data

Broussard, Mary Snyder.
  Snapshots of reality : a practical guide to formative assessment in library instruction / Mary Snyder Broussard, Rachel Hickoff-Cresko, and Jessica Urick Oberlin.
    pages cm
  Includes bibliographical references and index.
  ISBN 978-0-8389-8689-9 (paperback : alkaline paper) 1. Information literacy--Study and teaching--Evaluation. 2. Library orientation--Evaluation. 3. Academic libraries--Relations with faculty and curriculum. 4. School librarian participation in curriculum planning. 5. Educational evaluation. 6. Educational tests and measurements. I. Hickoff-Cresko, Rachel. II. Oberlin, Jessica Urick. III. Title.
  ZA3075.B76 2014
  028.7071--dc23

Copyright ©2014 by Association of College and Research Libraries, a division of the American Library Association. All rights reserved except those which may be granted by Sections 107 and 108 of the Copyright Revision Act of 1976.

Printed in the United States of America.

18 17 16 15 14   5 4 3 2 1

TABLE OF CONTENTS

PREFACE v

PART I   **Understanding Formative Assessment**
1. Introduction to Formative Assessment 3
2. Are Academic Librarians Doing Formative Assessment? 17
3. Embedding Formative Assessment into Library Instruction: The Advantages and Challenges Ahead 43

PART II   **Using Formative Assessment in the Academic Library Classroom**
4. Introduction to Part II: Guided Implementation, from Theory to Practice 65
5. Formative Assessment Snapshot Techniques for Before Instruction 75
6. Formative Assessment Snapshot Techniques for During Instruction 95
7. Formative Assessment Snapshot Techniques for After Instruction 151

PART III   **Digging Deeper into Formative Assessment**
8. The Relationship between Formative Assessment for Student Learning and for Teaching Improvement 173
9. Technology and Formative Assessment in Student Learning 195
10. Formative Assessment in School Libraries and Media Centers 219
11. Working towards a Culture of Assessment 235

APPENDIX   **Formative Assessment Guided Implementation Template** 247

Preface

Formative assessment has been shown to be a powerful tool to improve student learning, yet there are very few resources that help librarians learn how to implement it in information literacy instruction. We wrote this book because we had a strong desire to have such a resource. It represents our exploration of formative assessment in our teaching, both what we have already implemented and what we are working towards. We believe this book will support formative assessment as it moves into the spotlight of library instruction discourse.

The main audience for this book is academic librarians in traditional face-to-face classrooms, although we believe school librarians and distance education librarians as well as public librarians who provide instruction will also find it useful. The three authors of this book, Mary Snyder Broussard, Rachel Hickoff-Cresko, and Jessica Urick Oberlin, have knowledge of educational theory and have varying backgrounds working in academic libraries and K–12 classrooms and libraries. While we have some experience with online learning, our institution does not have a distance education program, and we do not wish to present ourselves as experts in all areas in which this important topic applies. We will leave that to others with more expertise in those fields.

We have divided this book into three parts. Part I, "Understanding Formative Assessment," introduces the theory behind formative assessment, examines its use in library instruction, and discusses the benefits and challenges the one-shot library session has for adapting formative assessment. A simple implementation of a one-minute paper or the use of clickers in an instruction class does not exemplify formative assessment. Educators must be looking for evidence of student learning and be willing to instantly adapt strategies to improve that learning. We must be able to distinguish between *teaching* and *learning*.

Part II, "Using Formative Assessment in the Academic Library Classroom," is the application section. Readers will be introduced to designing classes based on learning targets and to specific Formative

Assessment Snapshot Techniques (FASTs) that lend themselves well to information literacy and research instruction. We have selected a wide range of FASTs as individual librarians teach in a variety of ways. Many of the suggested techniques fit within the library one-shot session with little collaboration with the instructor. For those who are starting with a more collaborative relationship with instructors or who are wishing to develop one will be given specific ideas they can implement or suggest. There are also varying degrees of technology use, from FASTs that require none to FASTs that use technology quite heavily. Each FAST explicitly states the amount of collaboration and technological requirements.

Part III, "Digging Deeper into Formative Assessment," explores special topics, including librarians using student assessment data to become better teachers over time, the use of technology to facilitate formative assessment, and formative assessment for school librarians. As will be evident in this section, there are areas in which librarians are already utilizing effective formative assessment techniques. These areas of strength can be used to develop a wider range of valuable formative assessment practice. The conclusion will provide practical suggestions on how to get started with formative assessment and explore the value of communities of assessment.

Finally, we should note that our experiences come from the perspective of a small, private college of approximately 1,400 students. We have a very strong instructional library program with approximately 150 sessions taught each year by three instruction librarians, with several classes taught by the library director. The instruction librarians meet weekly to discuss experiences in the classroom as well as trends in library instruction literature. The instruction librarians also participate in many campus-wide teaching effectiveness events. This is an ideal environment to test formative assessment practices because there is a basic level of familiarity with all full-time instructors and many students, particularly those involved in the library instruction program. We recognize that many institutions, due to size or structure of the institution, have more challenges in developing meaningful, effective relationships among faculty and students. It is important to note we believe the techniques presented in this book will indeed work in a variety of settings, but modifications may be necessary to make them most effective in each reader's unique learning environment.

PART I
Understanding Formative Assessment

Chapter 1

Introduction to Formative Assessment

> To be blunt, if... librarians are to call themselves teachers, then they too must ensure that students are learning, not just "doing."
>
> —Kristin Fontichiaro[1]

It is all too common for instruction librarians to be skeptical of their impact on student learning. We lament having so little time with them in the omnipresent library one-shot. We are often asked to do the impossible in a single hour and wind up focusing on the most immediate skills at hand, recommending the best databases and sharing some tips on how to use them well enough to stumble through the assignment an instructor has designed. We do not know the individual students or the personality of the class; often we do not even have much of a relationship with the instructor. The instructor's assignment may not be well suited to the library's collections. Above all, as librarians, we do not often get to see what students do with what we teach, and we do not often get to see the papers or bibliographies.

Sure, librarians are dedicated to assessment. At the end of many instruction sessions, we ask for student feedback on how the class went, or we give a short quiz on the key points. These assessments may show misunderstandings that frustrate us. We wish we had known they understood *that* during the session; if we had known, we would have addressed it or fixed it. Or we wonder what on earth the student meant in a comment that said, "Put hot chocolate or bathroom in library!" We often wish we could ask the student to elaborate when he or she asks for longer hours, and then ask the class if this opinion was widely held.

What if we told you that there was a secret many K–12 teachers and education professors were in on that can help alleviate many of these problems? There is, and it is a simple concept called "formative assessment." While many changes need to be made to improve the far-from-ideal library one-shot that is so prevalent in information literacy instruction, we can obtain a better idea of what our students are getting out of our lessons while they are still sitting in our classroom and while we still have time to correct misconceptions and improve our teaching for that individual group.

Many academic librarians are already doing this on a subconscious level, some even consciously, but the scholarly library literature shows it is not prevalent or intentional enough. Therefore, we must turn to education scholars. Because librarians do not teach under the same conditions as other instructors, the goal of this book is to help librarians put the ideas behind formative assessment to work in the library classroom—whether it is a for-credit class or a one-shot session—accommodating varying levels of collaboration with the class instructor. We will start with an in-depth introduction to the education literature and the theories behind formative assessment for the remainder of this chapter and provide advice for librarians throughout the rest of the book.

Assessment: A Five-Course Meal versus Bite-Sized Pieces

When most educators think of assessment of student learning, they think of tests and quizzes. These are mostly known as "summative assessments" as they are a summation of what students have learned after the fact. They are often associated with student grades or, in the K–12 field, with high-stakes standardized tests. Although summative assessments have historically been a key component of education at all levels, relying solely on such evaluation is problematic because evidence of poor student learning is received too late for it to be useful. For struggling students, summative evaluation is waiting for them to fail and then making decisions about how to correct their lack of learning. This type of assessment looks at the end result and is not used to facilitate further learning or development of a topic. Summative assessment may provide a learning credential, but it is not embedded in the learning process as a means of support for deepening or growing one's understanding of a topic.[2] By the time this data is collected, the class has usually moved on to another unit or the students have graduated from the class altogether.

In contrast, formative assessments are "ongoing assessments, reviews, and observations" that educators use to "modify and validate instruction."[3] They are small, frequent, and often informal assessments designed to help the educator get an understanding of students' current knowledge and what they have learned. The evidence collected is used to create timely feedback, which is used by the educator to adjust teaching strategies and by students to adjust learning strategies. These adjustments are made on the spot while learning is still taking place. In other words, formative assessments are "in-the-process-of-learning assessments" gathered for the sole purpose of improving.[4]

The past few decades have seen a shift in theories on learning, and we are finally starting to see the disappearance of the so-called "sage on the stage" approach where the teacher has all of the information and answers and the students are supposedly sponges that magically soak up all that is presented. The value of a learner-centered classroom where the teacher guides the students in learning and draws out their knowledge is being recognized more and more by practitioners. This pedagogy meshes with formative assessment, and together the two have the power to transform the teaching and learning that takes place in the classroom.

Formative assessment allows an instructor to view or have access to knowledge that otherwise may be hidden within the student. The instructor can then use this knowledge to facilitate further learning by providing additional instruction or thoughtful questioning, enabling further inquiry and deeper cognitive processing.[5] Clark describes the formative assessment process as one that strategically adapts instruction to meet the needs of the learners and depends on a collaborative relationship between the instructor and learners, both having separate but important roles in the learning process.[6] This is what Nicol describes as moving from monologue to dialogue when he discusses how the trend of providing written feedback in higher education often lacks clarity and quality and leaves the student without specific suggestions and opportunities to improve their work.[7]

While summative assessment tends to be at the end of a unit, formative assessment often takes place in the beginning or middle of a lesson. However, a more accurate indication of whether an assessment is indeed "formative" is how the assessment will be used. Will the assessment's results be used to modify teaching and learning? If yes, then it is a formative assessment. A helpful analogy provided by Robert Stake (quoted in Scriven 1991, 168–69) captures this idea: "When the cook tastes the soup, that's formative; when the guests taste the soup, that's summative."[8]

We feel a more precise analogy in the context of education is in a culinary classroom where a master-chef tastes a soup being prepared by a chef-in-training and guides and/or prompts the student to identify ways to bring out some of the subtle flavors or make the flavor more robust. We believe this is a more precise analogy of formative assessment because it takes into account the teacher and student collaborating together to assess the current level of progress and determine the next steps to further the learning and/or meet the target. When the master-chef tastes the final product to evaluate the extent to which the student reached the target, he or she is making a summative assessment: The student cannot use the instructor's feedback to change the composition of that particular batch of soup. The student-chef can only use the instructor's feedback to help him or her with future cooking experiences. However, the master-chef may use the summative assessment to change the recipe to help future students produce a better soup, which is comparable to the way summative assessment may be used to change curriculum or instructional techniques for a future group of learners. In the case of the master-chef guiding his or her apprentice, the instructor is using evidence of the student's current performance to guide him or her in increasing the quality of the end product or learning target, which is formative assessment in action!

What Formative Assessment Is Not

It would be useful here to take a moment to address what formative assessment is *not*. It is not the casual use of active learning or questioning. Simply having students complete a task does not necessarily provide evidence that they have mastered the learning targets, nor is it likely that the librarian is collecting the evidence that is produced. Asking students factual questions to see if the one eager volunteer in the class knows the answer is also not formative assessment. This does not produce reliable evidence that the volunteer's knowledge is an adequate representation of the class or that the volunteer's knowledge of that one answer means that he or she actually knows how to *use* the information. Instead, formative assessment is a combination of purposeful learning activities strategically planned in advance and the flexibility to adapt to the assessment evidence on the spot.

Furthermore, solely requesting students to reexamine their work is not formative feedback because it does not assist them in learning how or why they are not meeting the learning target. For feedback to be considered formative, the learner must receive guidance on *how* to perform a task more effectively as opposed to receiving praise or punishment. Formative feedback should be used purposefully to enable students to progress their learning. In the next section, we will look at the characteristics of formative assessment in greater detail.

Characteristics of Formative Assessment

In 2006, the Council of Chief State School Officers (CCSSO) established a group called FAST SCASS (Formative Assessment for Students and Teachers and State Collaborative on Assessment and Student Standards), which reviewed current literature and related research to clarify the meaning of formative assessment and identify attributes of effective formative assessment. Formation of such a group indicates the widespread recognition by the education field that formative assessment can be a key component in improving teaching and learning.

The FAST SCASS group identified five attributes of effective formative assessment: (1) learning progressions, (2) learning goals and criteria for success, (3) descriptive feedback, (4) self- and peer-assessment, and (5) collaboration.[9] Let us briefly explore each.

Learning Progressions

Instructors have an overall picture of what their students need to learn and establish short-term goals to help students get to that final destination. Along the way, students hone existing skills that enable them to develop new skills. Formative assessment allows instructors to check for competency of each short-term goal before moving on, ensuring that students have the needed knowledge base to succeed. In recent years, educators typically refer to short-term goals as "learning targets" to provide a distinction from overall, long-term "lesson objectives." These learning targets are written in learner-centered language. Therefore, learning targets are mini-goals that provide the teacher and student common language to progress along a pre-determined sequence that will lead to thorough understanding of the learning objective.

Learning Goals and Criteria for Success

The second attribute consists of clearly identifying learning goals and criteria for success and communicating those to the learners. Using student-friendly language and providing students examples of work that both meet and do not meet the criteria assists the instructor and student in progressing toward the learning goals. A lack of clear purpose can allow a lesson to revolve around tasks that must be merely completed, thus creating a low-level measure of compliance as opposed to evidence of in-depth learning.[10] However, Marzano, Pickering, and Pollock caution that overly defined goals can cause students to focus too much on a specific piece of information and thus ignore related information that may allow them to draw on their existing schema.[11] Success in creating and sharing goals is an issue of finding balance: helping learners identify where they are going and what they need to do to get there but allowing them flexibility to choose the path that best suits their needs and learning styles.

Descriptive Feedback

Successful use of formative assessment requires providing students with specific, descriptive, evidence-based feedback. The feedback should focus on helping students understand the learning target, their relationship to the learning target, and, above all, how the student can close the gap between the two. Instructors should avoid comparisons between students' work; formative assessment is strictly focused on helping each individual learner meet the set learning target. We would add to this that feedback should be frequent and timely (if not immediate) so that it fits seamlessly into the flow of student learning.

Self- and Peer-Assessment

Students must have opportunities to think meta-cognitively about their learning, which the use of self- and peer-assessment provides for them. When instructors provide structure and support so students can be reflective of their own work and that of their peers, they are able to receive meaningful and constructive feedback that allows them to take an active role in planning, monitoring, and evaluating their own progress. Furthermore, the process of evaluating others' work encourages students to reflect on their own. Self- and peer-assessments should be directly linked to the identified learning goals and criteria for successful completion, but they should not be used in the formal grading process.

Collaboration

Formative assessment encourages a collaborative classroom culture where students and instructors are "bona fide partners in the learning process."[12] This partnership is accomplished through the other attributes such as sharing learning goals and success criteria with students and supporting them as they monitor their own learning. It is also important that instructors develop a non-threatening learning environment where students feel safe to experiment and take risks outside of their comfort zones.

While we believe FAST SCASS's five attributes are essential to K–12 formative assessment and are indeed relevant to the academic library classroom, we also feel there are three other notable components necessary in making these processes as effective as possible. First, students' beliefs about their academic abilities can affect their academic motivation, interest, and achievement.[13] Formative assessment is often associated with motivation. The feedback that students receive from their peers and instructor has the power to build their sense of efficacy and increase their motivation for academic learning. Because students perceive the instructor listening for their input, they realize they can drive instructional changes.[14] This is an empowering realization for students who are too often accustomed to being treated like sponges.

Second, formative assessments are flexible and individualized. Each group of students has a unique personality and unique learning needs. Gathering student data solely to improve teaching the next time the class is taught does not take this unique group dynamic into account. Formative assessment of student learning is administered and acted upon for the benefit of the same students who took the assessment. We can take advantage of spontaneous teachable moments that become apparent through formative assessments to confirm that we should proceed as planned or revise what we intended to adjust to our students' immediate learning needs. Students are able to use the feedback they receive to determine if they are going about the learning process in the correct way to achieve the task or target at hand.

Lastly, formative assessments can focus on cognitive or affective aspects of learning. Cognitive aspects of learning include what content students absorbed and what skills they have mastered. In contrast, affective aspects of learning include the emotional factors in the classroom that either facilitate or inhibit cognitive learning. While we recognize the importance of the affective aspects of student learning, this book primarily focuses on formative assessment of the cognitive aspects of student learning.

Exploring the Foundations of Formative Assessment

Formative assessment is not new. Educators have most likely utilized formative assessment throughout history.[15] Socrates used student responses to his probing and questioning to check for their level of understanding and respond with appropriate follow-up. While the Socratic method is still valued today for its use of questioning to promote dialogue and collaboration between the teacher and students, it was around the mid- to latter half of the twentieth century when the concept of formative assessment really began to develop in the field of education. We can find formative assessment rooted in the cognitive and social constructivist learning theories, two popular learning theories in the education field, which developed around this time period.

Cognitive constructivists believe learners actively construct their knowledge, and their ability to do so is dependent on their existing and unique background knowledge. Instructors facilitate learning by designing instruction that accounts for the learners' background knowledge and guides them towards the learning target by providing appropriate learning experiences. Jean Piaget, a well-known cognitive constructivist, believed learners understand new information by adapting and assimilating it to their previous knowledge. Although Piaget's theories are not currently accepted as widely as they were in the 1950s and 1960s, they have influenced later theories on learning.

One such example is social constructivism, which differs from cognitive constructivism in that it emphasizes the need for social interaction in order for learning to occur. The well-known social constructivist, Lev Vygotsky, referred to a learner's zone of proximal development (ZPD) as the distance between one's independent ability level and his or her potential level of ability that can be reached with the guidance of a teacher. Although the ZPD relies on cognitive concepts of learning, it is the collaboration with peers or the teacher that allows learners to reach their potential level. Interestingly, while Vygotsky did not live beyond the first half of the twentieth century, it was the latter half when his work was being translated to English and widely accepted in the education field. Effective educators recognize how crucial it is to know their students' abilities and to be able to provide instruction that is within their ZPD. They also recognize how collaboration between learners or between the learner and the teacher assist a student in reaching his or her potential level.

Constructivist learning approaches rely on formative assessment—the teacher gathering evidence of student learning and using it to structure instruction and/or learning activities that will allow the students to progress or further their potential level of achievement. Educators are aware that covering material students already know is a waste of precious class time and may lead to poor attitudes among students. They also know that covering content that is completely unfamiliar to students creates a missed opportunity for learning and causes frustration for learners because their lack of background knowledge prevents them from making necessary connections. Furthermore, educators recognize that *covering* content is not teaching. Not only is this supported by the theories of Vygotsky and Piaget, but John Dewey as well. Dewey advocated for progressive education where the teacher was not merely *pouring in* content, but instead *drawing out* the knowledge learners gain through purposefully designed content, learning experiences, and social interactions.[16]

Although the concept of formative assessment can be recognized in the learning theories we have just discussed, Scriven is known for being the first to use the *term* "formative evaluation" when he contrasted it with summative evaluation.[17] He described the differences in how the two types of evaluation could be used to impact curriculum changes: Formative evaluation can be used to refine the curriculum during instruction while summative results analyzed at the conclusion can reveal whether the entire curriculum was significantly effective.[18] Although Scriven first used the phrase "formative evaluation," the actual *application* of formative evaluation can be traced to Bloom, Hastings, and Madaus, where it was used to describe a type of evaluation that involved all parties (student, teacher, curriculum maker) and that was designed to help improve teaching and learning.[19]

Some of the first scholarly articles to report on the impact of formative assessment started to appear towards the end of the twentieth century. In 1988, Crooks reported that classroom assessment practices not only emphasized what is important to learn but positively affected student motivation as well.[20] Sadler is known for asserting that over time instructor-supplied feedback can help students develop self-assessment skills.[21] Most educational researchers credit Black and Wiliam's seminal article, "Assessment and Classroom Learning," in 1998 for thrusting the topic of formative assessment and its impact on learning into the spotlight of contemporary educational research.[22] This article found in an extensive literature review that formative assessment was the most powerful instructional change educators could make. Since then, there have been numerous reviews of recent research that have demonstrated the substantial power of formative assessment to increase learning.[23] Newmann, Bryk, and Nagaoka concluded that authentic classroom tasks that required learners to construct knowledge, utilize inquiry, and see a value beyond school allowed them to significantly outperform students who were not given such work.[24] Weurlander and colleagues conducted a study aimed at gaining insight into how students perceive formative assessment techniques, using individual written assessments and oral group assessments.[25] The results indicated that formative assessments motivate students to study and help them gain awareness of their own learning in terms of both processes and outcomes.

Application to Higher Education and to the Library Classroom

Interestingly, formative assessment has been a common topic in the K–12 education field for a few decades, but it is just beginning to grow in the further and higher education environments.[26] The single most influential work on formative assessment in higher education is Angelo and Cross's book, *Classroom Assessment Techniques*, first published in 1988 and then revised in 1993.[27] Angelo and Cross provide a background of classroom assessment techniques (CATs), which are simply structured formative assessment techniques, and then they share fifty CAT activities for instructors to use. This book is vital to anyone who teaches at a college or university and wishes to gain a better understanding of what their students know at a given time and thus will be discussed throughout this book as the CATs are applicable to the library classroom.

Has there been a true increase in formative assessment techniques utilized in the higher education now that two decades have passed since Angelo and Cross's fundamental book was published? Webber analyzed and compared responses from the 1993 and 2004 *National Study of Postsecondary Faculty* surveys, and she concluded that there has been an increase in the number of faculty members in the new millennium using learner-center assessment techniques as "an effective way to measure and promote learning."[28]

However, a special issue of the journal *Assessment and Evaluation in Higher Education*—"Approaches to Assessment That Enhance Learning"—published in 2010, illustrates how limited the interpretations of assessment remain and discusses the need to expand and diversify the typical forms of assessment used in higher education. In the editorial portion of this issue, Hatzipanagos and Rochon argue that institutions of higher education need to make assessment central to student learning, include a process of dialogue and feedback, and provide opportunities for the learner to monitor and identify what is needed to close the gap between the current level of performance and the learning target.[29] In this same issue, a commentary by Black and McCormick calls for studies in higher education to make use of K–12 literature on formative assessment and expands the contexts for the development of formative approaches, such as utilizing more oral dialogue, to provide feedback to students.[30]

Many colleges and universities have established committees, services, and specialized centers to support effective teaching practices, which would be a befitting environment to support the development and utilization of classroom assessment techniques. Instructors at other institutions have established less formal communities focused on improving as teachers. While the research evidence from the K–12 education field is strong in regard to the impact formative assessment has on student learning as is the anecdotal evidence from colleges and universities, there still is a need for more empirical data on the ways these ideas can translate most effectively to higher education.

Summary

Formative assessment techniques have been well established and their effectiveness highly regarded in the education field for the past few decades. Even so, there is still momentum building in education to increase the use of their most effective attributes. In recent years, instructors in the higher education setting are informing their practices of formative assessment through K–12 education research. Academic librarians have the power to provide college students with knowledge and skills that can enhance their entire college experience and offer them a background that will be utilized as they enter the work force. However, there can no longer be a mindset that instruction librarians are the experts who pour information into their students, and it is the students' responsibility to grasp, retain, and utilize it effectively. If academic librarians want to be respected as essential educators and if they want to have a true impact on student learning and success, the use of effective formative assessment techniques is a crucial step in doing so.

NOTES

1. Kristin Fontichiaro, "Nudging toward Inquiry: Formative Assessment," *School Library Monthly* 27, no. 6 (March 2011), http://www.schoollibrarymonthly.com/curriculum/Fontichiaro2011-v27n6p11.html.
2. Barbara Crossouard and John Pryor, "How Theory Matters: Formative Assessment Theory and Practices and Their Different Relations to Education," *Studies in Philosophy and Education* 31, no. 3 (2012): 251–63.
3. Douglas Fisher and Nancy Frey, *Checking for Understanding: Formative Assessment Techniques for Your Classroom* (Alexandria, VA: ASCD, 2007), 4.
4. Eva L. Baker and Girlie C. Delacruz, "Framework for the Assessment of Learning in Games," in *Computer Games and Team and Individual Learning 2007*, ed. Harry O'Neil and Ray Perez (Burlington, MA: Elsevier Science, 2007), 21–37.
5. Ian Clark, "Formative Assessment: Assessment Is for Self-Regulated Learning," *Educational Psychology Review* 24, no. 2 (2012): 205–49.
6. Ibid.
7. David Nicol, "From Monologue to Dialogue: Improving Written Feedback Processes in Mass Higher Education," *Assessment & Evaluation in Higher Education* 35, no. 5 (August 2010): 501–17.
8. Michael Scriven, *Evaluation Thesaurus* (London: Sage Publications, 1991), 168–69.
9. Council of Chief State School Officers, *Attributes of Effective Formative Assessment*, accessed January 6, 2014, http://www.ccsso.org/Documents/2008/Attributes_of_Effective_2008.pdf.
10. Douglas Fisher and Nancy Frey, *The Purposeful Classroom: How to Structure Lessons with Learning Goals in Mind* (Alexandria, VA: ASCD, 2011), 15.
11. Robert J. Marzano, Debra J. Pickering, and Jane E. Pollock, *Classroom Instruction That Works: Research-Based Strategies for Increasing Student Achievement* (Alexandria, VA: ASCD, 2001), 93–95.
12. Council of Chief State School Officers, *Attributes of Effective Formative Assessment*, 5.
13. Albert Bandura, Claudio Barbaranelli, Gian Vittorio Caprara, and Concetta Pastorelli, "Multifaceted Impact of Self-Efficacy Beliefs on Academic Functioning," *Child Development* 67 (June 1996): 1206–22.
14. Kathleen M. Cauley and James H. McMillan, "Formative Assessment Techniques to Support Student Motivation and Achievement," *Clearing House* 83, no. 1 (2009): 1–6.

15. Laura Greenstein, *What Teachers Really Need to Know about Formative Assessment* (Alexandria, VA: ASCD, 2010), 20.
16. Donna Ogle and James W. Beers, *Engaging in the Language Arts: Exploring the Power of Language* (Boston: Pearson, 2012), 5; Sharen Kucey and Jim Parsons, "Linking Past and Present: John Dewey and Assessment for Learning," *Journal of Teaching and Learning* 8, no. 1 (2012): 110.
17. Michael Scriven, "The Methodology of Evaluation," in *Perspectives of Curriculum Evaluation*, ed. Ralph W. Tyler, Robert M. Gagné, and Michael Scriven (Chicago: Rand McNally, 1967).
18. Dylan Wiliam, *Embedded Formative Assessment* (Bloomington, IN: Solution Tree, 2011), 33; Greenstein, *What Teachers Really Need to Know*, 21.
19. Benjamin Bloom, John Thomas Hastings, and George Madaus, *Handbook on Formative and Summative Evaluation of Student Learning* (New York: McGraw Hill, 1971) as cited in Paul Black and Dylan Wiliam, "In Praise of Educational Research," *British Educational Research Journal* 29, no. 5 (2003): 623.
20. Terry J. Crooks, "The Impact of Classroom Evaluation Practices on Students," *Review of Educational Research* 58 (1988): 438–81.
21. D. Royce Sadler, "Formative Assessment and the Design of Instructional Systems," *Instructional Science* 18 (1989): 119–44.
22. Paul Black and Dylan Wiliam, "Assessment and Classroom Learning," *Assessment in Education* 5, no. 1 (1998): 7–73; Paul Black and Dylan Wiliam, "Inside the Black Box: Raising Standards Through Classroom Assessment," *Phi Delta Kappa,* 80, no. 2 (1998): 139–48.
23. Dylan Wiliam, Clare Lee, Christine Harrison, and Paul Black, "Teachers Developing Assessment for Learning: Impact on Student Achievement," *Assessment in Education* 11, no. 1 (2004): 49–65.
24. Fred M. Newmann, Anthony S. Bryk, and Jenny K. Nagaoka, "Authentic Intellectual Work and Standardized Tests: Conflict or Coexistence? Improving Chicago's Schools," *Consortium on Chicago School Research*, (2001). ERIC (ED470299).
25. Maria Weurlander, Magnus Soderberg, Max Scheja, Hakan Hult, and Annika Wernerson, "Exploring Formative Assessment as a Tool for Learning: Students' Experiences of Different Methods of Formative Assessment," *Assessment & Evaluation in High Education* 37, no. 6 (September 2012): 747–60.
26. Crossouard and Pryor, "How Theory Matters," 251–63.
27. Thomas A. Angelo and K. Patricia Cross, *Classroom Assessment Techniques: A Handbook for College Teachers*, 2nd ed. (San Francisco: Jossey-Bass, 1993).
28. Karen L. Webber, "The Use of Learner-Centered Assessment in the US Colleges and Universities," *Research in Higher Education* 53 (2012): 223.

29. Stylianos Hatzipanagos and Rebecca Rochon, "Introduction to the Special Issue: Approaches to Assessment That Enhance Learning," ed. Stylianos Hatzipanagos and Rebecca Rochon, special issue, *Assessment & Evaluation in Higher Education* 35, no. 5 (August 2010): 491.
30. Paul Black and Robert McCormick, "Commentary: Reflections and New Directions," ed. Stylianos Hatzipanagos and Rebecca Rochon, special issue, *Assessment & Evaluation in Higher Education* 35, no. 5 (August 2010): 493.

Chapter 2
Are Academic Librarians Doing Formative Assessment?

As we saw in Chapter 1, "Introduction to Formative Assessment," there is an abundance of resources on formative assessment in K–12 education and a growing amount in higher education generally, but what about in academic libraries specifically? An initial search in the scholarly library literature for "formative assessment" leads to disappointingly few articles. Even when "classroom assessment techniques" or "assessment *for* learning" are added to a search, few relevant articles appear in the results. This chapter will analyze the literature for evidence that academic librarians are conducting formative assessment in their classes. We will look first at the publications with "formative assessment" or one of these synonyms in their titles, then at articles that explicitly mention it in the body of the text, and later those that provide evidence that formative assessment is happening in librarians' classrooms, even if that term is not used. Finally, we will look at articles that discuss "formative assessment" from the perspective of the librarian who wishes to improve his or her teaching.

Library Literature about Formative Assessment

In the scholarly library literature, only four articles, a book chapter, and a conference presentation were found that use the terms "formative assessment" or "classroom assessment techniques" in the titles and focus on assessment of *student* learning. In the earliest of these articles, Stewart summarizes Angelo and Cross's classroom assessment techniques (CATs), including the seven characteristics of CATs: learner-centered, teacher-directed, mutually beneficial, formative, context-

17

specific, continuing, and rooted in good teaching practice.[1] She also summarizes Angelo and Cross's five suggested exercises for educators who are just getting started with CATs: "Minute Paper" (CAT 6), "Muddiest Point" (CAT 7), "One-Sentence Summary" (CAT 13), "Directed Paraphrasing" (CAT 23), and "Application Cards" (CAT 24). Stewart acknowledges the challenge of providing feedback to CATs as librarians do not see the students again but suggests that librarians provide the students with written responses through the classroom instructor, "thus, the feedback loop is achieved without deviating from the Cross/Angelo Model and without undue effort."[2]

In a more recent article, Seely, Fry, and Ruppel worked with preservice teachers using a similar idea of formative assessment.[3] At the end of instruction, students were asked to write one thing they learned and one thing they were still confused about. Librarians also gave students written feedback, specifically addressing the quality of their preliminary lists of sources, which each student was required to submit. After these assessments had been evaluated, approximately a week after the library instruction session, the librarians scheduled a twenty-minute follow-up session in the students' regular classroom to address questions and misconceptions.

In their book *A Practical Guide to Information Literacy Assessment for Academic Librarians*, Radcliff et al. include a chapter on classroom assessment techniques. Again, they summarize Angelo and Cross and emphasize the recommendation to ease into formative assessment. They suggest four activities to begin with: one-minute paper or muddiest point, one-sentence summary, defining feature matrix, and an elaboration on the one-sentence summary.[4] The content of the chapter is rather superficial and does not sufficiently highlight the need to use student feedback to improve teaching. They suggest asking for an e-mail address on assessments as a way to provide individual feedback to students rather than selecting CATs that can be adapted to the library one-shot. Following up a library one-shot and responding to individual students by e-mail is low-level formative assessment.

We strongly feel that formative assessment can be much more powerful when it is more integrated into the learning process as described by Dunaway and Orblych.[5] They found that students' experience with information literacy skills varied widely, especially among graduate students who obtained undergraduate degrees at other institutions. They found that formative assessment could improve instruction in two sections of MBA students at the University of Michigan, Dearborn.

Their instruction process used a pretest to assess students' knowledge of libraries to tailor the class content to their needs and was followed by a clicker assessment during the class. Students had opportunities to test their knowledge and confront their misunderstandings while the librarians adapted their instruction based on the assessments' results. The results showed students to be much more engaged than in previous classes.

Broussard, one of the authors of this book, takes a more theoretical look at how eight critical traits of formative assessment align with critical traits of game-based learning (GBL).[6] The common traits include

- active learning—both require an environment of active learning;
- feedback—both emphasize the importance of frequent and timely feedback from the teacher (or game) to improve student understanding;
- motivation—both are associated with increased intrinsic motivation;
- moratoriums (safe learning spaces)—both encourage learning environments where students are free to experiment without harsh penalties;
- scaffolding—both build increasingly complex skills as students (or players) demonstrate levels of competence;
- critical thinking and self-assessment—both encourage learners to take control of their learning;
- social learning—both lend themselves to group work, allowing students (or players) to learn from each other;
- stealth assessment—both gather evidence of student learning and understanding often without students being aware that they are being assessed.

She describes how each of these qualities is demonstrated in two local information literacy games, one entirely online and one a hybrid online/physical game played in a library class for freshman composition students. She concludes that educational library games have the potential to be good environments for formative assessment.

In his Online Northwest Conference slides, Vidmar looks at using clickers as an interactive classroom assessment technique (iCAT).[7] He writes, "On-going formative assessment directs the course of instruction making sure students are achieving the desired outcomes." Vidmar gives suggestions on how to write questions, including focusing on what you really want to know, such as what is their background knowledge and what are their misconceptions or preconceptions, opinions, and reactions; he also encourages self-assessment and librarians to check-in with students about what they have just learned.

While there is scant coverage of formative assessment in the articles about academic libraries, there are a number of articles in school librarian publications. Because so many school librarians train first as teachers and second as librarians, it makes sense that formative assessment appears in their literature. In their book *Assessing for Learning: Librarians and Teachers as Partners*, Harada and Yoshina include useful descriptions of many types of formative assessments, ranging from individual research conferences to portfolios.[8] The use of worksheets, informal observation, and conversations with students was found by Edwards as an effective way to assess student learning and provide customized assistance.[9] Maniotes also uses various types of observations and guided learning through targeted questions or suggestions, turning the teaching process into a type of conversation between teachers and learners.[10] Furthermore, an online article by Fontichiaro is not only useful itself for the suggestions of index card feedback, mini-conferencing, and peer conferencing and editing but also for the additional formative assessment activity suggestions that appear in the article's comments.[11] Most of these comments suggest useful tools to facilitate formative assessment including Google Forms, Poll Everywhere, and Noodle Tools. There are many good ideas in this body of literature; however, it is clear that school librarians teach information literacy in very different circumstances and cultures from academic librarians. For this reason, formative assessment in school libraries will be discussed further in Chapter 10, "Formative Assessment in School Libraries and Media Centers."

Articles or Books That Mention "Formative Assessment:" The Good, the Bad, and the Ugly

There is no shortage of useful literature on library instruction and its assessment. However, few of these articles or books explicitly mention formative assessment of *student* learning. We strongly feel that formative assessment is an important piece of the overall assessment picture in library instruction and regret that the literature is not helpful to those wishing to know more about using this instructional method to immediately improve student learning. This section looks at those few articles and books that do explicitly mention "formative assessment," for better or worse.

Information Literacy Instruction, by Grassian and Kaplowitz, is one of the most-used textbooks on teaching information literacy.[12] Because formative assessment is so sparsely mentioned in the scholarly library literature, we were pleasantly surprised to find it sprinkled throughout their extensive book. They write that "formative assessment ... can occur at any point during instruction. Its main purpose is feedback—to the learner or to the teacher or to both. Formative assessment is used to improve the learning experience, to help learners reflect upon what they have learned, and, if necessary, to modify their methods and try again."[13] They go on to say that formative assessments "include the on-the-spot corrections that instructors make while teaching. They frequently rely on informal assessment techniques, such as observing verbal or nonverbal behavior during in-class exercises or activities. Feedback can be offered to learners during instruction itself to enhance the experience and to improve learning."[14] They additionally define classroom assessment techniques: "CATs generally take the form of exercises, worksheets, and other classroom activities interspersed within the instruction itself. CATs support learning by providing practice opportunities as well as feedback to both learner and teacher on how well the learners are performing."[15] Clearly, the authorities on library instruction hold the idea of formative assessment in high esteem.

Kaplowitz uses the term "learner-centered assessment" to describe formative assessment; and indeed formative assessment is always focused on the learner.[16] This type of assessment is critical to her book's overall topic, which is learner-centered teaching (LCT). She writes,

> The goal of learner-centered assessment is two-fold—as a way for learners to exhibit what they have accomplished and as a means to provide feedback to them. Feedback, in the learner-centered assessment paradigm, not only provides information on whether learners "got it right or wrong," but also offers constructive comments about how learning can be improved. So, in a way, learner-centered assessment becomes part of the instructor-learner conversation that is the cornerstone of LCT.[17]

Throughout the book she emphasizes other key traits of successful formative assessment, including conducting broad needs assessments of an overall student population, assessing specific students before or at the beginning of an information literacy class, adapting to students' needs on the spot during a class, giving students time to respond, and showing respect for their answers even when incorrect.

Two of the (arguably) most prominent authorities on library assessment, Debra Gilchrist and Megan Oakleaf, give some information on formative assessment in articles that focus on other types of library assessment. Gilchrist and Zald define formative assessment as "assessment that is done for the purpose of immediate evidence of student learning or for immediate feedback to the student.... We believe that formative assessment is also formative for the instructor, in that the information allows the teacher to repeat, reinforce, or rejoice."[18] They go on to suggest a number of active-learning exercises that obviously lend themselves to formative assessment such as having students write an initial sample Boolean search phrase at the beginning of the library class, revising it at the end of the class, and then explaining why it is improved. Oakleaf gives a brief definition of formative assessment in an article about the assessment cycle for librarians to improve as teachers and writes that during learning activities, "librarians may gather fast formative feedback about student learning using comprehension checks and other classroom assessment techniques."[19] Librarians may use this data to revise learning activities "on the fly."[20]

Whitlock and Nanavati demonstrate clear evidence of formative assessment when they talk about the importance of *informal* assessment.[21] They give the example of discussing the difference between magazines and scholarly journals, then holding up *Pro Wrestling Illustrated* and asking for a show of hands to vote on whether it was a magazine or a journal. If the librarians see many hands indicating that it is scholarly, "we immediately backtrack and reconsider how to teach that particular skill."[22] They do specifically mention formative assessment and give a valuable explanation about how the lines between formative and summative assessments blur. While an assessment may be summative at the end of the unit, it may be formative over the course of the semester. Or a summative term paper in freshman composition is formative in the student's academic career. One of the activities described in this article is feedback given on students' research logs in a for-credit information literacy course. In an e-mail correspondence, Whitlock clarified that the log is collected at the end of each unit. So it is a summative assessment for each unit but formative for the final annotated bibliography.

Additional authors use the term "formative assessment" ambiguously. Knight briefly mentions formative assessment, but she does not elaborate on what it means when she says, "To increase the formative nature of the assessment, the target population became first-year students, rather than seniors."[23] Ross and Furno report using "post-class formative assessments," but they do not indicate any feedback provided to students, so it is unclear what they mean by this phrase.[24] Bennett and Brothen write about "formative and summative instruction measures," but they do not provide a definition or explanation.[25] Sonntag and Meulemans say that CATs can be formative or summative, without defining either.[26] Their treatment of CATs is superficial, simply saying that CATs have the advantage of being easy to administer but do not adequately measure student learning.

Alarmingly, there is a trend to outright misuse the term "formative assessment" in the library literature in ways that cannot be found elsewhere. Tancheva, Andrews, and Steinhart seem to say that formative assessments are multiple-choice while summative ones are short-answer or open-ended questions, concluding "as difficult as it may seem, a summative approach is appropriate for evaluating single-session library instruction if one is concerned with learning outcomes."[27] Merz and Mark and Colborn and Cordell associate formative assessment with "affective assessment," or assessment of student attitudes rather than student learning. In contrast, measurement of student learning is "summative assessment."[28] A correct definition is provided initially by Gustavson, but even this definition evolves into formative assessment as an attitudinal survey, and from this she concludes that ultimately formative assessment "is an ineffective method for assessing an information literacy instruction program and student learning."[29] Other than Gustavson, who cites Colborn and Cordell as well as Tancheva, Andrews, and Steinhart, none of these articles provide a citation for their incorrect definitions of formative assessment nor do any talk about adapting instruction on the spot based on assessments.

Articles That Show Evidence or Imply Formative Assessment

Students need to be engaged in active learning to generate evidence of their understanding, although not all active learning includes formative assessment. The educator must be using the activity to generate evidence of student understanding, then provide feedback and encourage students to adjust their own learning strategies if necessary. We suspected and confirmed that formative assessment is happening in library classrooms as part of active learning even if librarians are not aware of this term.

Kerbel writes about instruction as a dynamic process, including the need to be adaptable during an instruction session.[30] She elaborates with an example of a class of new graduate students in which it quickly became clear that their goals for the library class did not match her chosen learning targets. She quickly adapted the class to meet their objectives, writing, "If I had ignored the interests of the students, I would have defeated the overall goal of instruction."[31] Just like Whitlock and Nanavati's research log assignment described above, both Smith and Mulherrin are explicit that they give feedback over time, which is used by the students to improve the quality of their final research project.[32] Smith elaborates on the value of these research journals:

> In my own experience, students who keep a research journal where they get regular feedback from instructors and librarians have a more positive experience with the research process and with the writing process. The journal helps them think through what they are doing, saves time and energy, and helps organize their work.... The journal also sets up an important collaborative tool for the librarian and composition instructor as they seek to maintain continuous dialogue with researchers.[33]

Several authors got to the heart of formative assessment but credited its key attributes to other closely related teaching methodologies such as cooperative learning or active learning. Allen writes, "Involving students leads toward unpredictability, and demands that teachers listen carefully to students, both to what is said, and what goes unsaid, and to remain alert and flexible to explore a student's learning path."[34] Another example is when Ragains discusses his implementation of active learning, writing, "active learning ... stresses giving students the freedom to voice initial ideas (including misunderstandings) openly, allowing instructors to answer the appropriate questions, elaborate on students' previous statements, and make necessary corrections."[35] What he is describing—collecting evidence and making adjustments based on this evidence—is formative assessment.

Orf and Hageman write, "The librarian should have some means by which to evaluate whether the students are grasping the concepts covered in the session."[36] They suggest using icebreaker questions to assess student understanding throughout the instruction session and "either adjust instruction or make use of more experienced students who could help others who need additional assistance."[37] They go on to describe a number of activities that lend themselves well to formative assessment and also point out that taking a moment to "debrief" through discussion after an activity allows the class to review what was just covered and check their understanding. Furthermore, they suggest beginning the class by asking students to create a wish list of what they would like to be covered in the session, "and then the session could be adapted on the spot to include those topics."[38] We feel this could be done even more efficiently by asking the instructor to collect these wish lists from students and deliver them to the librarian several days before the library class is scheduled. Formative assessment is always a balance between strategic planning and flexibility. In the case of students creating a wish list, on-the-spot adaptation will only allow the librarian to adapt superficially to their needs. At times this may be appropriate, but having a few days to plan will allow for the ability to build meaningful learning activities to more deeply satisfy their requests.

Angelo and Cross's "Background Knowledge Probe" (CAT 1) is designed to "help teachers determine the most effective starting point for a given lesson and the most appropriate level at which to begin instruction."[39] Starting out with a good picture of students' previous knowledge on a topic is an important part of formative assessment. Sobel and Sugimoto write that "[librarians] understand that determining what our students bring with them to the instruction lab and what they learn during the hour we teach them helps improve teaching."[40] However, we find very little evidence of this in the library literature. We believe that librarians most often rely on instructors' stated needs to build library one-shot lesson plans. Unfortunately, this information is frequently based on instructors' assumptions of students' research capabilities rather than evidence collected from formative assessments. The previously discussed article by Dunaway and Orblych is the only article we can find that uses a pretest to inform instructional design for a particular class.[41] An online assessment was conducted by Getselman and White to measure the existing knowledge of the entire incoming class at a medical school.[42] It is unclear as to how much the results informed their instructional design, but they drew examples to use in class from students' answers on the pretest. Most of the other articles mentioning pretests only use the results to compare with a posttest.[43]

A benchmark survey designed by Helmke and Matthies was used to gain understanding of their incoming freshmen's background knowledge of and attitudes towards libraries to inform the instructional design of a library tutorial.[44] While the assessment was not focused on a specific class, the survey population was the intended audience for the projected instruction. Additional authors describe other benchmark surveys to better understand their students. Klentzin surveyed students to find out more about their attitudes towards research.[45] Lycoming College, the home institution of the authors of this book, have published the results of two such surveys one looking at incoming freshmen's knowledge of plagiarism and one looking at how all students use social media for research.[46] While these are very useful as a broad starting point for instructional design, specific results of any of these surveys will vary from one class to the next, and they should not be overly relied on as an accurate representation of an information literacy class.

Additionally, Ivanitskaya et al. explored the use of pretests for motivation.[47] While they did not use the results to inform their instructional design, they hypothesized that students would pay more attention to areas where they demonstrated weakness. Indeed, the study's results showed the surveyed students performed better on the subjective parts of the posttest than did the control group. Broussard and McDevitt suggest using Library *Jeopardy!* as a pretest at the beginning of a library session to help students identify their weak areas.[48] This use of pretests to encourage adjustment on the students' side fits with the formative assessment literature where instructor feedback helps promote student self-assessment and the need to be self-directed learners.[49]

Numerous authors describe background knowledge probes within the classroom, most often with the aid of clickers or some other form of classroom response system. Zdravkovska et al. mention using laser pointers for "ascertaining prior knowledge," but do not elaborate on this.[50] Kautzman uses the first five minutes of class to ask a quick series of questions to gauge the class's knowledge of library research, and then she uses the data to adjust the class content as needed.[51] Mestre facilitates a class entirely based on student questions about research, therefore being very aware of students' current needs.[52] She collects the students' questions, organizes them onto the board, and facilitates discussions and demonstrations where students answer as much of each other's questions as possible. The librarian's role is to "reinforce, tactfully correct, or expand on students' ideas."[53] As questions are answered, they are checked off, and she follows up with any unanswered questions after class.

Discussion is also a frequently suggested formative assessment technique in the education literature, where the instructor uses students' comments to evaluate their collective understanding and correct misconceptions if needed.[54] Based on the literature, the use of discussions for library instruction is frequent, and it happens in a number of ways.[55] Angelo and Cross's CAT 3 is a misconception or preconception check.[56] They believe that prior knowledge can be the biggest block to learning. Dabbour opens classes with a discussion of students' stereotypes of libraries and librarians and a discussion of the anxieties these stereotypes produce.[57] Petrowski provides another good example of addressing affective barriers.[58] She opens her class with upper-level students by allowing them to share their concerns and anxieties related to their upcoming project on small pieces of paper. She collects the slips of paper and reads them aloud, recording each with a dot organized under predetermined categories. This provides a visual record of which categories are the most problematic, and the librarian can use those results to inform how to lead the remaining class discussion. If a librarian opens the class with an icebreaker activity about students' preconceptions, listens well to the students, and responds appropriately, students' affective barriers to library research are likely to be greatly reduced. Such an activity would be an example of how valuable respecting the affective aspects of learning can be.

Some librarians lead discussions after an active learning exercise, such as why students chose a particular resource or discussions arise after student presentations.[59] After a few student groups report, those who follow have already incorporated the feedback given into what they were going to report, which is evidence of the self-assessment that is important to formative assessment.[60] Jacobson and Mark describe several activities that seem to contain formative assessment.[61] In one activity to help students learn to narrow their topics to something manageable, students are required to submit preliminary ideas. The librarian assembles these ideas into a list and then leads a class discussion. As a class, they test keywords in the databases and work out the problems that arise, which they find much more effective than the unrealistically neat sample searches librarians tend to pick for instruction. At the end, they do a think-pair-share exercise, where students have to speculate and discuss their ideas on the purpose of the activity. While many of these authors do not explicitly say what the librarian's role is in such discussions, Ragains stresses correcting misunderstandings, confusion, or difficulties, and we assume from personal experience that other librarians do the same.[62]

Other authors turn the entire class into a conversation where the librarian's role is to ask key questions to direct the lesson towards important learning targets. Harris empowered students to learn from each other when she acted like a student, raising her hand to ask strategic questions to make sure the class was covering the necessary content.[63] Inspired by constructivism theory, Cooperstein and Kocevar-Weidinger turned the class over to students, guiding the class to the learning targets through questions.[64] They include periodic questions to check students' understanding, and they remain flexible so that if students show evidence of understanding the basics, they move on to more advanced concepts and skills. Mabry transformed the entire information literacy session into a think-pair-share exercise, where students begin with five minutes of individual writing on how to conduct library research, then share with small groups, and then discuss as a whole class.[65] Again, the librarian leads with occasional, strategic questions but mostly lets students be in charge of the class. She finds that most of the wrong answers have been weeded out before they reach the class-wide discussion.

Finally, some librarians combine other methods of formative assessment with discussion, using the results of the assessment as a launching point for a class-wide conversation. Abate, Gomes, and Linton use the results of clicker questions and students' contributions through the comments feature of the library blog to collect information and lead discussions in large medical classes.[66] Collins, Tedford, and Womack and Connor also describe class discussions of clicker results.[67] Getselman and White used example answers given in a pre-class assessment to generate class discussions.[68] Petrowski leads a discussion after an assessment on student anxieties.[69] Discussion is a very flexible way to adapt one's instruction based on assessment results.

Countless library articles indicate that a librarian circulates during hands-on practice to answer individual questions.[70] During the class time set aside for practice, librarians also often look over students' shoulders to observe what they are doing and provide help if students seem to be struggling. This could be considered formative assessment if the librarian listens, asks good questions, and provides helpful, individualized feedback.

Because one of the most difficult parts of translating formative assessment to the library classroom is the time constraint of the one-shot, it is useful to look at the literature to see how other librarians provide formative feedback to students. One idea is to schedule a short session with the students in their regular classroom a week after the library instruction.[71] In response to a five-minute letter exercise where students reflected on what they learned and still had questions about, Hurlbert responded by writing a formal follow-up letter to the class summarizing their responses and answering their questions.[72] She was careful to use their names if the question was not embarrassing. More individualized options that might be considered when appropriate are to e-mail individual students regarding their specific questions or to follow up on an end-of-class writing assessment.[73] Grassian and Kaplowitz have multiple suggestions for providing feedback to a one-minute paper, including students presenting their papers orally with a chance for the librarian to respond at the end of class, having the librarian respond on a bulletin board or by e-mail, or using students' questions to create a frequently asked questions (FAQ) web page.[74] If done as an FAQ, they suggest having subsequent classes read these FAQs before the library class and come prepared to share one thing they learned from them. Of course, librarians occasionally have the luxury of meeting with a class more than once, and we can open the second session with a discussion that answers students' questions from the assessment, making the activity double as a review before covering additional material or allowing students to ask questions about their individual research projects.

A few active learning exercises have the formative feedback built into the activity, which can be particularly satisfying to students and potentially lead to greater learning, though these can be difficult to design. For example, a treasure hunt activity that asks students to locate a particular book by title and call number, or a book specifically marked for the activity, in the stacks provides students positive feedback.[75] Smith and Chang describe a jigsaw activity where each student develops knowledge of their assigned organism as they complete a library activity.[76] Once students have completed their individual research, they realize their organisms fit into categories. In other words, completing the jigsaw activity helps them see a bigger picture. Finally, many online tutorials, quizzes, and educational games provide formative feedback, giving immediate praise for correct answers and mini-tutorials for wrong answers, often accompanied by an invitation to try again.[77]

Formative Assessment and Clickers in Libraries

There is a quickly growing body of literature on using clickers or other student response systems for information literacy instruction. Because of the volume of this literature and the obvious-to-us potential that clickers have for facilitating formative assessment, we feel it deserves its own subheading in this chapter. Clickers have the advantage of providing immediate, quantitative assessment that the students can see visually. Yet they are only a technological tool, not a methodology in and of itself. Briggs and Keyek-Franssen point out the need to use clickers in "educationally sound ways" and that clickers are most beneficial when the educator follows through on the assessment cycle.[78] In other words, they are most useful when used for formative assessment where the instructor adapts to the students' results.

Most of the studies in libraries indicate that use of clickers led to student enjoyment, engagement, and participation, but the few that look at actual learning remain skeptical.[79] However, many seem to miss clickers' potential as learning tools by not coupling them with formative assessment or following through on the assessment cycle. In the most heavily cited article on clickers in libraries, Dill's "Do Clickers Improve Library Instruction?," the control group and experimental group remained identical for the sake of the study, with clickers being the only variable.[80] Dennis, Murphey, and Rogers also reported working from a script, indicating librarians were not dynamically adjusting class content based on feedback from students.[81] Neither found clickers to be beneficial to student learning.

Yet other librarians are acknowledging the enormous potential of clickers. Collins, Tedford, and Womack report revisiting questions that many participants chose the wrong answer to and noticing students tend to pay more attention to feedback when they find they had selected the wrong answer.[82] Chan and Knight write, "As students responded to the questions, the librarian could gauge their current understanding of concepts, correct any misconceptions, and reemphasize major points."[83] Furthermore, clickers can "act as a gauge for instructors needing to reinforce concepts that might otherwise have been overlooked in traditional lecture or demonstration settings."[84] An additional use of clickers is to test for the misconceptions students bring into the library classroom that can hinder future growth.[85]

Osterman goes into further detail about using clicker feedback to "dynamically adjust … [ ] to the needs of the students at hand.… The goal is that the class becomes tailored, not one-size-fits-all.… Asking questions and getting useful information in response can allow for greater adjustment to the small components, including covering a concept with which the students are already comfortable."[86] She goes on to describe how clickers can be used to foster discussion as a prediction game or as an icebreaker. She stresses that each class is different, and clickers allow you to adapt to those particular students.

Conclusions of these articles are mixed. Most of the experiments using clickers with scripted instructions are not successful. In contrast, experiments using the clickers with formative assessment are successful. However, some articles test student learning and others assess the affective aspects of the learning experience. Many, if not most, clicker systems are limited to multiple-choice questions. This limitation should be taken into account for the most effective classroom use. Some report using clickers to facilitate discussion, thus ameliorating these limitations.[87] Clickers and other technologies that facilitate formative assessment will be discussed in greater detail in Chapter 9, "Technology and Formative Assessment in Student Learning."

Formative Assessment for Teaching Improvement

The main focus of this book is formative assessment of student learning. However, in our exploration of the literature, we found a number of authors using "formative assessment" to describe their own learning as educators. Many of the assessments described were conducted at the end of a library instruction session and not for the intent of providing immediate feedback to students. These librarians have taken a summative assessment of student learning to use as formative feedback to inform their own efforts to improve their teaching. These assessments provided feedback to the librarian on what worked and what did not so they can decide what to change in future semesters.

Oakleaf, a leading authority on library assessment, introduced the Information Literacy Instruction Assessment Cycle (ILIAC) in a relatively recent but already heavily cited article.[88] This seven-stage process includes (1) reviewing learning goals, (2) identifying learning outcomes, (3) creating learning activities, (4) enacting learning activities, (5) gathering data to check learning, (6) interpreting data, and (7) enacting decisions. She describes a case study at North Carolina State University that used ILIAC to evaluate and improve an online information literacy tutorial required by all students taking English 101. It is important to note that the seven stages make a loop, and that Stage 7 and Stage 1 of the next cycle overlap in this continual process of assessment and improvement.

The idea of the "Minute Paper" from Angelo and Cross inspired Choinski and Emanuel to use the results to identify areas in which the librarian needed to improve.[89] Along this line, Lahlafi, Rushton, and Stretton had students post sticky notes on the wall on the way out of class, each note indicating something they would stop doing, start doing, and continue doing as a result of the library session.[90] This information was intended for use on improving following semesters. Fenske and Roselle gave students two surveys, one the day after the library session and one two weeks later after the assignment was completed.[91] Based on the results, they added additional hands-on practice to the next session and were able to negotiate more instruction time with the students. Bennet and Brothen used assessment results from a citation analysis to argue for more institutional administrative support for the promotion of information literacy skills and to improve an online tutorial.[92] Swoger used pre- and posttests to develop more appropriate goals for the library portion of a freshman writing/critical thinking program at her institution.[93] Carter uses "formative assessment" throughout her article on using worksheets to assess students' ability to select appropriate keywords.[94] Worksheets are collected and scored with a rubric and used to inform librarians' future interactions with students and instructors, particularly about the topic development process.

The value of keeping a reflective teaching journal was explored by Tompkins when she kept records of class planning and correspondences as well as objective and reflective records of how the class went.[95] At the end of fall semester, she asked herself big-picture questions, like "How can I do a better job in engaging students?" She then used the journal for guidance in designing her classes in the spring. Changes she made included eliminating her short PowerPoint due to students' lack of interest. Instead, she started with active learning exercises and found that improved engagement. Many of her students spoke English as a foreign language and struggled with spelling in the database search exercises, so she included the words in a printed handout. She found that the journal greatly improved her communication with faculty, colleagues, and, above all, her students.

A new assessment program at Virginia Tech required librarians to assess 80% of their classes, the results of which would only be used for teaching improvement.[96] They used 3-2-1 cards (asking students to list three things they learned, two remaining questions, and one thing they would change about the class), OpScan surveys, and teaching portfolios. The results were used to adjust the assessment tools as well as to "intensify the collaborative relationships with faculty based on student feedback."[97]

There are a number of articles on peer observation or peer coaching programs in academic libraries. Levene and Frank provide helpful descriptions and advice on a successful peer-coaching program.[98] Samson and McCrea discuss a peer review of teaching program with eleven librarians at the University of Montana.[99] Alabi et al. describe a very similar program limited to seven pre-tenure librarians at Indiana University-Purdue University Indianapolis.[100] These programs differ in level of structure and formality. They often involve some kind of training or discussion group as a whole, then the librarian wishing to be observed has the opportunity to choose which other participant he or she would like to work with. Most of these articles stress the formative nature of these programs, which are voluntary, confidential, and non-threatening. The feedback generated in these programs should be used only for instruction improvement and not for personnel decisions. Surveys of participants were always positive, with all of the expected benefits as well as many that were unexpected.

A peer observation program described by Arbeeny and Hartman encouraged the more widespread use of formative assessment of student learning throughout their information literacy instruction program.[101] They write that as observers, program participants learned techniques to tackle problems in their own classes such as "asking questions to create an interactive dynamic and to discover the students' needs and interests … [and] being conscious of when students are not following you, and get them back on track without derailing the lesson."[102] This example shows that peer observation programs may help promote formative assessment of librarian's teaching and of student learning at the same time.

There is no shortage of articles in the library assessment literature of assessment data being used to improve teaching over time.

This section highlights some representative examples. Despite a lack of emphasis on library instruction in graduate programs, instruction librarians clearly have a genuine desire for continuous improvement as instructors.[103] We are learners, just as our students are. This deserves special attention, and Chapter 8, "The Relationship between Formative Assessment for Student Learning and for Teaching Improvement," will go into greater detail on this idea.

Conclusion

Formative assessment is not frequently mentioned in the library literature, especially not explicitly. However, there are a number of articles that do mention formative assessment by name or by describing its key traits. With at least most of the literature on active learning including individual assistance during hands-on practice or discussion and student presentations, we can conclude with confidence that formative assessment is happening in varying degrees in the library classroom. Librarians are using classroom assessment activities such as discussion, background knowledge probes, misconception checks, and one-minute papers.

However, as a whole, librarians are not using these tools as effectively as possible. Many of the examples provided here require some assumptions to count them as formative assessment, or they are low-level formative assessment. Clearly, many good library instructors are not aware of the principles of formative assessment. With the suggestions in the following chapters, we can learn from the education literature, do formative assessment more intentionally, and become better teachers.

NOTES

1. Thomas A. Angelo and K. Patricia Cross, *Classroom Assessment Techniques: A Handbook for College Teachers*, 2nd ed. (San Francisco: Jossey-Bass, 1993); Sharon Lee Stewart, "Assessment for Library Instruction: The Cross/Angelo Model," *Research Strategies* 16, no. 3 (1998): 165–74, doi:10.1016/S0734-3310(00)80002-6.
2. Stewart, "Assessment for Library Instruction," 169.
3. Sara Robertson Seely, Sara Winstead Fry, and Margie Ruppel, "Information Literacy Follow-Through: Enhancing Preservice Teachers' Information Evaluation Skills through Formative Assessment," *Behavioral & Social Sciences Librarian* 30, no. 2 (2011): 72–84.
4. Carolyn J. Radcliff, Mary Lee Jensen, Joseph A. Salem Jr., Kenneth J. Burhanna, and Julie A. Gedeon, "Classroom Assessment Techniques,"

in *A Practical Guide to Information Literacy Assessment for Academic Librarians* (Westport, CT: Libraries Unlimited, 2007), 33–46.
5. Michelle K. Dunaway and Michael T. Orblych, "Formative Assessment: Transforming Information Literacy Instruction," *Reference Services Review* 39, no. 1 (2011): 24–41.
6. Mary J. Snyder Broussard, "Using Games to Make Formative Assessment Fun in the Academic Library," *The Journal of Academic Librarianship* (forthcoming).
7. Dale Vidmar, "Interactive Classroom Assessment Techniques Using Clicker Technology" (presentation, Online Northwest 2013 Conference, Corvallis, OR, February 8, 2013), http://prezi.com/s5pk39m8ojyu/interactive-classroom-assessment-techniques-using-clicker-technology/.
8. Violet H. Harada and Joan M. Yoshina, *Assessing for Learning: Librarians and Teachers as Partners*, 2nd ed. (Westport, CT: Libraries Unlimited, 2010).
9. Valerie A. Edwards, "Formative Assessment in the High School IMC," *Knowledge Quest* 35, no. 5 (2007): 50-53.
10. Leslie K. Maniotes, "Teaching in the Zone: Formative Assessments for Critical Thinking," *Library Media Connection* 29, no. 1 (2010): 36–39.
11. Kristin Fontichiaro, "Nudging toward Inquiry: Formative Assessment," *School Library Monthly* 27, no. 6 (March 2011), http://www.schoollibrarymonthly.com/curriculum/Fontichiaro2011-v27n6p11.html.
12. Esther S. Grassian and Joan R. Kaplowitz, *Information Literacy Instruction* (New York: Neal-Schuman, 2009).
13. Ibid., 207.
14. Ibid., 210.
15. Ibid., 211.
16. Joan R. Kaplowitz, *Transforming Information Literacy Instruction Using Learner-Centered Teaching* (New York: Neal-Schuman Publishers, 2012).
17. Ibid., 102.
18. Debra Gilchrist and Anne Zald, "Instruction and Program Design through Assessment," in *Information Literacy Instruction Handbook*, ed. Christopher N. Cox and Elizabeth Blakesley Lindsay (Chicago: Association of College and Research Libraries, 2008), 175.
19. Megan Oakleaf, "The Information Literacy Instruction Assessment Cycle: A Guide for Increasing Student Learning and Improving Librarian Instructional Skills," *Journal of Documentation* 65, no. 4 (2009): .
20. Ibid., 544.
21. Brandy Whitlock and Julie Nanavati, "A Systematic Approach to Performative and Authentic Assessment," *Reference Services Review* 41, no. 1 (2013): 32–48.
22. Ibid., 34.

23. Lorrie A. Knight, "Using Rubrics to Assess Information Literacy," *Reference Services Review* 34, no. 1 (February 2006): 47, doi:101108/00907320510631571.
24. Alanna Ross and Christine Furno, "Active Learning in the Library Instruction Environment: An Exploratory Study," *Portal: Libraries and the Academy* 11, no. 4 (2011): 967.
25. Erika Bennett and Erin Brothen, "Citation Analyses as a Prioritization Tool for Instruction Program Development," *Journal of Library Administration* 50, no. 5-6 (July 2010): 426, doi:10.1080/01930826.2010.488585.
26. Gabriela Sonntag and Yvonne Meulemans, "Planning for Assessment," in *Assessing Student Learning Outcomes for Information Literacy Instruction in Academic Institutions* (Chicago: Association of College and Research Libraries, 2003), 6–21.
27. Kornelia Tancheva, Camille Andrews, and Gail Steinhart, "Library Instruction Assessment in Academic Libraries," *Public Services Quarterly* 3, no. 1-2 (2007): 33.
28. Lawrie H. Merz and Beth L. Mark, *Assessment in College Library Instruction Programs: CLIP Note #32* (Chicago: Association of College and Research Libraries, 2002); Nancy W. Colborn and Rosanne M. Cordell, "Moving from Subjective to Objective Assessments of Your Instruction Program," *Reference Services Review* 26, no. 3-4 (1998): 125–38.
29. Amy Gustavson, "Using ILIAC to Systematically Plan and Implement a Library Information Literacy Assessment Program for Freshmen Classes," *Public Services Quarterly* 8, no. 2 (2012): 110.
30. Sandra Sandor Kerbel, "The Self-Taught Instruction Librarian," in *Teaching Librarians to Teach: On-the-Job Training for Bibliographic Instruction Librarians*, ed. Alice S. Clark and Kay F. Jones (Metuchen, NJ: Scarecrow Press, 1986), 145–54.
31. Ibid., 148.
32. Whitlock and Nanavati, "A Systematic Approach"; Trixie G. Smith, "Keeping Track: Librarians, Composition Instructors, and Student Writers Use the Research Journal," *Research Strategies* 18, no. 1 (2001): 21–28; Elizabeth Mulherrin, "Teaching Information Literacy Skills to Undergraduates: The Electronic Research Log Model," in *Integrating Information Literacy into the College Experience: Papers Presented at the Thirtieth LOEX Library Instruction Conference*, ed. Julia K. Nims, Randal Baier, Rita Bullard, and Eric Owen (Ann Arbor, MI: Pierian Press, 2003), 183–86.
33. Smith, "Keeping Track," 27–28.
34. Eileen E. Allen, "Active Learning and Teaching: Improving Postsecondary Library Instruction," *Reference Librarian*, no. 51-52 (1995): 96.
35. Patrick Ragains, "Four Variations on Drueke's Active Learning Para-

digm," *Research Strategies* 13, no. 1 (1995): 42.
36. Jan Orf and Marianne Hageman, "Presentation Basics: Skills, Techniques, and Learning Styles," in *Theory and Practice: Papers and Session Materials Presented at the Twenty-Fifth National LOEX Library Instruction Conference*, ed. Linda Shirato and Elizabeth R. Bucciarelli (Ann Arbor, MI: Pierian Press, 1998), 65.
37. Ibid., 65.
38. Ibid., 68.
39. Angelo and Cross, *Classroom Assessment Techniques*, 121–25.
40. Karen Sobel and Cassidy R. Sugimoto, "Assessment of Learning during Library Instruction: Practices, Prevalence, and Preparation," *The Journal of Academic Librarianship* 38, no. 4 (2012): 245.
41. Dunaway and Orblych, "Formative Assessment."
42. Anna Getselman and Mia S. White, "Use of a Pre-Assessment Tool to Start a Meaningful Dialogue: New Paradigms in Library Instruction," *Medical Reference Services Quarterly* 30, no. 3 (2011): 245–56, doi:10.1080/02763869.2011.590414.
43. Tancheva, Andrews, and Steinhart, "Library Instruction Assessment"; Melissa R. Dennis, Rebecca M. Murphey, and Kristin Rogers, "Assessing Information Literacy Comprehension in First-Year Students," *Practical Academic Librarianship: The International Journal of the SLA* 1, no. 1 (2011): 1–15.
44. Jonathan Helmke and Brad S. Matthies, "Assessing Freshman Library Skills and Attitudes before Program Development: One Library's Experience," *College & Undergraduate Libraries* 11, no. 2 (December 2004): 29–50.
45. Jacqueline Courtney Klentzin, "The Borderland of Value: Examining Student Attitudes towards Secondary Research," *Reference Services Review* 38, no. 4 (2010): 557–70, doi:10.1108/00907321011090728.
46. Mary J. Snyder Broussard, Rebecca A. Wilson, Janet McNeil Hurlbert, and Alison S. Gregory, "Faculty and Undergraduate Perceptions of Expertise within Social Media," in *Social Software and the Evolution of User Expertise*, ed. Tatjana Takseva (Hershey, PA: Information Science Reference, 2013), 227–246; Mary J. Snyder Broussard and Jessica Urick Oberlin, "Using Online Games to Fight Plagiarism: A Spoonful of Sugar Helps the Medicine Go Down," *Indiana Libraries* 30, no. 1 (2011), 28–39.
47. Lana Ivanitskaya, Susan Duford, Monica Craig, and Anne Marie Casey, "How Does a Pre-Assessment of Off-Campus Students' Information Literacy Affect the Effectiveness of Library Instruction?" *Journal of Library Administration* 48, no. 3-4 (2008): 509–25.
48. Mary Snyder Broussard and Theresa McDevitt, "Fun Assessment: How to Embed Evaluation with Educational Games" (presentation, Library Orientation Exchange [LOEX] Conference, Columbus, OH, May 3–5,

2012), http://www.loexconference.org/2012/presentations/'LOEX2012_McDevitt'_LOEXPresentationfinal.pptx.
49. D. Royce Sadler, "Formative Assessment and the Design of Instructional Systems," *Instructional Science* 18, no. 2 (1989): 119–44.
50. Nevenka Zdravkovska, Maureen Cech, Pinar Beygo, and Bob Kackley, "Laser Pointers: Low-Cost, Low-Tech Innovative, Interactive Instruction Tool," *Journal of Academic Librarianship* 36, no. 5 (2010): 441.
51. Amy M. Kautzman, "Teaching Critical Thinking: The Alliance of Composition Studies and Research Instruction," *Reference Services Review* 24, no. 3 (1996): 61–66.
52. Lori Mestre, "Structuring a Session with Questions," in *Designs for Active Learning: A Sourcebook of Classroom Strategies for Information Education*, ed. Gail Gradowski, Loanne Snavely, and Paula Dempsey (Chicago: Association of College and Research Libraries, 1998), 50–51.
53. Ibid., 51.
54. Douglas Fisher and Nancy Frey, *Checking for Understanding: Formative Assessment Techniques for Your Classroom* (Alexandria, VA: Association for Supervision and Curriculum Development, 2007); Laura E. Abate, Alexandra Gomes, and Anne Linton, "Engaging Students in Active Learning: Use of a Blog and Audience Response System," *Medical Reference Services Quarterly* 30, no. 1 (2011): 12–18; Allen, "Active Learning and Teaching."
55. Orf and Hageman, "Presentation Basics"; Anne C. Osterman, "Student Response Systems: Keeping the Students Engaged," *College & Undergraduate Libraries* 14, no. 4 (2007): 49–57; Elizabeth Connor, "Using Cases and Clickers in Library Instruction: Designed for Science Undergraduates," *Science & Technology Libraries* 30, no. 3 (2011): 244–53; Candice C. Dahl, "Scenario-Based Active Learning in a Low-Tech Environment," *College & Undergraduate Libraries* 11, no. 2 (2004): 17–28.
56. Angelo and Cross, *Classroom Assessment Techniques*, 132–137.
57. Katherine Strober Dabbour, "Applying Active Learning Methods to the Design of Library Instruction for a Freshman Seminar," *College & Research Libraries* 58, no. 4 (1997): 299–308.
58. Mary Jane Petrowski, "Understanding Research as a Creative Process," in *Designs for Active Learning: A Sourcebook of Classroom Strategies for Information Education*, ed. Gail Gradowski, Loanne Snavely, and Paula Dempsey (Chicago: Association of College and Research Libraries, 1998), 156–158.
59. Van Houlson, "Getting Results from One-Shot Instruction: A Workshop for First-Year Students," *College & Undergraduate Libraries* 14, no. 1 (2007): 89–108; Jeanetta Drueke, "Active Learning in the University Library Instruction Classroom," *Research Strategies* 10, no. 2 (1992): 77–83.
60. Jeanne Davidson, "Library Research in the Sciences," in *Designs for*

Active Learning: A Sourcebook of Classroom Strategies for Information Education, ed. Gail Gradowski, Loanne Snavely, and Paula Dempsey (Chicago: Association of College and Research Libraries, 1998), 212–214.
61. Trudi E. Jacobson and Beth L. Mark, "Teaching in the Information Age: Active Learning Techniques to Empower Students," *Reference Librarian*, no. 51-52 (1995): 105–20.
62. Ragains, "Four Variations."
63. Amy Harris, "Active Learning for the Millennial Generation," *Georgia Library Quarterly* 47, no. 4 (2010): 13–14.
64. Susan E. Cooperstein and Elizabeth Kocevar-Weidinger, "Beyond Active Learning: A Constructivist Approach to Learning," *Reference Services Review* 32, no. 2 (2004): 141–48.
65. Celia Hales Mabry, "Using Cooperative Learning Principles in BI," *Research Strategies* 13, no. 3 (1995): 182–85.
66. Abate, Gomes, and Linton, "Engaging Students in Active Learning."
67. Bobbie L. Collins, Rosalind Tedford, and H. David Womack, "'Debating' the Merits of Clickers in an Academic Library," *North Carolina Libraries* 66, no. 1-2 (2008): 20–24; Connor, "Using Cases and Clickers."
68. Getselman and White, "Use of a Pre-Assessment Tool."
69. Petrowski, "Understanding Research."
70. Shelley Cudiner and Oskar R. Harmon, "An Active Learning Approach to Teaching Effective Online Search Strategies: A Librarian/Faculty Collaboration," *T.H.E. Journal* 28, no. 5 (2000): 52–57; Dave Kohut and Joel Sternberg, "Using the Internet to Study the Internet: An Active Learning Component," *Research Strategies* 13, no. 3 (1995): 176–81; Julia I. Smith and Lena Chang, "Teaching Community Ecology as a Jigsaw: A Collaborative Learning Activity Fostering Library Research Skills," *American Biology Teacher* 67, no. 1 (2005): 31–36.
71. Seely, Fry, and Ruppel, "Information Literacy Follow-Through."
72. Janet McNeil Hurlbert, "The Five-Minute Paper," in *Designs for Active Learning: A Sourcebook of Classroom Strategies for Information Education*, ed. Gail Gradowski, Loanne Snavely, and Paula Dempsey (Chicago: Association of College and Research Libraries, 1998), 23–24.
73. Radcliff et al., "Classroom Assessment Techniques"; Susan Ariew and Edward Lener, "Evaluating Instruction: Developing a Program That Supports the Teaching Librarian," *Research Strategies* 20, no. 4 (2005): 506–15.
74. Grassian and Kaplowitz, *Information Literacy Instruction*.
75. Dahl, "Scenario-Based Active Learning"; Mary J. Snyder Broussard, "Secret Agents in the Library: Integrating Virtual and Physical Games in a Small Academic Library," *College & Undergraduate Libraries* 17, no. 1 (January 2010): 20–30; Alison S. Gregory and Mary J. Snyder Broussard, "Unraveling the 'Mystery' of the Library: A 'Big Games' Approach

to Library Orientation" (paper presented at the Association of College and Research Libraries Conference, Philadelphia, PA, March 30–April 2, 2011), http://www.ala.org/acrl/sites/ala.org.acrl/files/content/conferences/confsandpreconfs/national/2011/papers/unraveling_the_myste.pdf.
76. Smith and Chang, "Teaching Community Ecology."
77. Broussard, "Using Games"; Cudiner and Harmon, "An Active Learning Approach."
78. Charlotte L. Briggs and Deborah Keyek-Franssen, "Clickers and CATs: Using Learner Response Systems for Formative Assessments in the Classroom," *EDUCAUSE Quarterly* 33, no. 4 (2010, http://www.educause.edu/ero/article/clickers-and-cats-using-learner-response-systems-formative-assessments-classroom.
79. Examples: Emily K. Chan and Lorrie A. Knight, "Clicking with Your Audience," *Communications in Information Literacy* 4, no. 2 (2010): 192–201; Emily Dill, "Do Clickers Improve Library Instruction? Lock in Your Answers Now," *Journal of Academic Librarianship* 34, no. 6 (2008): 527–29; Dennis, Murphey, and Rogers, "Assessing Information Literacy Comprehension"; Patricia Keogh and Zhonghong Wang, "Clickers in Instruction: One Campus, Multiple Perspectives," *Library Hi Tech* 28, no. 1 (2010): 8–21.
80. Dill, "Do Clickers Improve Library Instruction?"
81. Dennis, Murphey, and Rogers, "Assessing Information Literacy Comprehension."
82. Collins, Tedford, and Womack, "'Debating' the Merits of Clickers."
83. Chan and Knight, "Clicking with Your Audience," 196.
84. Ross and Furno, "Active Learning in the Library Instruction Environment," 959.
85. Christina Hoffman and Susan Goodwin, "A Clicker for Your Thoughts: Technology for Active Learning," *New Library World* 107, no. 9-10 (2006): 422–33.
86. Osterman, "Student Response Systems," 53.
87. Connor, "Using Cases and Clickers in Library Instruction."
88. Oakleaf, "The Information Literacy Instruction Assessment Cycle."
89. Elizabeth Choinski and Michelle Emanuel, "The One-Minute Paper and the One-Hour Class," *Reference Services Review* 34, no. 1 (February 2006): 148–55.
90. Alison E. Lahlafi, Diane Rushton, and Erica Stretton, "Active and Reflective Learning Initiatives to Improve Web Searching Skills of Business Students," *Journal of Information Literacy* 6, no. 1 (2012): 34–49.
91. Rachel Fenske and Ann Roselle, "Proving the Efficacy of Library Instruction Evaluation," *Research Strategies* 16 (1998): 175–85.
92. Bennett and Brothen, "Citation Analyses as a Prioritization Tool."
93. Bonnie J. M. Swoger, "Closing the Assessment Loop Using Pre- and

Post-Assessment," *Reference Services Review* 39, no. 2 (2011): 244–59.
94. Toni M. Carter, "Use What You Have: Authentic Assessment of In-Class Activities," *Reference Services Review* 41, no. 1 (2013): 49–61.
95. Elizabeth K. Tompkins, "A Reflective Teaching Journal: An Instructional Improvement Tool for Academic Librarians," *College & Undergraduate Libraries* 16, no. 4 (2009): 221–38.
96. Ariew and Lener, "Evaluating Instruction."
97. Ibid., 512.
98. Lee-Allison Levene and Polly Frank, "Peer Coaching: Professional Growth and Development for Instruction Librarians," *Reference Services Review* 21, no. 3 (January 1993): 35–42.
99. Sue Samson and Donna E. McCrea, "Using Peer Review to Foster Good Teaching," *Reference Services Review* 36, no. 1 (2008): 61–70, doi:10.1108/00907320810852032.
100. Jaena Alabi, Rhonda Huisman, Meagan Lacy, Willie Miller, Eric Snajdr, Jessica Trinoskey, and William H. Weare, "By and for Us: The Development of a Program for Peer Review of Teaching by and for Pre-Tenure Librarians," *Collaborative Librarianship* 4, no. 4 (October 2012): 165–74.
101. Pam Arbeeny and Chris Hartman, "Empowering Librarians to Be Better Teachers: The Value of Peer Coaching to Library Instruction," *Colorado Libraries* 34, no. 4 (October 2008): 39–45.
102. Ibid., 43.
103. Heidi Julien, "Education for Information Literacy Instruction: A Global Perspective," *Journal of Education for Library and Information Science*, no. 3 (2005): 210–16.

Chapter 3

Embedding Formative Assessment into Library Instruction: The Advantages and Challenges Ahead

The available literature on formative assessment is principally written by and for instructors who see students over the course of a semester or year. While many instructional improvement methods can be easily transferred from the broader education literature to the library classroom, others, including formative assessment, pose more of a challenge because librarians do not teach under the same conditions as other instructors. Many, if not most, of Angelo and Cross's fifty classroom assessment techniques (CATs) require time to process student data and provide feedback.[1] Instructors can take students' "Minute Papers" (CAT 6) back to their offices after class to process and use their conclusions of student progress and remaining needs to inform their future lesson plans.[2] For librarians teaching for-credit information literacy courses, this model continues to work, and this book will be useful for its theory and research-focused formative assessment techniques.

Yet much of information literacy instruction in higher education takes place in library one-shots. Because of the time constraints, these one-to-two-hour library classes tend to be tool-focused, focusing on the most immediate learning target: facilitating students' ability to complete the instructor-assigned research project. Librarians often wish that there were more time for the kind of information literacy skills students can transfer to other assignments or to the "real world." These weaknesses of the one-shot are well documented in the library literature.[3] Badke writes, "Yet all too often the task seems like a charade where the skilled teach the reluctant, resulting in something (as opposed to nothing) but signifying little."[4] These discussions on the ineffectiveness of the one-shot model are often integrated with expressions of frustration about giving up precious face time with students for assessment.

However, the course-integrated information literacy sessions have an important advantage over for-credit information literacy classes. This type of instruction is most valuable when it is attached to a real assignment based in an academic discipline. What librarians teach needs to have a context for students; information literacy cannot effectively be taught in a vacuum. "Since most college courses require students to find, evaluate, and present information, it is logical to integrate information literacy skills in the general coursework."[5] Furthermore, an instructor placing value on library instruction can be a powerful endorsement to students. The key to effective research instruction is building strong, collaborative relationships with instructors and incorporating formative assessment data of student learning.

The library one-shot, for better or worse, is not going away any time soon. Furthermore, if it does eventually evolve, it will only be because concrete assessment data prove to instructors and administration that our students need something better. While gathering evidence that improvement is necessary can be done through any kind of assessment, formative assessment has several advantages. First, it does not necessarily require additional time as many active learning activities can provide evidence of student learning. Secondly, because formative assessments are quick and easy to implement, they can be implemented in more classes. While each formative assessment is only a small snapshot of a particular skill, cumulatively, they can paint a powerful picture of students' strengths and weaknesses over time. We believe it is time for instruction librarians to bring formative assessment into the library classroom in an intentional and systematic way.

Now that we have briefly looked at how teaching differs between classroom instructors and librarians, it is time to begin transforming the theory and the formative assessment techniques from the education literature into something that works for librarians. Because the library one-shot model is so prevalent in information literacy instruction, this chapter will look at what aspects of the library one-shot lend themselves well to formative assessment and what aspects necessitate adaptations. The chapter will then look beyond the one-shot to more effective models of information literacy instruction that would enhance librarians' ability to gather formative assessment data in richer and more advanced ways.

Time Constraints

The biggest difference in how instructors and librarians teach is the amount of time spent with students. Many authors have shared their frustrations with giving up precious time in the one-shot to conduct assessments.[6] Much of librarians' distaste for assessment in general is due to their extremely limited time with students, which constrains their ability to assess student knowledge and skills. When librarians are asked to do so much in the course of a single meeting, with no other contact time with students, giving up ten minutes for assessment is a high price to pay.

Indeed, our limited time with students creates the biggest challenge to adapting formative assessments from the education literature to the library classroom because much of what is described requires time outside of class to reflect on and react to student data. In a regular course, students' learning process is stretched out over weeks or months while the librarian's part of the learning process lasts approximately an hour. To conduct formative assessment effectively in the library one-shot, librarians need techniques, advice, and tools to help them perform bite-sized assessments where the entire assessment process (collection, analysis, and reaction) can happen multiple times within an hour. We have put an emphasis on these types of assessments—formative assessment snapshot techniques (FASTs)—in Chapters 5–7 to help librarians get started with bite-sized formative assessment.

For an example of such a mini-assessment is the Scavenger Hunt (FAST 31), which assesses two learning targets for a library class: Students can use the online catalog and read Library of Congress call numbers to find a book. Students are divided into groups, and each group is given a book title and asked to find the physical book. Even with little prior knowledge or instruction, students working together can usually figure this out with little help from the librarian. The students find the book in the catalog, use the library directory to determine where the book is, confirm the location with the librarian as they leave the room, and go retrieve their book from the stacks. Finding the requested book is satisfying to students and confirmation to the librarian that they have met the learning target. At each step in this process, the librarian is rotating to help any students who are struggling. This includes the librarian going into the stacks to be available for questions (it is helpful to give students titles of books in the same physical area). This treasure hunt only takes about five minutes and provides ample opportunity for adjustment on the part of the librarian and students to modify teaching and learning as needed until the learning targets are met.

As this example illustrates, one of the biggest benefits of formative assessment for librarians is that it brings assessment into the primary activity, which is *learning*. Formative assessments are often the active learning exercises librarians already assign students, but the evidence elicited from these tasks can be most effective if they are *immediately* utilized to steer the teaching and learning process. When doing a treasure hunt activity like the one described above, students probably do not even realize they are being assessed. They are also unlikely to realize that the librarians' instruction may have been slightly different from another section of the same class an hour before or even from the group on the other side of the room; they just think the librarian is being helpful. Yet even when students are unaware they are being assessed, librarians can be collecting evidence for immediate teaching improvement as well as data to be shared at a later time with the instructor, instruction program supervisors, or even institutional administrators.

It is important to realize that any one formative assessment is not meant to reveal the big picture of a student's ability. For this we still need the larger, more invasive, and time-consuming assessment tools. Instead, a particular formative assessment paints a current picture of students' relationships to a specific learning target. We do not necessarily have to sacrifice instruction time for assessment; learning and assessing processes can overlap. Likewise, because formative assessments are designed to be quickly (or sometimes immediately) processed and reacted upon, assessing becomes a seamless part of the learning process from the students' point of view.

Getting to Know Your Audience

Because instructors get to know students in the first few weeks of the semester, they often call on students randomly by name as a way to stimulate student engagement. Many instructors also understand that each class has its own personality.[7] They may teach two sections of the same class in a semester, but they know one may be very talkative, needing little encouragement to participate, while the other may be quietly reflective, requiring the instructor to use more skills to get students to share their thoughts aloud. Furthermore, as departments build their curriculum, instructors know what foundation skills are taught in lower-level courses that serve as prerequisites for the upper-level courses. An instructor in a senior research methods course can be confident that his or her students were exposed to certain skills in those previous courses. This allows instructors in each department to scaffold important disciplinary skills.

For librarians, it can be a challenge to intellectually engage a class for a session without knowing students' names or the class's personality. Likewise, few academic libraries have done an institution-wide curriculum map of where specific information literacy skills are taught. When a librarian walks into an information literacy class, he or she cannot always count on knowing how many library classes the students have attended before. Furthermore, some students may have been to many library classes while others have been to none. This makes scaffolding information literacy skills difficult; and it is also difficult to have a good understanding of students' baseline skill level for instructional design planning.

Formative assessment can help because it facilitates getting to know students' knowledge and skills in a short amount of time. It enables the librarian to adjust on the spot for the benefit of those same students. Diagnostic surveys with individual classes can help librarians understand what previous knowledge students have when they arrive for information literacy instruction. These can take place before the class, at the beginning of the class, or throughout the class. As we saw in Chapter 2, "Are Academic Librarians Doing Formative Assessment?," there is little evidence in the library literature that librarians are conducting class-specific diagnostic surveys to inform their instructional design. Just as there is evidence that instructors overestimate students' information literacy skills, we suspect that librarians may be underestimating those same skills. As a result, librarians teach the same introductory skills to all class levels because these skills are fundamental to student success with library research, yet this causes students to be bored and complain that library instruction is repetitive. Knowing what skills a specific group of students already has can help librarians spend the precious time with students wisely and help relieve student boredom.

Because we do not know students' names, many librarians rely on volunteers who raise their hands to answer questions or participate in class discussions. However, formative assessment scholars urge us to break away from this model of participation. Wiliam states, "By allowing [students] to raise their hands to show they have an answer—[instructors] are actually making the achievement gap worse, because those who are participating are getting smarter, while those avoiding engagement are forgoing the opportunities to increase their ability."[8] Librarians often find themselves calling on the same three or four students throughout the class while the remaining students look away and zone out, knowing they will not be called on.

Formative assessments can help librarians create an atmosphere that emphasizes that there are no opt-outs for student engagement. The librarian can have students create a short piece of writing on a prompt, then switch papers with classmates. Students may be more likely to volunteer if they do not have to reveal their own potential inadequacies while the owner of the response can remain anonymous. Similarly, after assigning a Think-Pair-Share (FAST 33), the librarian can call on a group at random. Whatever group member volunteers to speak will have the confidence of representing their group rather than their own thoughts. All students can be asked to respond with hand signals (FAST 18: Fist-to-Five). They are more likely to be looking up at this point, so the librarian can more easily call on a student and to share his or her choice. If the librarian gets an "I don't know" response or another refusal to participate, he or she can come back to that student later to ask, "What did you think of that answer given by another student?" Formative assessments can help students realize that they are not off the hook and that engagement can facilitate further formative assessment. This is something academic librarians can implement immediately.

Throughout our lessons, formative assessments can help us customize our teaching to the specific needs of the students in front of us, even if we did not know the students before the beginning of class. Formative assessments facilitate understanding the previous knowledge and skills students have when they arrive and recognition of when students meet our classes' learning targets. When students do not meet the targets, we can quickly provide individual help or lead a class discussion to get them back on track. Even though librarians do not know the students in the same way instructors come to know them, smaller assessments help us make the most out of our time with them by helping us know their previous knowledge and the current state of their developing knowledge at check-in points throughout the class; these assessments enable us to be flexible to adapt to the class personality.

Critical Feedback

Formative assessment revolves around sharing information through feedback, and "feedback is most helpful when provided early and often in the learning process."[9] Educators assign activities to students that generate feedback to the educator on students' understanding. Educators then give feedback to help students' identify their strengths and weaknesses in regards to the learning targets. Students take the feedback they receive to adjust their learning strategies. Adjustment is needed on both sides to maximize student learning.

The feedback from students comes in many forms, including written, verbal, or non-verbal. Sometimes the feedback is explicit; at other times it is subtler. While the student data may be recorded for later analysis, it can also be analyzed and reacted to on the spot without being recorded. The feedback from the educator may also be written, verbal, or non-verbal. It may also happen in the form of a redirected lesson, or the instructor's feedback may even be worked into an activity so that a pattern is revealed when students have demonstrated competence (such as finding the book in the treasure-hunt example discussed above). No matter how the pedagogical conversation takes place, this feedback is critical for student learning.

Formative assessment emphasizes timely feedback. In fact, immediate feedback is ideal. Timely feedback fits seamlessly into the learning process from the students' perspective, and it becomes an engagement and motivation tool. From the instructor's perspective, frequent timely formative feedback is more than a Band-Aid on misunderstandings; it prevents misunderstandings from becoming too engrained in students' understanding of the material. Small misunderstandings are corrected while students are still forming their conceptions of the new material or new skills. The emphasis on timely feedback challenges librarians to select techniques that can provide fast yet meaningful feedback. Fortunately, there are such activities that allow for feedback within the library one-shot. While we realize the idea of adapting instruction on the fly may seem daunting, it should be remembered that librarians already demonstrate this flexibility in the information literacy instruction that happens at the reference desk where we must always "think on our feet."

One fairly low-tech form of formative assessment is Epstein Educational Enterprise's Immediate Feedback Assessment Technique (IF-AT) Forms (FAST 24).[10] These forms are small cards that look like standardized test bubble sheets, but instead of filling in the correct answer, students scratch off the film covering the correct answer, revealing a star. The form also shows how many attempts students made before finding the correct answer.

Figure 3.1. Using an IF-AT form by Epstein Educational Enterprise, students scratch off a film covering the correct answer, revealing a star. The form also shows how many attempts students made before finding the correct answer.

Cotner et al. describe using IF-AT forms in their classes.[11] They predicted this type of formative assessment would foster student engagement, encourage collaboration, and provide immediate feedback for student understanding. In their testing of the forms, they found that students valued immediate feedback because "it reveals misconceptions and improves their exam preparation."[12] In another study using the IF-AT forms, results clearly show that students strongly prefer this immediate feedback method over other assessment techniques, stating that it is easy to use, makes the test feel more like a game, lets them know the right answer to every question, and, most importantly, allows them to learn more.[13] Authors conducting the study inferred that this immediate feedback was the reason students claimed they had learned more.

At our institution's library, we have found IF-AT forms to be an effective activity in combination with a Think-Pair-Share (FAST 33) where students first take the paper quiz individually, then work in groups to come to a consensus on which answer to scratch off the IF-AT forms, which helps ensure that small groups stay on task and hold meaningful discussions. Groups earn more points if they require fewer attempts to find each correct answer. Once all groups have completed the IF-AT forms, the librarian leads a class discussion, spending the most time on the items students most struggled with. During this activity, immediate feedback is provided twice: when students scratch off an answer to find whether it contains the star and when the librarian spends time with the class discussing incorrect and correct answers.

Clickers also have the advantage of facilitating immediate feedback, even in very large classes. Clickers allow the librarian to "monitor student learning and to immediately respond to students' needs for clarification or additional practice."[14] Briggs and Keyek-Franssen looked at how clickers can facilitate Angelo and Cross's fifty CATs. They found that thirteen CATs could be done with clickers without modification; another ten could be adapted for clickers. This means that nearly half of the CATs can be combined with clickers to facilitate immediate feedback, which would enable even more CATs to be conducted in the library one-shot.

In addition to these techniques that fit within the one-shot, there are also advanced assessments that allow librarians to provide written feedback outside of class. For example, librarians can provide comments on annotated bibliographies in collaboration with the course instructor. This book gives a number of ideas for providing feedback that will work with varying degrees of instructor collaboration both later in this chapter and in Chapters 5–7.

Non-Threatening Environment

One of the requirements for formative assessment is a safe learning space. At the most basic level, this means students are not graded on the quality of their work for formative assessment activities. Their purpose is to make students feel safe to experiment and draw conclusions. Trial-and-error learning is extremely powerful, but it cannot take place if students fear their initial failures will affect their grades. In other words, providing a non-threatening learning environment removes many of the affective barriers of trial-and-error learning. The number of times this appears in the education literature on formative assessment would suggest that instructors may struggle with this. Yet librarians are not accustomed to assigning grades in the one-shot, so this is less of a temptation. This is the area where librarians will have the least trouble adapting formative assessment.

However, there is more to creating a safe learning environment than simply eliminating grades. Librarians can concentrate on welcoming students as they arrive to the library classroom to set a friendly tone for the class. Furthermore, librarians can work to develop the type of questions for which the formative assessment literature advocates. Like other educators, we tend to ask students factual, close-ended questions like "What database allows you to find current newspaper articles?" Many students could not possibly know the only right answer to this question if they have never had library instruction before. Such questions set students up for failure. Furthermore, librarians often are unable to deal with unexpected answers from students. Instead, librarians should work on using more open-ended questions. Mabry based an entire class on the single question "How do you conduct library research?"[15] There are many right answers to this question, even beyond those the librarian can anticipate. Likewise, if a student supplies something that needs correcting, the librarian can point out what is right before gently correcting the part that is not.

Finally, creating a safe learning environment can help librarians relieve the affective barriers that prevent students from gaining information literacy skills or effectively performing college-level research. Library anxiety is a powerful force in preventing students from using library resources or asking library staff for help. They are terrified of looking "stupid" or "incompetent." This fear may drive students to use web resources of questionable reliability, whether allowed or not, and to seek help from their peers instead of library staff.[16] Obviously, library anxiety can create a huge emotional barrier to students' ability to conduct research in the way educators want them to. Mellon describes how an emphasis on being friendly in library instruction greatly reduces library anxiety.[17] Vidmar describes how a short pre-session that acknowledges the feelings in the research process helps relieve the anxiety as can an icebreaker discussion on perceptions of libraries.[18] Librarians showing that they are listening to students describe their anxieties, looking for evidence of what knowledge students still need to be successful, and providing students encouraging feedback can set in motion a more personal, open relationship with students.

More than the One-Shot

There are two growing trends in librarianship that have the potential to greatly improve information literacy instruction efforts in higher education and allow librarians to conduct more sophisticated formative assessments: collaboration and flipped classrooms. For some readers, collaboration and flipped classrooms may already be a reality while they are only a dream for many others. This book is designed for librarians starting with isolated one-shots as well as those with stronger collaborations with instructors.

Collaboration and flipped classrooms are related to formative assessment in two ways. First, additional time with students provides additional time for formative assessment. Second, formative assessment results from one-shots, while primarily gathered to improve student learning within that lesson, have the secondary benefit of providing evidence for how instruction can be improved overall. This may mean that recorded formative assessment data provides evidence that students' information literacy skills can greatly benefit from collaborative assignment design and additional time with librarians. Let us look at each of these.

Collaboration

Outside of for-credit information literacy classes, librarians' access to students is through some degree of collaboration with instructors. On the *high* end of the collaboration spectrum, embedded librarians have much more interaction with students in and outside of the classroom. Fortunately, formative assessment can happen at any level of librarian-instructor collaboration. In the library one-shot session, instructors give up approximately an hour of class time for the students to learn skills that will assist them with their research projects. Sometimes the librarian has an on-going relationship with the instructor; sometimes their only contact is through a request form for library instruction. Regardless, this *low* level of collaboration is distinguished by no librarian involvement with students or the instructor outside of the one-shot session.

However, the librarian-instructor collaboration is capable of so much more. Each recognizes the other's importance: The instructor is an expert in the academic subject while the librarian is the expert in research skills and the library's resources. They work together to develop students' subject-integrated information literacy skills. The librarian often has more than one hour to spend with students to focus on more hands-on practice, and the instructor assigns library-related homework. The librarian may also be a grading partner, whether it is for effort points or as part of the students' final grades on their research projects. The instructor demonstrates how important information literacy skills are to his or her students by giving time to their development and rewarding students' demonstrations of research competence. Furthermore, the instructor works with his or her departmental colleagues to enable systematic scaffolding of information literacy skills within the department's curriculum. The librarian and instructor become true partners in supporting student learning.

Developing, maintaining, and improving this level of relationship with instructors requires a lot of effort, and an embedded librarian model is not appropriate or possible for every class. Not every assignment requires extensive library instruction. Over time, discussions of assessment results among librarians and with collaborating instructors can help inform what kind of information literacy instruction would best serve students completing that assignment. Fortunately, there are many models of instructor collaboration between the two extremes.

Some models involve negotiating more contact time with students. Gandhi found assessment results of student learning improved greatly when librarians moved from a one-shot to five separate twenty-five to thirty minute sessions with an emphasis on providing meaningful practice opportunities.[19] She also reports instructor-librarian collaboration is a key element in establishing strong librarian-student relationships as well—students see that the instructor is endorsing what the librarian is teaching.

Librarians can be meaningful partners in assignment design without requiring more time for information literacy instruction. An instructor may approach the librarian with a prescribed lesson based on assumed levels of student competency or with inefficient ideas on how to promote research skill development. Tuttle and McKinzie describe a co-teaching experience where the librarian and instructor worked together in assignment design.[20] In addition to the standard end-of-semester research paper, students were instructed to keep a "record of research" that included search results from library databases, abstracts, full-text printouts, notes, citations, and a personal explanation of what was happening throughout the research process. This record was worth 10–40% of the final project grade, the exact percentage to be chosen by the student. The librarian created a class-specific research portal that not only gave students a starting point but also helped the instructor prepare for the library classes, which the two educators co-taught like "tag team wrestlers."[21]

Furthermore, librarians are sometimes asked to support hands-off research assignments. Many instructors design research assignments that have a library one-shot when the research project is first assigned and a due date, without any structured guidance in between. These instructors may be frustrated when they receive poorly constructed papers at the end of the semester and wonder what is wrong with the students or what is wrong with their teaching. The librarian can step in with his or her knowledge of the research process and suggest a "process-based" assignment. This involves breaking a term paper or research presentation into mini-assignments such as annotated bibliographies, drafts, thesis statements, and research logs. Each piece of the assignment has its own due date, and it is an opportunity for instructors to make sure students are on the right path, give them feedback, and monitor their progress on the assignment over time. These process-based assignments have been shown to be effective in preventing plagiarism as completing the assignment in the way the instructor intends is easier than working backwards from a bought paper.[22]

Instructor-librarian collaboration can also come in the form of assessment partnerships. In any of the mini-assignment examples, librarians and instructors can provide individual feedback in their respective areas of expertise. We cannot find an example of co-grading in the academic library literature, but it is found in some of the articles from school librarians. Edwards offered to grade the library-related portion of class tests.[23] In a comment on *School Library Monthly*'s blog, librarian Giselle Boyadjian writes that librarians at her school collaborate with biology teachers, grading note cards for format, note-taking, and sources.[24] They similarly help grade the library portion of students' thesis statements, outlines, and works-cited pages throughout the research paper writing process. Harada and Yoshina argue that school librarians and teachers should work as partners throughout the assessment process to improve student learning.[25] Academic librarians can learn from school librarians in their efforts to develop meaningful collaborative relationships with instructors.

In higher education, librarians often seek instructors' assistance with assessing information literacy skills. This either involves instructors' collaboration to have access to students for assessment or their expertise in assessment design. Brown and Kingsley-Wilson describe how collaboration with journalism instructors created an authentic assessment that benefited both the library and the journalism department.[26] Knight asked instructors for assistance in creating a rubric to help evaluate 260 annotated bibliographies from freshmen.[27] Such reliance on instructors to have access to this kind of student information and for assistance in assessment design is not uncommon in the information literacy assessment literature.

Because librarians and instructors are partners in student learning, results from formative assessments of information literacy skills should be openly communicated with instructors. This gives instructors tangible evidence that the library lesson is effective and worthwhile or needs to be improved. Looking at assessment results as a partnership can increase future collaboration. If an instructor is not satisfied with final results, or if the librarian approaches an instructor with assessment results from a one-shot, together they can make changes that may greatly improve student learning. Forming collaborative relationships with instructors will ultimately improve formative assessment implementation and the overall success of the instruction program and student learning.

Many instructors simply do not know how much more the librarian can contribute beyond performing as a guest lecturer. Communication with instructors is the key to establishing successful collaborations and determining what is most appropriate for any given group of students. Instructors do not need to come to the librarian with a fully formed idea of how they would like him or her to approach the lesson. It is the librarian's job to provide instructors with an idea of the range of possibilities that exist in how we can fully support our mutual goals of turning students into information-competent researchers. Formative assessment results can inform collaborators on best practices for meeting their mutual goal of developing students' subject-embedded information literacy skills.

Flipped Classrooms

A flipped classroom is any educational setting where students' first exposure to the content happens before class, and class time is spent on applying that knowledge and getting feedback from peers and the instructor. The idea behind flipped classrooms is not new, but there is growing discussion on how to make the most of this model. Modern implementations often involve watching educational videos or streamed lectures before class, though Schell stresses that flipped classrooms are about pedagogy, not technology.[28] Because this model of instruction places a heavy emphasis on active learning, practice, and feedback to allow students to check their understanding, it is apparent why flipped classrooms and formative assessment go hand in hand.

Flipped classrooms have a lot of potential for library instruction. Students often do not have the necessary foundational knowledge to devote an entire library session to active learning and application; usually some lecture is necessary. Flipping a library one-shot would allow librarians to make the lecture homework before the session, allowing the entire session to be spent on application to turn students' new knowledge into usable skills. Students are used to having homework to prepare for a regular class session—it is not asking too much of them to prepare for a library session. This can happen through a paper-based pre-class activity or through pre-recorded lectures delivered through course management systems.

There is very little literature on flipped classrooms for library instruction. Datig and Ruswick describe a project at Mary Baldwin College, where librarians implemented flipped classrooms so they could focus on active learning activities while in the library classroom.[29] The authors reported that the activity led not only to student learning but also to a good deal of student engagement. Four video lessons or reading assignments were given before each class: the first focusing on searching the databases, the second on keyword searching, the third on website evaluation, and the fourth on identifying source types. Each of these lessons was followed in the classroom with group activities, student presentations, and class discussions, providing an opportunity for formative assessment and feedback in each case. In the end, students found the experience engaging and effective.

Schell addressed educators' skepticism in the likelihood that students would actually complete the homework and come to class prepared.[30] She says, "If you assess it, they will come." Lectures should be "chunked" with small tests in between. Chunks should be between seven and fifteen minutes long, meaning each chunk could represent an individual learning target within a library lesson. The tests can be a few multiple-choice questions, but they should be questions that students have to think about and not just simply recall an answer. These questions hold the students accountable for the homework and also reward students for their efforts.

Librarians interested in flipping classrooms do not necessarily have to record their own videos. ResearchReady is a new tutorial service from the makers of EasyBib that combines short, customizable information literacy lessons with multiple-choice and short-answer questions. Results can be easily reviewed by the instructor and librarian. There are also high-quality information literacy videos freely available on the Internet like Costal Carolina University's information literacy videos and many institution-neutral online tutorials in Association of College and Research Libraries' PRIMO database.[31] These can easily be combined with online tests by embedding them in a course management system so that the instructor can see the results before class.

Furthermore, flipped classrooms expand librarians' ability to provide students with meaningful feedback. For end-of-library-class formative assessments such as the One-Minute Paper (FAST 44), librarians struggle with providing feedback that is still part of students' learning process. If students were already familiar with an online platform through a flipped library class, the librarian can respond to students' one-minute papers in a way that is integrated into their learning process. For example, if students saw an e-book listed in the catalog during the class activity, but the lesson did not go into as much detail as some students desired, the librarian could create a brief JING video on how to open and download e-books. He or she could also combine additional assessment questions to hold students accountable for the after-class content as well.

Clearly, flipping a library one-shot class requires collaboration with the instructor because the instructor is the one who will be requiring the homework. Students will look to their instructors for guidance about the value of such an experience. The librarian must be able to trust the instructor to not only require the pre-class homework but to convince students of its value towards completing their research assignment and learning the overall course content. In this case, flipped classrooms have the potential to crack open the one-shot library instruction model and create something that can help educators effectively and efficiently turn facts about library tools into valuable information literacy skills.

Summary

Librarians are well aware of the importance of information literacy skills. We also are mindful of the need to find more effective ways of teaching these skills than the isolated library one-shot. Formative assessment has been shown in the education literature to be one of the most effective educational techniques for improving student learning. It is time to bring formative assessment to the forefront of discussions on library instruction improvement.

Because of the prevalence of the library one-shot model of information literacy instruction, it is not always self-evident how the education literature on formative assessment can be applied in the conditions in which librarians teach. The main hurdle is the limited time we have with students. However, with the suggested formative assessment snapshot techniques for low-level collaboration with instructors that are found in Chapters 5–7, librarians can begin implementing formative assessment within the one-shot.

We have also briefly looked at alternatives to the library one-shot model of information literacy, including collaboration with instructors and flipped classrooms. Our potential to truly influence students' information literacy skills is greatly enhanced with increased contact with the students. This can be through librarians and instructors working as partners in developing assignments, providing feedback, or freeing more class time for application of new knowledge. Furthermore, formative assessment results can help provide the necessary evidence to instructors that such partnerships are necessary and mutually beneficial.

NOTES

1. Thomas A. Angelo and K. Patricia Cross, *Classroom Assessment Techniques: A Handbook for College Teachers*, 2nd ed. (San Francisco: Jossey-Bass, 1993).
2. Ibid.,148–53.
3. Susan Ariew and Edward Lener, "Evaluating Instruction: Developing a Program That Supports the Teaching Librarian," *Research Strategies* 20 (2005): 506–15; Donald Barclay, "Evaluating Library Instruction: Doing the Best You Can with What You Have," *RQ* 33 (1993): 195–202; Patrick Ragains, "Evaluation of Academic Librarians' Instructional Performance: Report of a National Survey," *Research Strategies* 15, no. 3 (January 1997): 159–75; Smiti Gandhi, "Faculty-Librarian Collaboration to Assess the Effectiveness of a Five-Session Library Instruction Model," *Community & Junior College Libraries* 12, no. 4 (2004): 15–48.
4. William Badke, "Ramping Up the One-Shot," *Online* 33, no. 2 (2009): 47.
5. Gandhi, "Faculty-Librarian Collaboration."

6. Barclay, "Evaluating Library Instruction," 195–202; Ariew and Lener, "Evaluating Instruction," 506–15; Ragains, "Evaluation of Academic Librarians' Instructional Performance," 159–75.
7. Angelo and Cross, *Classroom Assessment Techniques*, 5.
8. Dylan Wiliam, *Embedded Formative Assessment* (Bloomington, IN: Solution Tree, 2011), 81.
9. Charlotte Briggs and Deborah Keyek-Franssen, "Clickers and CATs: Using Learner Response Systems for Formative Assessments in the Classroom," *EDUCAUSE Quarterly* 33, no. 4 (2010), http://www.educause.edu/ero/article/clickers-and-cats-using-learner-response-systems-formative-assessments-classroom.
10. "Order IF-AT Forms," Epstein Educational Enterprises, accessed January 7, 2014, http://www.epsteineducation.com/home/order/default.aspx.
11. Sehoya H. Cotner, Bruce A. Fall, Susan M. Wick, J.D. Walker, and Paul M. Baepler, "Rapid Feedback Assessment Methods: Can We Improve Engagement and Preparation for Exams in Large-Enrollment Courses?" *Journal of Science Education and Technology* 17, no. 5 (October 2008): 537–43.
12. Ibid., 442.
13. David DiBattista, Johan O. Mitterer, and Leanne Gosse, "Acceptance by Undergraduates of the Immediate Feedback Assessment Technique for Multiple-Choice Testing," *Teaching in Higher Education* 9, no. 1 (January 2004): 17–28, doi: 10/1080.1356251032000155803.
14. Briggs and Keyek-Franssen, "Clickers and CATs."
15. Celia Hales Mabry, "Using Cooperative Learning Principles in BI," *Research Strategies* 13, no. 3 (1995): 182–85.
16. Ibid.
17. Constance A. Mellon, "Library Anxiety: A Grounded Theory and Its Development," *College & Research Libraries* 47, no. 2 (March 1986): 160–65.
18. Dale J. Vidmar, "Affective Change: Integrating Pre-Sessions in the Students; Classroom Prior to Library Instruction," *Reference Services Review* 26, no. 3-4 (September 1998): 75–95.
19. Gandhi, "Faculty-Librarian Collaboration."
20. James B. Tuttle and Steve McKinzie, "Reconstructing the Research Project: A Case Study of Collaborative Instruction," in *Information Literacy Collaborations That Work*, ed. Trudi Jacobson and Thomas P. Mackey (New York: Neal-Schuman Publishers, 2007), 109–21.
21. Ibid., 117.
22. Janet McNeil Hurlbert, Cathleen R. Savidge, and Georgia R. Laudenslager, "Process-Based Assignments: How Promoting Information Literacy Prevents Plagiarism," *College & Undergraduate Libraries* 10, no. 1 (June 2003): 39.

23. Valerie A. Edwards, "Formative Assessment in the High School IMC," *Knowledge Quest* 35, no. 5 (2007): 50–53.
24. Giselle Boyadjian, "Score along the Way," in Kristin Fontichiaro, "Nudging toward Inquiry: Formative Assessment," *School Library Monthly* 27, no. 6 (March 2011), http://www.schoollibrarymonthly.com/curriculum/Fontichiaro2011-v27n6p11.html.
25. Violet H. Harada and Joan M. Yoshina, *Assessing for Learning: Librarians and Teachers as Partners* (Santa Barbara, CA: Libraries Unlimited, 2010).
26. Carol Perruso Brown and Barbara Kingsley-Wilson, "Assessing Organically: Turning an Assignment into an Assessment," *Reference Services Review* 38, no. 4 (2010): 536–56, doi:10.1108/00907321011090719.
27. Lorrie A. Knight, "Using Rubrics to Assess Information Literacy," *Reference Services Review* 34, no. 1 (February 2006): 43–55, doi:101108/00907320510631571.
28. Julie Schell, "Flipping the Classroom: How to Turn Your Student's World Right Side Up," (webinar, Turning Technologies, August 8, 2013), https://turningtechnologies.webex.com/ec0701l/eventcenter/recording/recordAction.do?theAction=poprecord&AT=pb&isurlact=true&renewticket=0&recordID=61038892&apiname=lsr.php&rKey=b533f94f29bf8115&needFilter=false&format=short&&SP=EC&rID=61038892&siteurl=turningtechnologies&actappname=ec0701l&actname=%2Feventcenter%2Fframe%2Fg.do&rnd=7453049057&entactname=%2FnbrRecordingURL.do&entappname=url0201l.
29. Ilka Datig and Claire Ruswick, "Four Quick Flips: Activities for the Information Literacy Classroom," *College & Research Libraries News* 74, no. 5 (May 2013): 249–51, 257.
30. Schell, "Flipping the Classroom."
31. Kimbel Library Instructional Videos, Coastal Carolina University, last modified September 18, 2011, http://www.coastal.edu/library/videos/.

PART II
Using Formative Assessment in the Academic Library Classroom

Chapter 4
Introduction to Part II: Guided Implementation, from Theory to Practice

This section of the book is designed to help readers transfer the theory discussed in Part 1 into practice. One of the most important recommendations we can make when it comes to applying these ideas is to maintain simplicity when planning and implementing the techniques. For the assessment data collected to be as accurate a representation of student learning as possible, the librarian must be comfortable with implementing Formative Assessment Snapshot Technique (FAST). Students are very aware of activities and teaching techniques with which educators are not at ease, and that recognition can negatively impact the learning process. Furthermore, learning new assessment techniques is useless if they are unsustainable.

The greatest value of FASTs is that each one focuses on a tiny part of student learning throughout a lesson. Most of the FASTs in this section, particularly in Chapters 5 and 6, are very easy to implement with little planning, and they consume little class time. Because FASTs are so quick to plan, implement, interpret, and react to, several can easily be performed in each library session, and many can be repeated to monitor students' progress towards the learning target. Some FASTs assess factual knowledge while others address students' ability to evaluate, synthesize, and apply knowledge in authentic contexts. FASTs do not add much work to a librarian's instructional design process and are therefore very sustainable.

Chapters 5–7 describe forty-eight bite-sized assessment techniques for information literacy instruction. Chapter 5, "Formative Assessment Snapshot Techniques for Before Instruction," discusses FASTs that begin either before students meet with the librarian or at the start of the library session. They offer a variety of ways to determine students' existing background knowledge, reinforce or check for understanding of recently learned information, or set the stage for new learning by helping the students focus in on the learning target(s). Chapter 6, "Formative Assessment Snapshot Techniques for During Instruction," contains techniques that take place in the midst of the library session. It is the longest chapter in this section because it represents the time when librarians have the most contact with students and the most opportunities for the results that can drive instruction. Techniques that can be performed after or at the end of library instruction are included in Chapter 7, "Formative Assessment Snapshot Techniques for After Instruction." Unlike most of the FASTs in Chapters 5 and 6, many of the FASTs in Chapter 7 require a higher amount of collaboration with the course instructor and more of the librarian's time. However, they allow the librarian an in-depth look at the quality of learning the students have reached, and, in some cases, the long-term impact the session has on the student learning. Because these do take more time and effort to implement, the assessments in Chapter 7 should be selected with these considerations in mind.

Within each FAST description, we address a number of important aspects that are specific to the technique. The required level of collaboration between the librarian and course instructor is an important consideration when choosing a FAST. If an assessment can easily be implemented in a library instruction class with little collaboration with the instructor, it is labeled as "low." If the instructor must assign the assessment as homework and/or the instructor must facilitate communication between the students and librarian outside of class, it is labeled as "medium." If the assessment requires intensive coordination with the instructor, it is labeled as "high."

It is common, even in "low" levels of instructor-librarian collaboration, for the instructor to send the librarian the research assignment details. This is an ideal time to ask the instructor for specific information in regards to the group of students that will be receiving information literacy instruction. The librarian should ask the instructor if there are any students with special needs. This includes not only those with disabilities but also English language learners and nontraditional students. The instructor can even describe the class personality such as whether the students tend to easily participate in whole-class discussion or whether they prefer individual learning activities. The librarian can use this information to select appropriate FASTs, making any necessary adaptations.

Taking audience size into consideration is also critical for successful implementation of FASTs. All assessments in Chapters 5–7 are suitable for small (1–15) and medium-sized (16–35) classes. We have made a special notation for FASTs that are suitable for large audiences (36+). Those that require adaptation for large audiences are designated with an asterisk (*). Look in the "Ideas for Adapting" section for details on how to make the FAST work with a large class.

Another aspect that deserves special consideration is the feedback level. Formative assessment can gather data at different levels. While individual feedback is ideal, and most of Angelo and Cross's fifty classroom assessment techniques gather data on individual students' understanding, this is not often practical in the library classroom.[1] Due to time limits, data in a library session must usually be collected, interpreted, and utilized to inform instruction on the spot. Asking students to discuss a concept within small groups and report to the class is often more practical and provides an opportunity for students to pool their individual knowledge and learn from each other. Other assessments demonstrate the class's understanding as a whole. Many FASTs can be adjusted, depending on goals and time, to various feedback levels.

Formative Assessment Guided Implementation Template

To help librarians transition concepts of theory into practice, we have created a lesson plan template that can be used to organize formative assessment techniques. With a process similar in structure to what Wiggins and McTighe refer to as "backwards design," our template starts with identifying the learning targets for the library session and the evidence that will show the target has been met, and it ends with the librarian's post-instruction reflection.[2] The template in this chapter is completed with a lesson plan that is used at our institution. We have also included a blank template in the book's appendix that can be copied for readers' individual use when designing library instruction to incorporate formative assessment. Allow us to briefly explain each of the template's five sections.

Learning Target(s)

The first section of the template has the librarian identify the learning target(s) for the session. The learning target should answer the question "What should students know or be able to do by the end of the class?" We recommend limiting the number of learning targets to two or three for a library one-shot session and matching the FASTs to those goals to check for student understanding. For some of the more-involved FASTs in Chapter 7, such as the Annotated Bibliography (FAST 38), it may be beneficial to show students examples of quality student responses to encourage them to understand the difference between mere task completion and learning-target achievement. At the very least, the librarian should determine what exemplifies meeting the learning target(s) before the instruction takes place. Finally, this section of the template should include a plan for sharing the learning targets with students during the lesson so they understand the purpose of the assessment.

Association of College and Research Libraries (ACRL) Information Literacy Competency Standards for Higher Education[3]

Identify the ACRL Standard(s) the lesson will address. The standards are as follows:
- **Standard 1:** The information literate student determines the nature and extent of the information needed.
- **Standard 2:** The information literate student accesses needed information effectively and efficiently.
- **Standard 3:** The information literate student evaluates information and its sources critically and incorporates selected information into his or her knowledge base and value system.
- **Standard 4:** The information literate student, individually or as a member of a group, uses information effectively to accomplish a specific purpose.
- **Standard 5:** The information literate student understands many of the economic, legal, and social issues surrounding the use of information and accesses and uses information ethically and legally.

Formative Assessment Snapshot Technique(s)

Once it is determined when students need to show evidence of their understanding, the librarian can choose which chapter to pull an appropriate FAST. It may be helpful to determine what evidence will show that the students have met the learning targets identified and find a FAST that can be adapted to create such a confirmation of understanding. Finally, the lesson plan should indicate if the FAST will follow a lecture or other learning activity or if the students will be learning the desired content directly from the FAST.

Plan to Use Formative Assessment Results

As we discussed in Chapters 1–3, formative assessment is only effective if the librarian uses the results to further impact student learning. Formative assessment is a delicate balance between planning and flexibility. The librarian should predict how students will respond in this section of the template and should be prepared for a variety of outcomes that he or she must adapt to on the fly. We believe anticipating what students will easily master and what they will find challenging can assist the librarian in using the results effectively. However, when evidence of student understanding is wildly off from what the librarian predicted, discussion is the most flexible remediation tool. Additionally, the instructional design should include a plan for the support of students as they reflect on their learning so they can answer the following three questions: "Where am I going? Where am I now? How can I close the gap?"

Notes for Next Use

Librarians should plan to reflect on their use of formative assessment by taking a few minutes to jot down ideas on what went well and what needs to be changed in future classes. This reflection should make use of both personal reflection and the student data collected from FASTs.

Table 4.1. Formative Assessment Guided Implementation Template	
Learning Target(s):	An education instructor is having students select an issue in special education to research and write a paper on. They must use only peer-reviewed articles from the past five years. **Learning Targets:** • Working understanding of what constitutes a peer-reviewed article • Basic familiarity with the education and psychology databases, the two databases recommended by the instructor • Selection of keywords When I introduce myself, I will share the overarching goal of helping them learn about resources for their upcoming paper. I will highlight the requirements of the paper and how they relate to what they will learn in this class.
ACRL Standard(s):	**Standard 2:** The information literate student accesses needed information effectively and efficiently. Standard 3: The information literate student evaluates information and its sources critically and incorporates selected information into his or her knowledge base and value system.

Table 4.1. Formative Assessment Guided Implementation Template

Formative Assessment Snapshot Technique(s):	This library one-shot class will have no planned lecture. The class handout will guide the class, with a FAST to teach and assess each learning target. **Learning Target 1: Drawing/Visual Assessment (FAST 17)** Students will be asked to draw their understanding of the peer-review process. **Learning Target 2: Grid/Matrix/Semantic Feature Analysis (FAST 21)** Students will be asked to complete a matrix comparing key features of the education and psychology databases with particular emphasis on the features that relate the instructor's assignment. **Learning Target 3: Guided Practice Template (FAST 22)** Several open-ended questions will be asked that require students to brainstorm appropriate keywords, test how to combine the keywords to match their topic, assess the effectiveness of their searches in the database, and analyze how their searches will differ depending on which of the two recommended databases they are using.
What do I anticipate they will master easily? How will I encourage them to go beyond this?	Most students will have already taken the introductory psychology course, so they should be familiar with the basics of that database.
What do I anticipate they will be challenged by? How will I provide additional support?	They will probably be less familiar with the education database, and not all will understand peer-reviewed journals. I do not know how well they will select keywords.
Plan to use formative assessment results:	Each FAST will conclude with a debriefing activity involving a class discussion. This allows me to continue collecting data on their understanding while giving me a chance to provide feedback and encourage students to give each other feedback. Also, if I see groups struggling with certain issues, I could give short mini-lessons.

Table 4.1. Formative Assessment Guided Implementation Template

How will the learners reflect on the process?	Exit Slip (FAST 41): Before leaving the room, students will show me the last two questions on their class handouts, which will be— • How will you determine if a journal article you find in a database is peer-reviewed? • How will your keywords change as you move from the psychology to the education database and vice versa? If we run out of time for individual checks, I will collect the papers, give feedback, and promptly return them to the instructor for redistribution.
Notes for next use:	Overall, I liked the handout and activities chosen for the class. However, I misjudged the level of previous knowledge the students had on doing research. Most were where I assumed they would be, but others had no experience with electronic databases before, and I didn't want to leave them behind. Knowing now that students in this class have varying backgrounds, I may ask the professor to do a Pre-Assessment (FAST 9) or Admit Slip (FAST 1) before the class. Also, many didn't understand my directions about illustrating the peer-review process with the directions: 1. **This assignment requires you to use only peer-reviewed journal articles. In the space below, draw a diagram that represents your understanding of the peer-review process.** Many drew the peer-review process of student papers even though the prompt said journals. I will need to clarify this for next time. But many of the drawings or diagrams students made were excellent. I had one student come put her drawing on the board. Next time I will ask several students to share theirs with the class.

The resulting class handout that includes the four FASTs:

Library Resources for SPED 230

1. This assignment requires you to use only peer-reviewed journal articles. In the space below, draw a diagram that represents your understanding of the peer-review process.

2. Complete the following table that compares the two recommended databases for this assignment.

	ERIC	PsycINFO
What academic discipline does this database cover?		
Does it contain articles from scholarly, trade, or popular journals?		
Is there a way to limit to peer-reviewed journals? If so, how?		
Is there a way to limit to just articles from the past five years? If so, how?		
How do you get the full text of an article?		

3. Brainstorm some keywords for your topic.
4. Now select the best keywords and create a structured search.
5. Try the search in one of the recommended databases. Are you satisfied with your result? ☐ YES ☐ NO
6. If your answer was no, how can you improve your search?

Before you leave the classroom, please show your responses to the following two questions to the librarian.

7. How might your keywords differ depending on which database you are using (PsycINFO vs. ERIC)?
8. How will you determine if an article you found in a database is peer-reviewed?

NOTES

1. Thomas A. Angelo and K. Patricia Cross, *Classroom Assessment Techniques: A Handbook for College Teachers*, 2nd ed. (San Francisco: Jossey-Bass, 1993).
2. Grant P. Wiggins and Jay McTighe, *Understanding by Design* (Alexandria, VA: Association for Supervision and Curriculum Development, 2005).
3. Association of College and Research Libraries, "Information Literacy Competency Standards for Higher Education," ACRL, last modified January 18, 2000, http://www.ala.org/acrl/sites/ala.org.acrl/files/content/standards/standards.pdf.

Chapter 5

Formative Assessment Snapshot Techniques for Before Instruction

The nine formative assessment snapshot techniques (FASTs 1–9) in this chapter are designed to be used before class or at the start of class. For more information about the technology suggested in some of these FASTs, see Chapter 9, "Technology and Formative Assessment in Student Learning."

FAST 1: Admit Slips

Description: Students complete admit slips to assess their existing background knowledge, reinforce or check for understanding of recently learned information, or set the stage for new learning.

Instructor Collaboration: Low

Audience Size: Small, medium, or large*

Feedback Level: Individual, small group, or whole group

Time Frame: 3–10 minutes

Materials/Technology: Admit slip worksheet

Standards:
  ACRL Information Literacy Standards: Any
  Standards for the 21st-Century Learner: Any

How: Select key concepts (or facts) you want students know before beginning the lesson and make an admit slip to check for student understanding of such concepts at the start of class. Once students have completed their slips, ask students report their responses to the whole class or in small groups as you rotate around the room to listen to groups' conversations. After listening to students' responses, make a quick summary of what was discussed and state how it connects to the lesson's learning target(s). If the students' previous knowledge greatly differs from what you anticipated when you designed the lesson plan, adjust your plan as needed.

Ideas for Adapting: Combine admit slips with flipped classrooms so that students complete an assignment before the library class. Then begin class by asking students to respond to a prompt relating to the completed assignment. This holds them accountable for the assignment and sets the stage for the lesson.

*****Ideas for Adapting for Large Audiences:** Use a technological tool, such as Google Forms, Socrative, clickers, or Poll Everywhere, that allows students to enter text and enables you to quickly review many student responses, giving you an overall picture of the class's understanding and a report of trends that can be addressed during the lesson.

Example:

> What is your favorite database to use for history research and why?
>
> Now that you have completed the Goblin Threat plagiarism game (http://www.lycoming.edu/library/instruction/tutorials/plagiarismGame.aspx), name one thing that you learned about plagiarism that you didn't know before.

Figure 5.1. Admit Slips

FAST 2: Anticipation Guides

Description: Students complete anticipation guides to help focus student attention on the learning target(s), assess or activate background knowledge on the topic, or stimulate interest in the topic.

Instructor Collaboration: Low

Audience Size: Small, medium, or large*

Feedback Level: Individual, small group, or whole group

Time Frame: 3–10 minutes

Materials/Technology: Anticipation guide or clickers

Standards:
    ACRL Information Literacy Standards: Any
    Standards for the 21st-Century Learner: Any

How: Prepare an anticipation guide—a list of statements, facts, or opinions that connect to the learning target of the lesson. Ask students to respond by indicating whether they think each statement on the guide is true or false or whether they agree or disagree with the statement. At the end of class, re-administer the assessment and lead a class discussion on the questions where many students changed their minds over the course of the class.

    Tip: Keep this assessment simple—include no more than seven statements, facts, or opinions that are directly connected to the learning target(s).

    ***Ideas for Adapting for Large Audiences:** Use a technological tool, such as Google Forms, Socrative, clickers, or Poll Everywhere, that allows students to enter a response and enables you to quickly review many student responses, giving you an overall picture of the class's understanding and a report of trends that can be addressed during the lesson.

Example:

Before Lesson			After Lesson	
Agree	Disagree		Agree	Disagree
		ERIC is a major database of education-related articles.		

Before Lesson		After Lesson	
	Scholarly journals in education have articles written by well-respected researchers.		
	Trade Magazines in education report the most recent research studies conducted in the field.		
	If I switch around the words from a sentence in an article to form a new sentence and cite the source I am **not plagiarizing**.		

Figure 5.2. Anticipation Guide

FAST 3: Boolean Improvement

Description: Students practice writing effective search phrases, and the Boolean Improvement technique serves as a quick and easy pre- and posttest that assesses students' ability to select keywords and demonstrate understanding of Boolean operators.

Instructor Collaboration: Low

Audience Size: Small, medium, or large*

Feedback Level: Individual, small group, or whole group

Time Frame: 5 minutes

Materials/Technology: None required, though students may benefit from Internet access to test their search phrase's effectiveness

Standards:
   ACRL Information Literacy Standards:
      Standard 2: The information literate student accesses needed information effectively and efficiently.
   Standards for the 21st-Century Learner:
      Standard 1: Inquire, think critically, and gain knowledge.
      Standard 2: Draw conclusions, make informed decisions, apply knowledge to new situations, and create new knowledge.

How: At the beginning of an information literacy class (or even before, with instructor collaboration), ask students to write search phrases for their topics using both AND and OR. Walk around and quickly review students' search phrases to assess their current level of understanding and make decisions about the extent to which you will address this topic is addressed in class. Towards the end of the class, instruct students to write new search phrases using what they have learned during the lesson and explain why the new phrases are better. If students have Internet access, they can test the effectiveness of their search phrases in databases. This activity is best done as a small group so that students can correct each other. At the end, facilitate a whole group discussion to provide reinforcement or correction as needed.

   Ideas for Adapting: Use TodaysMeet and Google Forms to allow students to submit their searches and explanations anonymously. Display them at the front of the classroom and read them aloud to the class and provide any necessary feedback or demonstrations.

***Ideas for Adapting for Large Audiences:** Use a technological tool that allows students to enter text (Google Forms, Twitter, TodaysMeet, Socrative, blog comments) and enables you to quickly review many student responses, giving you an overall picture of the class's understanding and a report of trends that can be addressed during the lesson.

NOTE

Debra Gilchrist and Anne Zald, "Instruction and Program Design through Assessment," in *Information Literacy Instruction Handbook*, ed. Christopher N. Cox and Elizabeth Blakesley (Chicago: Association of College and Research Libraries, 2008), 164–92.

FAST 4: Brainstorming

Description: Students create a mental map of ideas or strategies for information literacy concepts, allowing the librarian to see the thought process as students brainstorm on a task, concept, or idea.

Instructor Collaboration: Low

Audience Size: Small or medium

Feedback Level: Individual

Time Frame: 10+ minutes

Materials/Technology: Guided Practice Template (FAST 22) or Graphic Organizer (FAST 20) or blank paper

Standards:
    ACRL Information Literacy Standards:
        Standard 1: The information literate student determines the nature and extent of the information needed.
    Standards for the 21st-Century Learner:
        Standard 1: Inquire, think critically, and gain knowledge.
        Standard 4: Pursue personal and aesthetic growth.

How: Using a Guided Practice Template (FAST 22) or Graphic Organizer (FAST 20) that specifically supports students' brainstorming process, ask students to write all thoughts that come to mind for their research topic. This allows you to see what students are thinking about their assignments or research projects. Students may not be sure on how to start a project or which library sources they should be using. By doing the brainstorming assessment, both you and the students see what students already know about researching their topic or what they may struggle with. This assessment helps you and the students most effectively focus their efforts in completing the early stages of the research process.

    Tip: Help students get the most out of this assessment by giving them a list of topics they can brainstorm about; use a blank piece of paper for a more open-ended assessment.

    Example: Students in a psychology class were asked by their instructor to research common proverbs, such as "Love is blind" and "Absence makes the heart grow fonder," within a psychological context. Students' goals of the research paper were to support or refute the main idea of each proverb with empirical studies and peer-reviewed articles. The instructor explained to the librarian that she was frustrated by the fact that students simply typed the proverb into the search box and then reported that they could not get any results. To steer students away from this habit, the librarian created a simple guided practice template asking students to pick out certain concepts about their proverb before even searching a database or conducting research.

As students filled in concepts and brainstormed with partners in the class, the librarian walked around the room, helping students define keywords and correcting any misunderstandings about which terms were likely to work in the databases.

Below is an example of the guided practice template used for a brainstorming technique designed to help students research a common proverb within a psychological context. This example was completed by student Bryanna Garnett at Lycoming College.

> Bryanna Garnett
> **"What is Research, but a Blind Date with Knowledge"**
> –British chemist, *William J. Henry* (1774-1836)
> **Social Proverb Research in Snowden Library**
> Dr. Norton   PSY 220   September 30, 2013
>
> Proverb/Saying: <u>Every rose has its thorn</u>
> (Circle main terms that could be used in the databases)
>
> **Brainstorming Keywords**
>
> For each area, write as many key terms that will help you search the databases.
>
> What does the saying actually mean?/Interpretation (Circle key words)
> Everything or everyone that is (beautiful) also has (flaws) – every (relationship) has (pain) – what is perceived may not be true.
>
> Off the top of your head:
> beauty, attraction, negatives, friendships/marriage, suffering, struggle/effort
>
> Psychology terminology:
> interpersonal relationships, idealize, perfection, impressions, attributions (happy vs unhappy) dysfunctional beliefs
> ↳ getting to know someone, familiarity
>
> Textbook words (Are there chapters in your textbook that encompass to this proverb?):
> Attribution theory, impression management, idealism
>
> Synonyms/Antonyms (Sometimes searching the opposite works!):
> Attraction, imperfections, interactions or associations, ache, struggle/ ugly, strength, *enemy, pleasure or wellness
>
> More key terms found after initial research:
> * adult attitudes * marital conflicts * self-monitoring

Figure 5.3. Brainstorming Technique Template Use Example.

FAST 5: Crystal Balls or Wish Lists

Description: Students are given a short amount of time at the beginning of an information literacy class to guess what the lesson will be about or to make a list of what they want to learn.

Instructor Collaboration: Low

Audience Size: Small, medium, or large*

Feedback Level: Individual, small group, or whole group

Time Frame: 5 minutes

Materials/Technology: Paper or poster board

Standards:
    ACRL Information Literacy Standards: Any
    Standards for the 21st-Century Learner: Any

How: This assessment is likely to reveal preconceptions, anxieties, or students' own learning targets that you can address and incorporate into the lesson. Set aside the first five minutes of class for students to quickly write what they think the class will be about. They can also be encouraged to write any specific topics or questions they have. You can indicate which ideas will be met with the planned lesson and incorporate discussions or demonstrations to meet students' additional learning targets.

You can collect student responses in multiple ways. Through Think-Pair-Share (FAST 33), give students a short time to quietly reflect and then talk in small groups. Later, ask each group to share their ideas with the class. Or instruct students to write their questions and ideas on a sheet of poster board at the front of the room where you can mark off questions as they are addressed during the lesson. Finally, record individual responses through Google Forms or TodaysMeet and then shared with the class through a projector.

*****Ideas for Adapting for Large Audiences:** Use a technological tool that allows students to enter text (Google Forms, Twitter, TodaysMeet, Socrative, blog comments) and enables you to quickly review many student responses, giving you an overall picture of the class's expectations for the lesson and a report of wishes that can be addressed during the lesson.

Example: Below is a crystal ball assessment completed by education students at Lycoming College.

> How to find reference books in the library.
>
> What are kid friendly databases?
>
> Are technology or book references more important to teach?
>
> How to find books when given the number of where it is
>
> How do you know sources are credible?
>
> How to determine if websites are age/grade appropriate?
>
> How do you keep kids interested in the research project?

Figure 5.4. Crystal Ball Exercise Example.

NOTE

Douglas Fisher and Nancy Frey, *Checking for Understanding: Formative Assessment Techniques for Your Classroom* (Alexandria, VA: ASCD, 2007), 68.

FAST 6: KWL Charts

Description: Before a lesson, students fill out a chart with what they think they **k**now regarding the learning target(s) and what they **w**ant to know. Later, they fill in what they **l**earned.

Instructor Collaboration: Low

Audience Size: Small or medium

Feedback Level: Individual

Time Frame: 15+ minutes

Materials/Technology: KWL chart

Standards:
  ACRL Information Literacy Standards: Any
  Standards for the 21st-Century Learner: Any

How: Before class, or at the beginning of class, ask students to complete a chart, describing what they already **k**now about the learning target(s) in the K column of the worksheet and what they **w**ant to know about their topic in the W column. If students do not know much about their topics yet, instruct them to look their topics up in a reference book to complete the first two columns. Then give them class time to search for articles and books on their topic, encouraging them to carefully read abstracts and summaries along the way.

Move around the classroom, reading what students have written in the K and W columns and giving tips to individuals as necessary. During the last ten minutes of the class, ask students to record a brief summary of what they **l**earned from the research done during the class and about the skills and tools they used to find it. Additionally, ask them to note any areas or skills or tools where they feel their understanding is weak. Then lead a discussion with students to cement their understanding of concepts learned and to respond to any areas where the students identify as needing more information.

You can also collect the worksheets, provide written responses in the form of tips or encouragement, and return them to the instructor in a timely manner to be redistributed to the students.

Example: In an upper-level math course, students had to research a math concept by looking at its history and/or its development using library materials. For example, a student may want to research how using statistics in gambling began, its popularity, and how it is utilized. The librarian asked students to tell her what they **k**now about library resources at the beginning of class. With this information, she was able to see the math students' lack of knowledge about the library materials. Since students already had their topics, they were then able to describe **w**hat they would need to know about the library to succeed in accessing materials. At the end of the class, the librarian had students describe resources they **l**earned about and students presented their findings to the class.

(K) What I Know	**(W) What I Want to Know**	**(L) What I Learned**
The library books are on the third floor. Reference books are on the first floor.	Which call numbers are usually associated with math books? Does the library carry encyclopedias that can give me better ideas on a possible topic?	There are also books on the fourth floor. Books starting with the call number "QA" deal with math topics. I can search the library's catalog and limit by subject area to refine my topic. The library has multiple encyclopedias to help me with research ideas, but also I can use Reference Universe to search for other reference book articles.

Figure 5.5. Sample KWL Chart

FAST 7: Library Jeopardy!

Description: Students play Library *Jeopardy!*, a fun trivia game, to help the librarian assess students' background knowledge.

Instructor Collaboration: Low

Audience Size: Small or medium

Feedback Level: Whole group

Time Frame: 10–15 minutes

Materials/Technology: Preferably a projector and *Jeopardy!* PowerPoint template. Buzzers such as "Me First" Personal Answer Domes™ help definitively determine which team buzzed in first. However, this technique can be done with questions printed on paper, taped to the wall face down, and hand-raising or squeaky toys

Standards:
    ACRL Information Literacy Standards: Any
    Standards for the 21st-Century Learner: Any

How: Introduce the game and divide the class into the desired number of teams. Arrange the questions in a grid so that columns represent categories and rows have increasing point values. Instruct teams to take turns selecting a category. Read the question and call on the team that buzzes in (or raises hands) first to answer. If the answer is correct, the game continues. If it is incorrect, the question is open to other teams. Take quick notes on your observations of the class's knowledge. If students ask questions about an answer they do not understand or disagree with, lead a mini-discussion without overly disrupting the flow of the game. Use the information gathered on students' previous knowledge to refer to for the remainder of the class.

    Tips:
- Ask the instructor to keep track of scoring and be in charge of determining which team responded first if buzzers are unavailable.
- Deviate from the official *Jeopardy!* rules. At our institution, we do not penalize for wrong answers; we do not require respondents to form answers in the phrase of a question; and we have teams take turns choosing the question rather than the winner of the previous question, which can partially alleviate one team dominating the entire game.

- Lead the affective aspects of the game experience and make all efforts to keep the competition friendly.

Ideas for Adapting: Pre-assessment trivia games can be done in many ways. At our institution, Use a 5 x 5 tic-tac-toe grid drawn on a poster board and laid on the floor. The class was divided into two teams, each one represented by a type of individually-wrapped candy. The librarian took turns reading each team a trivia question relating to completing library research in that academic discipline. If the team got the answer correct, they were directed to place a piece of their candy on a square of their choosing. If they answer incorrectly, the other team has a chance to answer the question. The goal for each team is to capture four squares in a row. As the games are completed quickly, we often conducted at least two rounds of the game. At the end of the game, all students are invited to eat the candy.

Example:

Reference Books	Articles	Library Policies	Help Resources	Plagiarism
1	1	1	1	1
2	2	2	2	2
3	3	3	3	3
4	4	4	4	4

Figure 5.6. Example of Library Jeopardy! Completed Board.

Sample Questions:

Reference Books for 1:
Encyclopedias and dictionaries are examples of what type of resource?

Reference Books for 2:
On which floor of the library is the Reference Department?

Reference Books for 3:
What call numbers contain most of the psychology resources in the Reference Department?

Reference Books for 4:
Why can't you do all your research using Reference Resources?

NOTES

Billie E. Walker, "This is *Jeopardy!* An Exciting Approach to Learning in Library Instruction," *Reference Services Review* 36, no. 4 (November 2008): 381–388.

Guy J. Leach and Tammy S. Sugarman, "Play to Win! Using Games in Library Instruction to Enhance Student Learning," *Research Strategies* 20, no. 3 (2005): 191–203.

FAST 8: Predicting

Description: Students predict the results before performing a task. They then perform the task and compare their prediction to what actually happened.

Instructor Collaboration: Low

Audience Size: Small, medium, or large

Feedback Level: Individual, small group, or whole group

Time Frame: 2–10 minutes

Materials/Technology: Predicting worksheet

Standards:
   ACRL Information Literacy Standards:
      Standard 3: The information literate student evaluates information and its sources critically and incorporates selected information into his or her knowledge base and value system.
   Standards for the 21st-Century Learner:
      Standard 1: Inquire, think critically, and gain knowledge.
      Standard 2: Draw conclusions, make informed decisions, apply knowledge to new situations, and create new knowledge.

How: This technique is based on students' critical reflection on the scientific process. Ask students to write a prediction about what they expect to happen after a stated task or action. For example, you can ask how the number of results in a database is likely to be affected when you add additional keywords with AND or OR. Students can verbally respond "more" or "less," or you can request that they raise hands to indicate their prediction. You can also ask students to record written predictions in more detail while exploring recommended resources with a partner. You can also give students a search phrase and ask them to predict how effective it will be. Students can then perform the search, evaluate the results, and reflect on how those results confirm or refute their prediction. At the end of the assessment, lead students in a discussion of their results and draw conclusions about how the tools or concepts work. This discussion allows you to determine whether students have met the learning target or need more practice.
   Example: At the beginning of a capstone business class, the librarian asked students to reflect on their past experiences with business

databases and to use that knowledge to predict which databases would be useful for their current information needs. In this example, they each determined their own research needs based on their individual internship experiences. They then had time to test how successful each database was in meeting their chosen needs. The librarian then reassembled the class and led a discussion on students' conclusions about how well each database gave the predicted results.

> I. Think about your research skills. What information projects have you completed during your junior and senior years? Describe the course and any library databases you recall using.
>
> *In my junior year, I took BUS244 which helped with my management research skills. To find out how a company could best enter a new market in a foreign country, I used Business Source Premier to research successful companies in China. I also used LexisNexis to read current newspapers that talked about China's coffee and tea industry. I feel I excel now in reading industry reports and trade news to help any company I work with in the future.*
>
> II. Thinking about your current internship, what information would you take to your supervisor to show your research expertise? Which library databases do you predict will have the best information on this topic?
>
> | Topic/Information Needed | Databases: |
> |---|---|
> | A. *Best practices in website development* | A. *LexisNexis Academic* |
> | B. *Trends in purchasing clothing online* | B. *Hoover's* |
> | C. *Competing companies* | C. *Hoover's* |
> | D. *Financial statements of Company X* | D. *Reference USA* |
>
> III. Now use a computer to see how well your database meets each information need. Which databases met your need? Which did not? Record your observations below and be prepared to discuss with the class.
>
> *Hoover's was not the best resource for showing trends. It only showed minimal information. It does show competing companies. However, I was looking for United States information, not the foreign countries Hoover's showed. Business Source Premier had better trends information in trade publications. The other databases provided the predicted information.*

Figure 5.7. Business Capstone Example.

FAST 9: Pre-Assessments

Description: Pre-assessments are simple surveys conducted before class to find out what students know before they receive library instruction.

Instructor Collaboration: Medium

Audience Size: Small, medium, or large

Feedback Level: Individual or whole group

Time Frame: Takes place before the library class

Materials/Technology: Survey, which can be facilitated with tools such as Google Forms, SurveyMonkey, or course management software

Standards:
    ACRL Information Literacy Standards: Any
    Standards for the 21st-Century Learner: Any

How: After analyzing the instructor's assignment, design a survey based on relevant library tools and skills students will need to be successful. Then send the survey to the instructor approximately a week before the library class is scheduled. The instructor asks students to complete the survey as homework, and then collects the responses and returns them to you. Tally students' responses into three categories:
    1. Does not understand
    2. Shows some understanding
    3. Understands

Determine which areas are the strongest and weakest. If all students know what tool to use to find books, do not include it in the lesson. If most show understanding on a topic but some do not, briefly touch on that topic or include it in a handout, but do not focus on in it in class. Focus on areas where students are the weakest. Use students' answers, without displaying names, as examples to discuss in class, making the learning experience more authentic.

    Tip: Ask one question at a time. We have found that if we ask a question such as "What database helps you find reference book articles and what are they good for?" students only answer one of the two questions.

Example:
The following survey was conducted with a 300-level criminal justice class approximately two weeks before they were scheduled to come into the library.

---

1. What is the primary database for scholarly articles on criminal justice at the Snowden Library?
2. What database helps you find newspaper articles and legal information?
3. What are newspaper articles good for when writing a scholarly paper?
4. What database helps you find individual articles in reference books?
5. What are reference book articles good for in the research process?
6. What online tool helps you find books at the Snowden Library?
7. What database helps you find books that you can order through Interlibrary Loan?
8. What secondary database might you find useful for criminal justice because it covers sociology?
9. What search words would you type into the database if you were looking for information on how gender affects the rates of criminals repeating their illegal behaviors after being released from prison?

Figure 5.8. Sample Survey

The first semester this was implemented, students demonstrated almost no understanding of keyword creation, with most students providing a long phrase for Question 9. The class spent some time on the recommended research tools and learned how to use newspaper articles in a scholarly paper, but the majority of class time focused on keyword selection.

NOTE:
Thomas A. Angelo and K. Patricia Cross, "Background Knowledge Probe," in *Classroom Assessment Techniques: A Handbook for College Teachers*, 2nd ed. (San Francisco: Jossey-Bass, 1993), 121–125.

Chapter 6

Formative Assessment Snapshot Techniques for During Instruction

The twenty-seven formative assessment snapshot techniques (FASTs 10–37) in this chapter are designed to be used during class. For more information about the technology suggested in some of these FASTs, see Chapter 9, "Technology and Formative Assessment in Student Learning."

FAST 10: 10:2 Reflections

Description: Every ten minutes, students take two minutes to reflect on what they are learning.

Instructor Collaboration: Low

Audience Size: Small, medium, or large*

Feedback Level: Individual, small group, or whole group

Time Frame: 12+ minutes

Materials/Technology: Pre-made template, sticky notes or blank paper for students to record responses

Standards:
    ACRL Information Literacy Standards: Any
    Standards for the 21st-Century Learner: Any

How: Before class, determine what type of reflection is desired from the students (summary, analysis, clarification, or a combination of all three). After ten minutes of the lesson passes, pause to ask students to respond using the chosen type of reflection. Have students discuss and clarify their responses as appropriate—contribute to the discussion when necessary. Then continue the lesson, incorporating student feedback.

Tip: Try just one 10:2 reflection per class until you feel comfortable using the student responses to determine the next steps in the lesson.

Ideas for Adapting:
- Vary the amount of time between assessments, teaching for fifteen minutes and having students reflect for three minutes.
- Ask students to reflect individually, with a partner, or in small groups. Divide the lesson into chunks based on learning targets.
- After each chunk of material, pause and ask students to reflect on what they have just learned before moving on.

*****Ideas for Adapting for Large Audiences:** Use a technological tool that allows students to enter text (Google Forms, Twitter, TodaysMeet, Socrative, blog comments) and enables you to quickly review many student responses, giving you an overall picture of the class's understanding and a report of trends that can be addressed during the lesson.

Example:

Now that we have looked at the recommended resources for this topic, match the topic with the kind of resource that would be best (each topic have more than one appropriate resource).	
1. Sports	1. Books
2. History	2. Newspaper articles
3. Biographies	3. Biography Resource Center
4. Current events	

Figure 6.1. Resource Matching

FAST 11: Bingo

Description: Students play bingo as a fun way to check for understanding of key concepts and terms.

Instructor Collaboration: Low

Audience Size: Small, medium, or large

Feedback Level: Whole group

Time Frame: 5–15 minutes

Materials/Technology: Blank bingo cards, bingo chips, and a list of key terms and descriptions

Standards:
  ACRL Information Literacy Standards: Any
  Standards for the 21st-Century Learner: Any

How: Give students a list of key terms and a bingo card and direct them to randomly write the terms on the card's blank squares. Then read a term's definition or description and have students place a bingo chip on the corresponding term. When a student shouts "Bingo!" to signal he or she has five chips in a row, he or she reads the five *terms* to the class while you check whether his or her answers are correct. When the winner has been confirmed, re-read each *description*. Ask the rest of the class to give a thumbs-up or thumbs-down to indicate whether they knew the corresponding term. This helps you check each individual's level of understanding, not just the winner's. If you notice a significant number of students had difficulty matching a term with its description, provide more discussion and examples to support students' understanding.

  Ideas for Adapting:
  - To save class time, create the bingo cards before class—be sure each card is different. To make this less time-consuming, ask students to complete the cards the first time, then collect the cards for use in future classes.
  - Using bingo cards with key places and people in the library, instruct students to find those places and people and have the appropriate person initial "their" square to show the student correctly found the location.

FAST 12: Blog Comments

Description: Students use the comment feature of the library blog to contribute to class discussions individually or in pairs. (This technique is from Abate, Gomes, and Linton.)

Instructor Collaboration: Low

Audience Size: Small, medium, or large

Feedback Level: Individual or small group

Time Frame: 5–10 minutes

Materials/Technology: Internet access, computers or tablets, and blog with question posted

Standards:
   ACRL Information Literacy Standards:
      Standard 3: The information literate student evaluates information and its sources critically and incorporates selected information into his or her knowledge base and value system. This assessment could be adapted to address other standards.
   Standards for the 21st-Century Learner: Any

How: This exercise is particularly good for large classes with tablets or in a computer lab where individual participation is difficult to manage. Before class, post a question on a blog. In the post, provide links to two websites for students to compare. Then instruct students to use the comment feature of the blog to vote for the more credible of the two sites and provide the reasoning behind their decisions. Quickly evaluate the results from the front of the room and lead a class discussion.

   Tip: Use the library's main blog so that the students can find it easily from the library website. Abate, Gomes, and Linton did this, and right after the class, they deleted the post so other visitors to the blog did not see it.

NOTE
Laura E. Abate, Alexandra Gomes, and Anne Linton, "Engaging Students in Active Learning: Use of a Blog and Audience Response System," *Medical Reference Services Quarterly* 30, no. 1 (2011): 12–18.

FAST 13: Boolean Operators Shading

Description: Students complete a Venn diagram showing their understanding of Boolean operators.

Instructor Collaboration: Low

Audience Size: Small, medium, or large

Feedback Level: Individual

Time Frame: 1–2 minutes

Materials/Technology: Boolean operator graphic organizer

Standards:
  ACRL Information Literacy Standards:
    Standard 2: The information literate student accesses needed information effectively and efficiently.
  Standards for the 21st-Century Learner:
    Standard 2: Draw conclusions, make informed decisions, apply knowledge to new situations, and create new knowledge.

How: The advantage to this assessment is that you can judge each student's understanding in a fraction of a second. When discussing how AND and OR work in databases, direct students to the worksheet (see example below). Ask them to pretend that each dot represents an article and the circles represent which articles can be retrieved for a particular keyword search in a database. Instruct students to shade the areas that represent the articles that would be retrieved for a particular search using Boolean operators. Move around the classroom to look at their results or ask students to hold up their papers. A quick glance allows you to judge their understanding and provide individual feedback for those who require it.

Example:
Each dot represents an article in a database. Shade the area that would represent the list of results that would be retrieved for the search ATHLETES AND HEART RATE

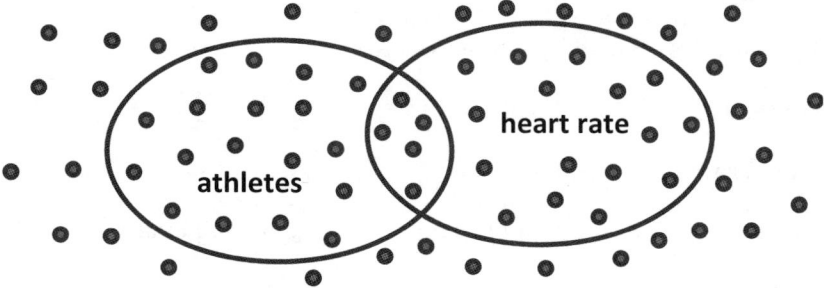

Figure 6.2. "Athletes and Heart Rate" Search Results

Shade the area that would represent the list of results that would be retrieved for the search CIGARETTES OR SMOKING

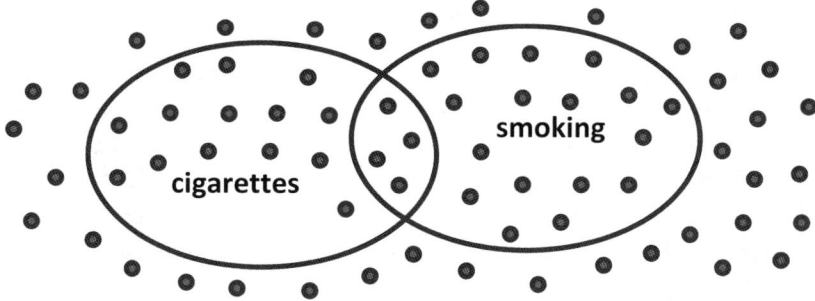

Figure 6.3. "Cigarettes or Smoking" Search Results

FAST 14: Checklists

Description: Students use checklists to initiate self-assessment and metacognition to determine what they need to do to reach learning targets based on their current level of knowledge or understanding.

Instructor Collaboration: Low or medium

Audience Size: Small, medium, or large*

Feedback Level: Individual

Time Frame: 5 minutes

Materials/Technology: Checklist

Standards:
   ACRL Information Literacy Standards: Any
   Standards for the 21st-Century Learner: Any

How: First, determine the types of skills, strategies, or thinking the students need to gain as a result of the lesson and create a corresponding checklist. Share this checklist with the students at the start of the lesson so they are aware of the lesson's learning target(s) and so you can refer to it as the lesson progresses. Periodically, ask students to identify what they feel they have grasped and what they still need to know. Use student feedback to gear the teaching and learning toward their needs. This activity also encourages students to practice the type of thinking they need to become independent in the learning process.

This assessment relies on students' ability to self-assess. While it does not directly demonstrate their ability to meet the learning targets, it indicates their level of confidence in their abilities. If students are not confident, they will not check the box, which will either cause them to raise their hand and ask for help during individual work time, or they will not check the box, which will prompt you or the instructor to ask if they need help in that area.

Ideas for Adapting:
- Do this technique outside of the library one-shot with instructor collaboration. Ask students to periodically turn in checklists indicating their confidence in their ability to meet goals appropriate to various stages of the research process. Provide a space under each of the checklist's categories for comments or

questions, allowing you and the instructor an opportunity to provide assistance.
- Use checklists as Exit Slips (FAST 41) where students must have all boxes checked before they can leave class.

***Ideas for Adapting for Large Audiences:** Use a technological tool that allows students to enter text (Google Forms, Twitter, TodaysMeet, Socrative, blog comments) and enables you to quickly review many student responses, giving you an overall picture of the class's understanding and a report of trends that can be addressed during the lesson.

Example:

Before leaving class today, please confirm you agree with the following statements by checking the corresponding boxes:
☐ 1. I have decided on my research topic and it fits the instructor's assignment criteria.
☐ 2. I can explain what my research topic is and how it meets the instructor's assignment criteria.
☐ 3. I can explain how I will begin searching for information related to my topic.
☐ 4. I can explain how two sources I found provide information that supports my topic.
☐ 5. I can explain how one source I found contradicts my topic/thesis.

Figure 6.4. Exit Slips

NOTE
Violet H. Harada and Joan M. Yoshina, *Assessing for Learning: Librarians and Teachers as Partner* (Santa Barbara, CA: Libraries Unlimited, 2010), 20–22.

Formative Assessment Snapshot Techniques for During Instruction **103**

FAST 15: Citation on Walls

Description: Students work in teams to assemble citations on the classroom's walls.

Instructor Collaboration: Low

Audience Size: Small or medium

Feedback Level: Small group

Time Frame: 20 minutes

Materials/Technology: Citations printed on colored paper, punctuation marks on another color, photocopies of the relevant citation manual pages with helpful examples highlighted, a physical copy of each source to be cited, and tape

Standards:
    ACRL Information Literacy Standards:
        Standard 5: The information literate student understands many of the economic, legal, and social issues surrounding the use of information and accesses and uses information ethically and legally.
    Standards for the 21st-Century Learner:
        Standard 1: Inquire, think critically, and gain knowledge.
        Standard 2: Draw conclusions, make informed decisions, apply knowledge to new situations, and create new knowledge.

How: Before class, locate subject-relevant sources that fit the assignment criteria and create a citation for each source using a word processor. Enlarge the citations to 100-point font on "landscape" orientation, then print each citation on a different color of paper. Next, print all necessary punctuation marks on a color not being used by any of the citations. Cut the citations into strips, removing punctuation. Then tape each piece of the citation (author, article title, journal title, etc.) together to make one strip of paper. For example, if an author's name is in two parts, "Smith" and "John," tape them together. If there are multiple authors, keep the authors' names on individual strips.

In class, divide students into teams and give each team a source to be cited, the strips of citation pieces for that source, a photocopy of the relevant page of the citation manual, and tape. Direct students to the pile of punctuation at a central location in the room. Ask students to spread out around the room and tape their citations to the wall. Rotate around the room and offer help as needed. When students are done assembling their citations, lead a class discussion about each citation, reviewing the rules, guiding students to correct their errors, and using the manual as a resource/reference.

Tips:
- Give yourself plenty of time to prepare for this technique—it takes a significant amount of time to get ready.
- Include at least one source that has multiple authors as this provides an opportunity to talk about students' common misperception that authors should be listed alphabetically.

Example:

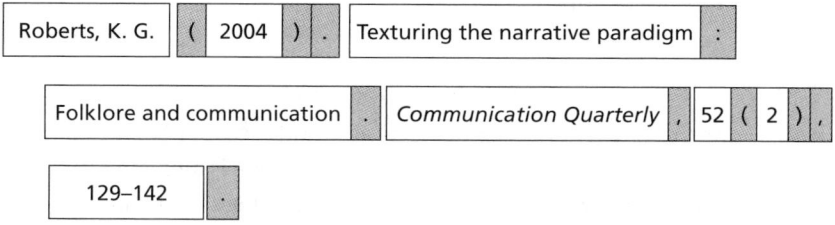

Figure 6.5. Citation exercise

FAST 16: Clickers

Description: Students use clickers to respond to respond to the librarian's questions. The immediate results can be interpreted immediately and the librarian can adjust instruction as a result.

Instructor Collaboration: Low

Audience Size: Small, medium, or large

Feedback Level: Individual or whole group

Time Frame: 10+ minutes

Materials/Technology: Clicker software and hardware and a projector

Standards:
    ACRL Information Literacy Standards: Any
    Standards for the 21st-Century Learner: Any

How: Create questions before class in PowerPoint or the clickers' software. Throughout the exercise, ask students questions and have them answer individually using their clickers. Questions can focus on previous knowledge or serve as comprehension checks after material is covered in lectures and activities. Be prepared to adapt the instruction based on the results. The easiest way to dynamically adjust lesson content based on students' needs is to lead a discussion after each result is posted if there is a clear misunderstanding or mixed results. Students may have misunderstood the question (which can be improved for next time), or a student who comprehends the concept can explain it in a way that is understood by those who were confused the first time. Clickers can also be used to debrief after a learning activity.

    Tip: Be sure to mix factual questions (low-level learning) with questions that require students to think critically about what they have just learned (high-level thinking).

    Ideas for Adapting:
- Use low-tech alternatives to clickers such as Fist-to-Five (FAST 18) and Response Cards (FAST 30). These alternatives are often more flexible and do not require special hardware or software.
- Use websites Poll Everywhere or Socrative instead of clickers. Poll Everywhere allows students to use their cell phones to report their answers. Socrative allows students to use any Internet-connected device (i.e. computer, smart phone, tablet, etc.)

to report their answers, and it also permits students to write responses to open-ended questions.
- Use clickers to debrief after a learning activity.

Example:

Question 1:
Larsen, L. (2012). A new design approach to game-based learning. *Journal of Interactive Learning Research*, 23(4), 313–323.

Is this a citation for a:
A. Book
B. Scholarly Article
C. Newspaper

Question 2:
According to the Centers for Disease Control, what percentage of Americans are overweight or obese?
A. 25%
B. 40%
C. 66%

Question 3:
You have an assignment to write a paper for your psychology class about babies' exposure to television and whether it is harmful. What are the best keywords for your search on this topic?

A. infants AND television
B. harmful AND TV
C. effects AND babies

Figure 6.6. Clicker Questions

Question 1: After the class's results were displayed, the librarian asked students to share what clues they used to make their selection.

Question 2: They were not expected to know the answer to this question. The point of this question is how surprising and powerful statistics are in creating an argument; therefore, they are worth looking for on government sites or polling databases.

Question 3: This is an example of a multiple-choice question where students have to think critically about part of a simulated research topic to choose an answer. The librarian showed the answer and led a discussion on how students came to choose the answers they did.

NOTES

Charlotte L. Briggs and Deborah Keyek-Franssen, "Clickers and CATs: Using Learner Response Systems for Formative Assessments in the Classroom," *EDUCAUSE Quarterly* 33, no. 4 (2010): n.p.

Bobbie L. Collins, Rosalind Tedford, and H. David Womack. "'Debating' the Merits of Clickers in an Academic Library," *North Carolina Libraries* 66, no. 1-2 (2008): 20–24.

Michelle Kathleen Dunaway and Michael Teague Orblych, "Formative Assessment: Transforming Information Literacy Instruction," *Reference Services Review* 39, no. 1 (2011): 24–41.

FAST 17: Visual Assessments

Description: Students create drawings or diagrams that represent their understanding of various information literacy concepts.

Instructor Collaboration: Low

Audience Size: Small or medium

Feedback Level: Individual or small group

Time Frame: 10+ minutes

Materials/Technology: Paper, markers, and rulers

Standards:
   ACRL Information Literacy Standards: Any
   For the examples show below—
      Standard 3: The information literate student evaluates information and its sources critically and incorporates selected information into his or her knowledge base and value system.
   Standards for the 21st-Century Learner: Any
   For the examples shown below—
      Standard 1: Inquire, think critically, and gain knowledge.
      Standard 2: Draw conclusions, make informed decisions, apply knowledge to new situations, and create new knowledge.

How: Instruct students to work individually or in groups to draw an example or diagram of information literacy concept. For example, ask students to draw a picture of a popular and a scholarly journal or a diagram of the peer review process. Rotate around the room answering questions and providing suggestions. Have groups take turns showing their examples to the class; ask group members questions and facilitate a class discussion to make sure the lesson content is covered, preferably by the students themselves.

This can be done with any information literacy topic. Students can be asked to draw an abstract representation of their understanding of an information literacy concept, such as the peer review process. The librarian can ask students for further explanation of their drawings as appropriate.

Tip: Set a time limit and remind students of it periodically—students tend to get carried away with their art work even after initial hesitation.

Formative Assessment Snapshot Techniques for During Instruction

Examples:

Figure 6.7. A drawing created by a group of education students at Lycoming College illustrating examples of scholarly, trade, and popular journals.

1. This assignment requires you to use only peer-reviewed journal articles, in the space below, draw a diagram that represents your understanding of the peer-review process:

Figure 6.8. A diagram of the peer review process created by Carly Brower at Lycoming College.

FAST 18: Fist-to-Five

Description: Students check their own understanding or assess their level of knowledge to help them develop metacognitive thinking skills.

Instructor Collaboration: Low

Audience Size: Small, medium, or large

Feedback Level: Individual, small group, or whole group

Time Frame: 1–5 minutes

Standards:
  ACRL Information Literacy Standards: Any
  Standards for the 21st-Century Learner: Any

Materials/Technology: None

How: Instruct students to give you a hand signal to indicate their level of understanding. The most basic hand signals are thumbs-up, thumbs-down, and thumbs-in-the-middle. You can ask students to indicate how they feel they are progressing towards the learning target(s), making a judgment call, or evaluating a resource. You can also ask students to rate their knowledge or confidence in using a show of fingers (one being low and five being very high). Evaluate student responses and conduct a class discussion to clarify any uncertain concepts. Once a discussion is held, conduct another fist-to-five assessment to ensure all the concepts were understood.

  Tip: Use fist-to-five to check students' understanding of simple learning targets—students are can accurately assess this level of knowledge.

  Ideas for Adapting: Use the rating systems described above to have students indicate their level of confidence that their response to a question or prompt is on target with what the librarian expects for thorough understanding.

Example:
Librarian: "Looking at this document from the National Center for Education Statistics, do you think it's a reliable source to use for your paper? Thumbs-up, thumbs-down, or thumbs-in-the-middle if you're not sure."

  Librarian: "Bobby has three tests and a paper due in the same week and falls behind. He has a paper he wrote for his freshman English class last year that would work for his anthropology class this semester. Would it be plagiarism for him to turn it in? Thumbs-up means yes, it would be plagiarism; thumbs-down means no, it would not be plagiarism; thumbs-in-the-middle means you're not sure."

Librarian: "You have to find a scholarly journal for this assignment. How confident do you feel in using the database to accomplish this? One finger means you don't know where to start; five fingers mean you are very comfortable."

NOTE

Douglas Fisher and Nancy Frey, *The Purposeful Classroom: How to Structure Lessons with Learning Goals in Mind* (Alexandria, VA: ASCD, 2011), 129–130.

FAST 19: Four Corners

Description: Students demonstrate their evaluation of a concept by physically moving to designated corners or locations in the classroom.

Standard 3: Share knowledge and participate ethically and productively as members of our democratic society.

Instructor Collaboration: Low

Audience Size: Small or medium

Feedback Level: Individual, small group, or whole group

Time Frame: 5+ minutes

Materials/Technology: Signs to label the four choices in the classroom, but they are not necessary

Standards:
  ACRL Information Literacy Standards:
    Standard 3: The information literate student evaluates information and its sources critically and incorporates selected information into his or her knowledge base and value system.
  Standards for the 21st-Century Learner:
    Standard 2: Draw conclusions, make informed decisions, apply knowledge to new situations, and create new knowledge.

How: Ask students to evaluate a concept. Then ask them to match their evaluation with one of four choices and demonstrate their choice by physically moving to a designated corner of the classroom. This requires all students to be actively involved, and it allows them to compare their own opinions or ideas with others in the class. As students make their choices, ask students to share why they chose what they did. Through this questioning, correct misconceptions or open up the floor to debate.

Example:
An instructor was frustrated that her students were keeping every article or resource they found while doing research. They needed help in determining which resources were best for their assignment. Also, their assignment required finding primary as well as secondary sources and students struggled in defining the difference. For the library class,

students were shown print and image resources along with citations. As students viewed the resource on display, they chose which corner of the room best suited their opinion on the resource. The four choices students had are represented here:

Primary Source— Good for my topic	Secondary Source— Good for my topic
Primary Source— Bad for my topic	Secondary Source— Bad for my topic

Figure 6.9. Four Corners

After the librarian saw which corner students chose, she had the students explain their reasoning and corrected any misconceptions. After a few class examples, students then used this same evaluation process in choosing their own articles for the assignment.

NOTE
Laura Greenstein, "Part 2: Using Formative Assessment," in *What Teachers Really Need to Know about Formative Assessment* (Alexandria, VA: ASCD, 2010), 48–55.

FAST 20: Graphic Organizers

Description: Students use graphic organizers to organize their thoughts in both a user- and reader-friendly format that is concise and allows the librarian to quickly check for understanding.

Audience Size: Small or medium

Feedback Level: Individual, small group, or whole group

Time Frame: 3–20 minutes

Materials/Technology: Graphic organizer worksheet

Standards:
  ACRL Information Literacy Standards: Any
  Standards for the 21st-Century Learner: Any

How: First, determine the lesson's learning target(s) and choose a graphic organizer that best allows students to document their thinking in regard to the target(s). There are numerous free, downloadable graphic organizers online, and you can easily create basic templates by using the Insert Shapes feature in Microsoft Word. When students complete the graphic organizer, ask them to show you their results so you can check for understanding. They can also discuss their organizers in small groups or with the entire class. Be ready to provide individual or aggregate feedback as necessary.

  Tip: Complete the graphic organizer with the target information to ensure it works for the content before using it with the class.

Examples:
  1. KWL Chart (FAST 6)
  2. Grid/Matrix/Semantic Feature Analysis (FAST 21)
  3. ISP (**I**nformation, **S**ource, **P**age) Chart for note taking (see example below)

Information	Source	Page
If the players get overwhelmed, they tend not to absorb new info in games, so designers broke the lessons down into smaller pieces, added "gating," where players cannot progress until they master a skill.	Schiller	361

| To use games for assessment, designers must answer these three questions:
• "What do we want trainees/students to learn?"
• "How do we know that they have learned? That is, what classes of actions against which criteria will suffice?"
• How good is good enough? | Baker & Delacruz | 24 |

Figure 6.10. ISP Chart

FAST 21: Grid/Matrix/Semantic Feature Analysis

Description: Students compare and contrast features of similar databases using a grid or matrix.

Instructor Collaboration: Low

Audience Size: Small or medium

Feedback Level: Individual, small group, or whole group

Time Frame: 5–15 minutes

Materials/Technology: Grid or matrix worksheet and access to resources being analyzed

Standards:
  ACRL Information Literacy Standards:
    Standard 3: The information literate student evaluates information and its sources critically and incorporates selected information into his or her knowledge base and value system.
  Standards for the 21st-Century Learner:
    Standard 1: Inquire, think critically, and gain knowledge.
    Standard 2: Draw conclusions, make informed decisions, apply knowledge to new situations, and create new knowledge.

How: Provide students with a worksheet that, for example, has a grid that lists traits along one axis and database names along another. Give students time to explore the databases on computers in small groups and record their comparisons on the grid. Survey the room as the worksheet is completed to quickly view students' results and correct any misunderstandings.

Ideas for Adapting:
- Use this technique to compare different features of similar tools or ideas such as the three ways to use other people's information (paraphrase, summarize, and quote). Ask students to give the name, definition, and whether they need to cite it. Use a matrix to facilitate and outline a class discussion.

Example:
The following table was used in an entry-level biology course to compare three of the subject-specific databases.

	Scholarly	How do you obtain full text if it's not in this database?	Can you limit it to peer reviewed?
PubMed	Yes	Periodicals A-to-Z on the library website	No
MEDLINE	Yes	"Check for Lycoming Access" link	No
Academic Search Elite	Mixed	"Check for Lycoming Access" link	Yes
Biological Abstracts (BIOSIS)	Yes	"Check for Lycoming Access" link	No

Figure 6.11. Database Comparison

NOTE

Thomas A. Angelo and K. Patricia Cross, "CAT 9: Defining Features Matrix," in *Classroom Assessment Techniques: A Handbook for College Teachers*, 2nd ed. (San Francisco: Jossey-Bass, 1993), 164–167.

FAST 22: Guided Practice Template

Description: Students are given guided practice templates (written instructions) that guide them through practicing new skills on sample topics or on starting research on their own topics.

Instructor Collaboration: Low

Audience Size: Small or medium

Feedback Level: Individual or small group

Time Frame: 10+ minutes

Materials/Technology: Guided practice template

Standards:
   ACRL Information Literacy Standards: Any
   Standards for the 21st-Century Learner: Any

How: Before class, create a guided practice template that helps students use the skills that are the lesson's learning targets. A template includes a series of instructions that facilitates students' exploration of new skills. At the start of class, introduce skills and allow students to practice the new skills using the template, or you can skip the introduction and let the template walk students through meeting the learning target(s). The template can focus on hypothetical research topics (good for lower-level classes or students who have not yet selected research topics), or it can guide students through the beginning stages of research on their chosen topics (recommended for upper-level students). If students are using their own topics, this technique enables them by the end of class to leave class having begun research on their topics. It can also encourage them to use the recommended skills or resources that were taught in the class. In other words, the guided practice template encourages students to research well and not just resort to what they already know or what is easiest. Survey the room throughout class and talk with students individually about their answers or lead a class discussion.

Example:

1. What is your language (circle one)—Spanish German French?
2. Find one relevant reference book or reference article on Spanish/German/French culture. What is the title and call number?
3. Use Reference Universe to find one relevant reference book article on your topic. What is the title of the reference book?
4. What is the name of the general encyclopedia for your language (see handout)?
5. Use the Snowden Library's Online Catalog to find one item in our collection (can be anything, though most of our foreign-language stuff is literature) that is in Spanish/German/French. What is the call number?
6. Does the Snowden Library have any books on your topic (any language)? Ask for help before saying "no." Give one title that looks useful.
7. What database helps you find books at other libraries (see handout)?
8. Go into this database and find at least one relevant book on your topic. What is the title?
9. Do any libraries in the United States own this item? YES NO
10. What database is most relevant to your topic? Use the Subject Links, Databases chart, or ask for help.
11. What are some possible ENGLISH keywords you could try to find scholarly research on violent video games in France/Spain/Germany?
12. In Snowden Super Search (on the library's home page), try your keywords. Did you find anything? If not, how could you revise your search?
13. In LexisNexis, go to News > Foreign Language. Find one article in your language on anything that interests you. Don't forget to select your language and use search terms in that language.
14. Because "Germany" and "German" are almost the same word, how could you do a search in the databases (excluding LexisNexis) using the asterisk symbol (see handout)?
15. Use ARTstor to find one relevant image for your topic and save it to your H Drive. (You must be registered and logged into ARTstor to download.)

Figure 6.12. Guided Practice Template

FAST 23: Human Boolean Exercise

Description: Students learn how to use understand Boolean operators AND, OR, and NOT by using themselves as "articles" in a database.

Instructor Collaboration: Low

Audience Size: Small, medium, or large

Feedback Level: Whole group

Time Frame: 2–3 minutes

Materials/Technology: None

Standards:
  ACRL Information Literacy Standards:
   Standard 2: The information literate student accesses needed information effectively and efficiently.
  Standards for the 21st-Century Learner:
   Standard 1: Inquire, think critically, and gain knowledge.

How: Create search phrases that can apply to students such as "blue jeans AND blond hair" or "tennis shoes OR sweat shirt." In class, ask students to stand up when they think a search phrase applies to them. Follow up the exercise with a brief discussion of how AND and OR seem to work. NOT can be added if it is relevant.

Tip: Use keywords that represent students' visual attributes such as eye color or length of hair. This will ensure that you can see the students who do not understand the learning target. If non-visible attributes are used, such as birthday month, you will not be able to observe whether students who should be standing are.

FAST 24: IF-AT Forms

Description: Students answer multiple-choice questions with scratch-off IF-AT forms, which reveal the correct answer.

Instructor Collaboration: Low

Audience Size: Small, medium, or large

Feedback Level: Individual, small group, or whole group

Time Frame: 10–15 minutes

Materials/Technology: Quiz and IF-AT forms, available at http://www.epsteineducation.com/home/order/default.aspx

Standards:
   ACRL Information Literacy Standards: Any
   Standards for the 21st-Century Learner: Any

How: Give students are individually given a short paper-based, multiple-choice quiz. After they have completed their quizzes, divide students into small groups and give each group an IF-AT form. Instruct them to work within their groups to form a consensus on which answer is correct, and then direct them to scratch off their answer on the form. If they choose correctly, a star is revealed. If they do not find the star, they know the answer they chose is incorrect and they need to discuss which answer to try next. The scratch-off form leaves a record of how many attempts it took each group to correctly answer each question. Throughout the process, rotate around the room to answer questions and listen to the students' conversations. When all groups have completed the IF-AT form, write the scoring scheme on the board. The exact numbers will depend on which package of IF-AT forms purchased (A–D or A–E), but an example scheme is—

- 1st try: 4 points,
- 2nd try: 2 points,
- 3rd try: 1 points,
- 4th try: 0 points.

At the end of the assessment, ask which group had the highest score. Then collect the forms and look at which questions groups struggled with the most. Use this information to lead a discussion and demonstration on those topics. If there is a group that answered a question on the first try when the rest of the class struggled, ask that group to explain or demonstrate how they came up with the correct answer.

Example:
Below is an example of IF-AT form by Epstein Educational Enterprise.

Figure 6.13. Example of IF-AT form by Epstein Educational Enterprise.

The following quiz was used in a 400-level biology course.

1. What is the browsing call number for medicine in the Library of Congress system?
   a. B
   b. F
   c. M
   d. R

2. What is the name of the SUBSCRIPTION medical database at Lycoming College?
   a. Snowden Super Search
   b. PubMed
   c. BIOSIS
   d. MEDLINE

3. What is the name of the GOVERNMENT-SPONSORED (a.k.a. free) medical database that you will continue to have access to after you graduate?
   a. Snowden Super Search
   b. PubMed
   c. BIOSIS
   d. MEDLINE

Formative Assessment Snapshot Techniques for During Instruction **123**

4. Which of the following words helps you connect two search terms with the goal of getting fewer, more specific results?
   a. OR
   b. NOT
   c. AND

5. BUT Which title is NOT a reference book?
   a. Gale Encyclopedia of Medicine
   b. Blood Transfusions: An In-Depth History
   c. Dictionary of Neurological Signs
   d. Thieme Atlas of Anatomy: Head and Neuroanatomy

6. What do you do when you find an article in the subscription database but don't see the full-text icon?
   a. Click on the "Is this article available at Snowden?" link to see if it's in another database or in print.
   b. Use the Interlibrary Loan link on the library's home page.
   c. Use the Periodicals A-to-Z link on the library's home page to find out if we have that journal title in full text.
   d. Call other libraries to have them send the article to you.

7. If you found an interesting citation in the government-sponsored medical database, and don't see the full text linked to it, what can you do?
   a. Click on the "Is this article available at Snowden?" link to see if it's in another database or in print.
   b. Use the Interlibrary Loan link on the library's home page.
   c. Use the Periodicals A-to-Z link on the library's home page to find out if we have that journal title in full text.
   d. Call other libraries to have them send the article to you.

8. You need to find the scientific abbreviation for a journal title for your citation, what do you do?
   a. Periodicals A-to-Z List link on the library website
   b. Scientific Journal Abbreviations in the reference collection
   c. Web of Science database
   d. Index Medicus freely available on the Internet

9. What is the name of the tool in the subscription database that gives you a list of "controlled vocabulary" for more efficient searching?
   a. Thesaurus
   b. Indexes
   c. MeSH
   d. LCSH

10. What is the only way you CANNOT contact a librarian for help with your research topic?
    a. At the Research Help Desk or in an office
    b. Text message
    c. Home phone numbers
    d. Telephone

Figure 6.14. 400-Level Biology Course Quiz

NOTE

Sehoya H. Cotner, Bruce A. Fall, Susan M. Wick, J.D. Walker, and Paul M. Baepler, "Rapid Feedback Assessment Methods: Can We Improve Engagement and Preparation for Exams in Large-Enrollment Courses?," *Journal of Science Education and Technology* 17, no. 5 (October 2008): 537–443.

FAST 25: Jigsaw Presentations

Description: Students, working in groups, independently explore one tool or learning target for the class. Groups then take turns presenting their "piece" of the "puzzle."

Instructor Collaboration: Low or medium

Audience Size: Small or medium

Feedback Level: Small group

Time Frame: 30+ minutes

Materials/Technology: None, but computers and/or presentation equipment are often useful depending on what students are asked to explore and demonstrate

Standards:
    ACRL Information Literacy Standards: Any
    Standards for the 21st-Century Learner: Any

How: Divide students into groups as they enter the classroom. Give each group approximately twenty minutes to explore its assigned tool or learning target. You can design and give them a worksheet to help students discover the most important features of the tool or learning target. Have groups then take turns presenting what they learned to the class. Ask questions to get student presenters to share all the necessary information, facilitate discussion, or provide any other tips.

    Ideas for Adapting:
- Have students do presentations outside of class in collaboration with the instructor. Have students use screen capture software such as Jing to record their presentations, and then link the presentations to the class page in the institution's course management platform.
- Record and upload to YouTube traditionally delivered presentations to share with the class. This allows presentations to be viewed by other students when they begin their research.
-

Example:
In an introduction to theatre class with an upcoming design project, students were divided into small groups of no more than five. Each group was given one of the following research tools to explore:

5. Google Books: Magazines
6. The library's print magazine collection
7. ARTstor
8. Free Sound Project

Groups were then given about ten minutes to explore their assigned resource. During that time, the librarian rotated between the groups and asked questions about special features, gave tips, and answered any questions. After the exploration time was completed, groups took turns sharing their assigned resource with the whole class. The librarian asked questions and made corrections as needed, and students were strongly encouraged to ask each other questions.

NOTES

Patrick Ragains, "Four Variations on Drueke's Active Learning Paradigm," *Research Strategies* 13, no. 1 (1995): 40–50.

Julia I. Smith and Lena Chang, "Teaching Community Ecology as a Jigsaw: A Collaborative Learning Activity Fostering Library Research Skills," *American Biology Teacher* 67, no. 1 (2005): 31–36.

FAST 26: Keyword Sorting Exercise

Description: Students think about how keywords need to be chosen and adjusted based on the database or finding tool being used in this technique.

Instructor Collaboration: Low

Audience Size: Small, medium, or large*

Feedback Level: Small or whole group

Time Frame: 5–10 minutes

Materials/Technology: A short newspaper article on a subject-relevant topic and a sheet of poster board divided into two columns, titled, for example, "Keywords for Scholarly Database" and "Keywords for Newspaper Database"

Standards:
    ACRL Information Literacy Standards:
        Standard 2: The information literate student accesses needed information effectively and efficiently.
    Standards for the 21st-Century Learner:
        Standard 1: Inquire, think critically, and gain knowledge.
        Standard 2: Draw conclusions, make informed decisions, apply knowledge to new situations, and create new knowledge.
        Standard 3: Share knowledge and participate ethically and productively as members of our democratic society.

How: This exercise has two parts. First, give pairs of students a short newspaper article and ask them to circle words that would be good keywords for a scholarly database and underline words that would be good for a newspaper database like LexisNexis. Walk around the room, talking with students as they identify keywords. If you see a student who is confused or going in the wrong direction, give brief instruction to get him or her back on track. Once students have read their articles and marked their keywords, ask each pair to send a representative to the front of the room to write their keywords on a sheet of poster board with two columns on it, one for each type of database (see example below). Then lead the class in a discussion about the terms they chose and how likely the keywords are to be effective in the databases.

*Ideas for Adapting for Large Audiences: Use a technological tool, such as Google Forms, Socrative, or Wordle, that allows students to enter text () and enables you to quickly review many student responses, giving you an overall picture of the class's understanding and a report of trends that can be addressed during the lesson.

Example:
For an upper level criminal justice class, students were asked to read a newspaper article and circle keywords that they would use to search Criminal Justice Abstracts and underline keywords that they would use to search LexisNexis.

This activity is designed to get you thinking about how keywords change depending on what database you use if you were to search for more information on this topic. Read the following newspaper article and circle the keywords that you would use in Criminal Justice Abstracts (a database of scholarly and trade journals) and underline the keywords that would work well for a newspaper database like LexisNexis.

Do violent (video games) lead to (violent) criminal behavior? There are many examples that support a connection, including 17-year-old Warren Leblanc who killed a boy in a park in 2004, Ryan Chinnery who (sexually assaulted) four women, and Eric Harris and Dylan Klebold who opened fire at Columbine High School in Colorado in 1999. Leblanc was obsessed with *Manhunt*, Chinnery with *Grand Theft Auto*, and Harris and Klebold with *Doom*. Would these young men have committed these crimes without this inspiration, or do these immensely popular games lead to real-life violent acts?

Paraphrased from "Inspired by Obsession," *The Mirror* (3 Star Edition), Apr. 4, 2012.

Figure 6.15. Keyword Sorting Exercise

Formative Assessment Snapshot Techniques for During Instruction

After reading the newspaper article and circling and underlining possible keywords, students were then instructed to come to the front of the room to write their chosen keywords on a piece of poster board, bringing their work into one central place so the librarian could check their understanding and lead a discussion.

Keywords for Scholarly Database	Keywords for Newspaper Database
Video games	Warren Leblanc
Violent/violence	Ryan Chinnery
Sexual assault (rape)	Eric Harris
	Dylan Klebold
	Manhunt
	Doom
	Grand Theft Auto

Figure 6.16. Keyword Sorting Exercise

FAST 27: Paraphrasing Practice

Description: Students read short nonfiction pieces to practice paraphrasing.

Instructor Collaboration: Low

Audience Size: Small or medium

Feedback Level: Individual, small group, or whole group

Time Frame: 10–30 minutes

Materials/Technology: A short nonfiction text

Standards:
   ACRL Information Literacy Standards:
      Standard 4: The information literate student, individually or as a member of a group, uses information effectively to accomplish a specific purpose.
   Standards for the 21st-Century Learner:
      Standard 2: Draw conclusions, make informed decisions, apply knowledge to new situations, and create new knowledge.

How: Give students a short nonfiction text and ask them to work individually or in small groups to paraphrase it. Move around the room to observe and answer questions as needed. Then direct students to take turns reading their paraphrases while you and the instructor and provide feedback.

    Tip: Create a Graphic Organizer (FAST 20) with a three columns labeled "Quote," "Paraphrase," and "in-Text Citation." Ask students to write an interesting part of a text, a quotation, in the quote column, then transform the quotation into a paraphrase, and then finally, write an in-text citation for both the quotation and the paraphrase. This organizer can help students see the evolution of finding relevant information and transforming it into their own writing.

	Quote	**Paraphrase**
Text	"Even more important, I learned that video games create what the psychologist Eric Erickson has called a psychosocial moratorium—that is, a learning space in which the learner can take risks where real-world consequences are lowered. After all, you can save the game and start back at the save point when you fail … None of this is to say that it does not bother or even frustrate players when they die or do not play part of a game well. It does indeed. Of course they care about how well they do—but the cost of caring is not prohibitive, as it so often is in school." (62–63). Gee, J. P. (2003). *What video games have to teach us about learning and literacy*. Gordonsville, VA: Palgrave Macmillan.	Video games are good at creating "psychosocial moratoriums," which are spaces where the "real-world consequences" of mistakes are reduced while players learn how to move or interact with the new material.
In-Text Citation (APA)	(Gee, 2003, p. 62-63)	(Gee, 2003)

Figure 6.17. Paraphrasing Practice

Examples:

The screenshot below is a sample paraphrasing assessment on our library's website (http://www.lycoming.edu/library/forms/paraphrasing.aspx). Students can go to this site, type their paraphrase, send it to one of the instructional services librarians for evaluation, and receive feedback within 24–48 hours. Its use remains a manageable workload at our institution. Librarians at large institutions may need to consider more sophisticated technology that can distribute student responses to multiple librarians to keep feedback sustainable.

PARAPHRASING ACTIVITY

In-Text Citation Exercise

* Name: [ ]
* Email: [ ]
Professor: [ ]

Read the following passage carefully. Then paraphrase the passage using your own words in the box provided.

While the Japanese attack of Pearl Harbor came as a shock to most Americans, the U.S. government had already investigated possible actions to take in case of war with Japan. Japanese Americans also had speculated on what would happen to them, fearing as early as 1937 that they would be "herded into prison camps – perhaps we would be slaughtered on the spot" (Daniels 1989). Some Nisei emphasized their loyalty and Americanism, which led to generational conflict with their Issei parents.

Useful terminology:

Figure 6.18. Sample Paraphrasing Assessment

The text for this paraphrasing activity comes from the first paragraph of "A Brief History of Japanese American Relocation during World War II," in *Confinement and Ethnicity: An Overview of World War II Japanese American Relocation Sites* (http://www.nps.gov/history/history/online_books/anthropology74/ce3a.htm).

In another example of how this technique has been implemented, 400-level biology students were asked to reexamine the abstract of an article they had already read in class. They were then instructed to write a two-sentence summary of that abstract. It was a small class of only five students, so each student took a turn reading his or her summary, which was quickly evaluated by the instructor with additional feedback from the librarian.

FAST 28: Periodical Sorting

Description: Students sort a pile of different types of periodicals into groups such as popular and scholarly.

Instructor Collaboration: Low

Audience Size: Small or medium

Feedback Level: Small group

Time Frame: 5 minutes

Materials/Technology: Mixed periodicals

Standards:
  ACRL Information Literacy Standards:
    Standard 3: The information literate student evaluates information and its sources critically and incorporates selected information into his or her knowledge base and value system.
  Standards for the 21st-Century Learner:
    Standard 1: Inquire, think critically, and gain knowledge.
    Standard 2: Draw conclusions, make informed decisions, apply knowledge to new situations, and create new knowledge.
    Standard 3: Share knowledge and participate ethically and productively as members of our democratic society.

How: Divide students into small groups. Give each group a pile of popular magazines, scholarly journals, and other discipline-appropriate types of publications such as trade journals and newspapers. Ask students to sort the periodicals into groups. When completed, lead a brief class discussion highlighting the features of each type.

  Tip: Combine this technique with a Grid/Matrix/Semantic Feature Analysis (FAST 21) so that students or groups can record their observations.

FAST 29: Quick Write

Description: Students complete a quick write, which is an informal writing technique that can be used during the library class to summarize key points, assess students' current understanding of the learning targets (similar to FAST 10: 10:2 Reflection), or respond to a prompt such as determining the best keywords to use when searching for a topic and why.

Instructor Collaboration: Low

Audience Size: Small, medium, or large*

Feedback Level: Individual, small group, or whole group

Time Frame: 3–10 minutes

Materials/Technology: None

Standards:
  ACRL Information Literacy Standards: Any
  Standards for the 21st-Century Learner: Any

How: Choose the key concepts that you want students identify at a desired point in the lesson. When the time comes, ask students to informally write their thoughts about the key concepts informally and then share with a partner or small group (FAST 33: Think-Pair-Share) as you rotate to observe the various discussions. After students share, synthesize the relevant main points discussed by students before moving on with the lesson.

  Ideas for Adapting:
  - Use quick writes before a lesson to activate students' background knowledge (similar to FAST 1: Admit Slips) or to make predictions.
  - Use quick writes to have students summarize key points of a previous class, video, or article in a flipped classroom setting.

  ***Ideas for Adapting for a Large Audience:** Use a technological tool that allows students to enter text (Google Forms, Twitter, TodaysMeet, Socrative, blog comments) and enables you to quickly review many student responses, giving you an overall picture of the class's understanding and a report of trends that can be addressed during the lesson.

FAST 30: Response Cards

Description: Students use response cards as a low-tech and flexible alternative to clickers, allowing for whole group cognitive engagement that serves as a check on each student's level of understanding before moving on to the next stage in the learning process.

Instructor Collaboration: Low

Audience Size: Small, medium, or large

Feedback Level: Whole group

Time Frame: 3+ minutes

Materials/Technology: Pre-printed response cards or blank cards

Standards:
    ACRL Information Literacy Standards: Any
    Standards for the 21st-Century Learner: Any

How: Before class, prepare response cards that include answer choices such as

- "True" or "False;"
- "Professional Journal," "Trade Magazine," or "Online Journal;"
- "Reference Section," "Periodical Section," or "Media Section."

Or plan to give students blank cards to write their own responses. During class, periodically ask students to respond to a question by holding up the response card that best represents their understanding at the time. Then use the evidence gathered from the response cards to determine if you should continue with the lesson or hold a class discussion to correct misunderstandings.

Tips:
- Hold all students accountable by waiting until all response cards are in the air before making a conclusion about the class's understanding.
- Take notice of any students who seem to wait to see a neighbor's response before responding themselves, indicating that they are not confident in their understanding.

FAST 31: Scavenger Hunt

Description: In a scavenger hunt, students find particular items or locations to show that they met the learning target.

Instructor Collaboration: Low

Audience Size: Small, medium, or large*

Feedback Level: Individual or small group

Time Frame: 5+ minutes

Materials/Technology: Scavenger hunt worksheet

Standards:
 ACRL Information Literacy Standards:
  Standard 2: The information literate student accesses needed information effectively and efficiently.
 Standards for the 21st-Century Learner:
  Standard 1: Inquire, think critically, and gain knowledge.
  Standard 2: Draw conclusions, make informed decisions, apply knowledge to new situations, and create new knowledge.

How: Ask students to find a book, journal, or location. This is often done with tools such as a handout explaining Library of Congress call numbers or a library directory and/or map. Finding the item or location is feedback to the students that they were able to navigate the library correctly. Instruct students to bring the items back to the class's meeting place or have them write down on their worksheets the code posted at each location. Students can also take pictures of items or locations with cell phones or tablets. Any of these methods provides evidence to you that students met the learning target. In addition to the help materials incorporated into the assignment, make yourself available to answer student questions as needed. This is a very flexible assessment. Students can be asked to look for a single item, such as a specific book title, or the whole class can hunt for several items.

Tips:
- Strive to create authentic finding experiences such as those described above.
- Ask students to find electronic items on the library website, in databases, or on the Internet. This requires you to be more creative in finding a way to gather proof that students found the desired electronic locations.

Formative Assessment Snapshot Techniques for During Instruction **137**

*Ideas for Adapting for Large Audiences: Scavenger hunts can be made for large audiences, though the assignment can easily become labor-intensive. Keep large numbers of students from looking for the same item at once by creating multiple tracks or directing students to start in different areas of the library. The other challenge to scavenger hunts with large audiences is collecting students back in one place for a debriefing activity such as a library one-shot. These large-scale scavenger hunts may be better suited for an asynchronous orientation activity (see Gregory and Broussard, 2011) or an activity students complete at their convenience before the one-shot.

Examples:
In a campus history game, "Lyco Map Game," the learning target was for students to learn the physical history of Lycoming College's campus. Posters with QR codes were posted around the campus, some on existing buildings, and others on easels to represent historical buildings that no longer exist. As groups of students located each one, they held up a cardstock avatar in front of each poster to show which team was taking the picture, took the picture, and used a QR code to upload it into the game's Picasa albums. Below is an image of a team avatar in front of the Eveland Hall poster in the Lyco Map Game

Figure 6.19. Lyco Map Game QR Code

In a second example, students from the physics colloquium visited the library for a very broad orientation to resources for their discipline. This game required participants to explore physical and digital library resources and record the answers to their clues in the crossword puzzle. The actual crossword puzzle was created with a free crossword puzzle creator online. Most of the clues required students to find items using the recommended tools and used an existing title or database name as the answer to be written down in the crossword puzzle. The librarian posted a code word "timetravel" at the physical location of the *American Journal of Physics* for 11 across.

Figure 6.20. Example Physics Crossword Puzzle

Across
5. The floor of the library which contains print journals
9. The recommended database for searching physics topics at the Snowden Library
11. Code word found at the print journal of American Journal of Physics
12. The title of the reference book found at Ref. QB501 .S627 2010

Down
1. Electronic tool on the library's home page that helps you find which journals the library has access to
2. American _____ Society provides us access to Physical Review A-E
3. The first author of the article titled "experimental and theoretical investigation into the worm-hole effect"
4. _____ Search Elite is the name of one of the databases that has the full text of the journal Chaos
5. The title of the book with the call number QC23.2.K35 2005, The Physics of _____
6. The floor of the library which contains the physics books (use the directory in this room)
7. If our library doesn't have an article in full text, you can get it through _____ Library Loan
8. The online tool that helps you find books in the Snowden Library
10. Link in databases that helps you find full text says "_____ for Lycoming Access"

NOTES

Mary J. Snyder Broussard, "Secret Agents in the Library: Integrating Virtual and Physical Games in a Small Academic Library," *College and Undergraduate Libraries* 17, no. 1 (January-March 2010): 20–30.

Alison S. Gregory and Mary J. Snyder Broussard, "Unraveling the 'Mystery' of the Library: A 'Big Games' Approach to Library Orientation" (paper presented at the Association of College and Research Libraries, Philadelphia, PA, March 31, 2011), http://www.ala.org/acrl/sites/ala.org.acrl/files/content/conferences/confsandpreconfs/national/2011/papers/unraveling_the_myste.pdf.

Monty L. McAdoo, "Scavenger Hunts," in *Building Bridges: Connecting Faculty, Students, and the College Library* (Chicago: American Library Association, 2010), 101–114.

FAST 32: Source Evaluation

Description: Students work in groups to evaluate a website or another type of information source.

Instructor Collaboration: Low

Audience Size: Small, medium, or large*

Feedback Level: Small or whole group

Time Frame: 5+ minutes

Materials/Technology: Printed copy of or access to source to be evaluated

Standards:
    ACRL Information Literacy Standards:
        Standard 3: The information literate student evaluates information and its sources critically and incorporates selected information into his or her knowledge base and value system.
    Standards for the 21st-Century Learner:
        Standard 1: Inquire, think critically, and gain knowledge.
        Standard 2: Draw conclusions, make informed decisions, apply knowledge to new situations, and create new knowledge.

How: Give students a research scenario. Ask them to work in pairs or small groups to evaluate a source as it relates to their given scenario. You can ask them to judge it for credibility, to compare it to another source to determine which is better for research, or to evaluate its content. Ask for volunteers or call on students to share their individual opinions. Then lead a class discussion as needed.

    Ideas for Adapting: If time is limited, display the source in the front of the room and ask students to indicate whether they agree or disagree by a show of hands that it is suitable for the given scenario.

    *****Ideas for Adapting for Large Audiences:** Use the iPad app iAnnotate. Using the app, students add comments, notes, arrows, photographs and audio clips to images of a resource. They can send their annotated image as a PDF to you and the instructor. You can then show representative evaluations on a projector and discuss as a class.

Example:
The following was a prompt used in a teacher education course when students visited the library for instruction.

Formative Assessment Snapshot Techniques for During Instruction 141

> Imagine that you are a fifth-grade teacher and you are creating a trivia game for your students to learn about the life and achievements of Martin Luther King, Jr. One of the top results in your Google search is www.martinlutherking.org.
>
> Evaluate the site for credibility by answering the following questions:
>
> 1. What biographical information does it contain?
> 2. Who is the author and what is their purpose in creating the site?
> 3. How does the content compare to other sources you have reviewed?
>
> How would you handle a student wanting to use www.martinlutherking.org for a class project?
>
> Can you think of another research scenario in which this would be a good resource?

Figure 6.21. Source Evaluation Prompt

FAST 33: Think-Pair-Share

Description: The librarian asks a question or provides a prompt to students to reflect on individually, then share with a partner, and then discuss as a whole group.

Instructor Collaboration: Low

Audience Size: Small or medium

Feedback Level: Individual, small group, or whole group

Time Frame: 1–3 minutes

Materials/Technology: None

Standards:
  ACRL Information Literacy Standards: Any
  Standards for the 21st-Century Learner: Any

How: Think-pair-share reduces students' perceived risk of sharing by allowing them to first confirm or revise their thinking with a peer before sharing with the class. Use a think-pair-share at any point in the lesson when you feel the need to check for understanding before progressing with the lesson. Provide feedback when partners are sharing and when students share as a whole group to clarify confusions.

  Tip: Label each table with a number to facilitate calling on groups to share their ideas.

  Ideas for Adapting: Because students often sit near familiar classmates, get them outside of their comfort zones by having them work with a partner they may not know as well. One way of doing this is to use an appointment-clock technique, which encourages students to talk with several different students who are not seated next to them. Direct students to find a partner at "12:00 o'clock" or at "6:00 o'clock" to discuss the prompt. Rotate around, listen to their discussions, and provide feedback as needed. Then ask students to share their ideas with the class.

FAST 34: Twitter

Description: Students use Twitter to comment on items learned during the lesson.

Instructor Collaboration: Low or medium

Audience Size: Small, medium, or large

Feedback Level: Individual or small group

Time Frame: 5+ minutes

Materials/Technology: Computers, tablets, or mobile devices and the library's Twitter account or student Twitter accounts

Standards:
    ACRL Information Literacy Standards: Any
    Standards for the 21st-Century Learner: Any

How: Before class, decide whether the class will share tweets with a shared hashtag (for example, #ENG106) or with a shared Twitter account where all students input their feedback at a central computer workstation. During class, use Twitter throughout the lesson to collect student feedback and to engage students in virtual classroom discussions. Twitter facilitates brainstorming, student questions, and group discussions. You can also use it as a classroom response system by asking a specific question to which students respond using their devices. Because Twitter limits tweets to 140 characters, you can ask students summarize their understanding at appropriate points in the lesson. Ideally, the Twitter discussion feed should be viewable by all students so you can to refer to it during the lesson. Pauses throughout the lesson to address tweets, confirm ideas, expand on the lesson, or answer questions. Additionally, students are monitoring their own and each other's learning and can answer each other's questions.

Tips:
- Keep in mind that not every student has a Twitter account. Ask students to team up with partners or require them to create an account before the class.
- Establish Twitter etiquette policies and expected behaviors at the beginning of the class.

Ideas for Adapting:
- Use the Twitter feed beyond the library one-shot lesson by allowing students to continue asking questions or discussing ideas via the class feed.
- Use TodaysMeet—it provides librarians with all of the advantages of Twitter without requiring students to have individual accounts or using their personal accounts for class. Simply set up a room within TodaysMeet and provide students with the room number.

NOTE

Julie Kent, "Library Instruction with Twitter," *Transliteracy Librarian* (blog), March 6, 2012, http://transliteracylibrarian.wordpress.com/2012/03/06/library-instruction-with-twitter/.

Formative Assessment Snapshot Techniques for During Instruction **145**

FAST 35: When to Cite Paragraph

Description: Students learn the rules about when an in-text citation is necessary in a text.

Instructor Collaboration: Low

Audience Size: Small, medium, or large*

Feedback Level: Individual, small group, or whole group

Time Frame: 10 minutes

Materials/Technology: A sample paragraph with citations removed and a box inserted into each place a citation *could* appear (regardless if it *should*)

Standards:
 ACRL Information Literacy Standards:
  Standard 5: The information literate student understands many of the economic, legal, and social issues surrounding the use of information and accesses and uses information ethically and legally.
 Standards for the 21st-Century Learner: Any

How: Give students a sample paragraph (see example below). Read each sentence to the class then ask the class to vote on whether it needs an in-text citation. If there is disagreement, lead a discussion. If the class concludes a citation is required, discuss what it should look like.
 Ideas for Adapting:
 - Have students complete this technique individually as homework or in small groups.
 - Collect the worksheets to provide individual feedback or go through each sentence as a class, randomly calling on an individual or group to share their conclusion for that sentence.

 ***Ideas for Adapting for Large Audiences:** Use a technological tool that allows students to enter text (Google Forms, Twitter, TodaysMeet, Socrative, blog comments) and enables you to quickly review many student responses, giving you an overall picture of the class's understanding and a report of trends that can be addressed during the lesson.

Example:
The following was an assessment used in a criminal justice class to help students understand when information needs in-text citations. Students had time to individually check where they believed a citation was needed, then the librarian read each sentence aloud, had students vote on whether the sentence needed a citation, and discussed why it did or did not need one.

In the following paragraph, place a letter X in every place that requires an in-text citation.

I believe that our society does not pay enough attention to women-on-women sexual violence ☐. Society tends to view women as inherently nurturing and incapable of committing sexually violent acts ☐. Despite the fact that approximately 10% of Americans are gay, many victims of same-sex violence perceive traditional rape support services as only for men-on-women assault ☐. Furthermore, very few seek justice through the police and court system ☐. Girshick found victims were depressed, even suicidal, and felt the need to quit driving or change jobs ☐. One victim described herself as "very vulnerable, insignificant, dehumanized, disrespected, confused, guilty, ashamed, dirty, weak, stupid, wary, untrusting, angry, betrayed ☐."

Works Cited
Girshick, L. B. (2002). No sugar, no spice: Reflections on research on woman-to-woman sexual violence. *Violence Against Women*, 8(12), 1500–1520.

Figure 6.22. Citation Assessment Activity

FAST 36: Whip Around

Description: Students summarize or analyze key points so the librarian can check for the level of understanding from the whole group before moving on to the lesson's next point. This technique gets all students cognitively engaged, eliminates the need for students to volunteer, and can be helpful when the librarian does not know all of the students' names.

Instructor Collaboration: Low

Audience Size: Small or medium

Feedback Level: Whole group

Time Frame: 1–5 minutes

Standards:
   ACRL Information Literacy Standards: Any
   Standards for the 21st-Century Learner: Any

Materials/Technology: None

How: Ask a question or read a statement. Have students respond by making a list of three to five ideas. Then ask all students to stand while you randomly call on one student at a time to share an idea they have written down. Other students check off any idea(s) on their own lists when someone else shares it. Each student sits down when all of his or her ideas have been said. Keep calling on students until all students are seated. Be sure to address each idea offered. Then lead a class discussion when the last student sits down about any unaddressed ideas worthy of consideration and help the class draw some overarching conclusions.

   Tip: Word your questions and statements broadly to allow for a variety of student responses.

   Ideas for Adapting: Do this technique at the end of class to summarize key ideas.

Examples:
- **Librarian:** "List five characteristics of popular magazines."
- **Librarian:** "List five databases that include primary sources."
- **Librarian:** "List five tips for avoiding plagiarism."

NOTE
Douglas Fisher and Nancy Frey. *Checking for Understanding: Formative Assessment Techniques for Your Classroom* (Alexandria, VA: ASCD, 2007), 34.

FAST 37: Word Sorts—Open or Closed

Description: Students sort key terms or concepts into categories that the librarian determines (closed sort) or into categories that they create (open sort).

Instructor Collaboration: Low

Audience Size: Small or medium

Feedback Level: Small or whole group

Time Frame: 1–5 minutes

Standards:
   ACRL Information Literacy Standards: Any
   Standards for the 21st-Century Learner: Any

Materials/Technology: Word cards

How: Divide students into small groups and provide them with cards that contain key terms or concepts. Instruct students organize the cards into categories and justify the organization. In a *closed* word sort, provide students with cards that have associated terms or concepts and ask students to sort them into designated categories and defend their reasoning. In an *open* word sort, provide students with cards that have key terms or concepts and ask students to sort them into categories they create and explain their reasoning. In both types, small groups explain to the whole group how they sorted their cards and provide reasoning behind their choices. Steer the discussion as necessary.

   Tip: Prepare the cards for each group in advance and separate them in envelopes.

   Ideas for Adapting: Do this technique at the beginning of class to gauge your students' current level of understanding or at the end of the class to summarize key ideas.

Example:
Towards the end of a library class on library resources, the librarian used a closed word sort to check for students' understanding of the lesson. Students worked in pairs to sort cards into assigned categories: reference, online catalog, interlibrary loan, and online database.

Formative Assessment Snapshot Techniques for During Instruction

REFERENCE	ONLINE CATALOG	INTERLIBRARY LOAN	ONLINE DATABASES
When you need background info to get started	To find books at our library	Use when the library doesn't have a book or article	Academic Search Elite or EBSCO
Credo or Reference Universe	Log in with a college I.D. to renew materials	Allows borrowing from other libraries or institutions	Scholarly collections of articles, dissertations, or reviews

Figure 6.23. Closed Word Sort

Chapter 7

Formative Assessment Snapshot Techniques for After Instruction

The ten formative assessment snapshot techniques (FASTs 38–48) in this chapter are designed to be used at the end of class or after class. For more information about the technology suggested in some of these FASTs, see Chapter 9, "Technology and Formative Assessment in Student Learning."

FAST 38: Annotated Bibliographies

Description: Students receive feedback on annotated bibliographies from both the instructor and the librarian.

Instructor Collaboration: High

Audience Size: Small, medium, or large

Feedback Level: Individual

Time Frame: Approximately one week after library instruction, plus time for librarian and instructor to respond to students

Materials/Technology: None

Standards:
  ACRL Information Literacy Standards:
    Standard 3: The information literate student evaluates information and its sources critically and incorporates selected information into his or her knowledge base and value system.
  Standards for the 21st-Century Learner:
    Standard 2: Draw conclusions, make informed decisions, apply knowledge to new situations, and create new knowledge.

How: Before meeting with students, discuss with the instructor about what your role will be in providing feedback. For example, you can comment on the scholarliness of sources and the quality of the citation format while the instructor looks at how appropriate each source is for the chosen research topic, thus sharing responsibility for evidence of critical thinking and reflection on each source.

After the library class, give students an appropriate amount of time to collect research materials. They must read and evaluate books and articles and create a one- or two-paragraph summary and evaluation of each resource. The evaluation focuses on the scholarliness of the source and the appropriateness of the content for the student's paper. A week later, have students submit the annotated bibliographies to their instructor. Both you and the instructor provide written feedback that will help them continue their research and write their papers.

Tips:

- Be sure to return students' annotated bibliographies quickly so they can make use of the feedback.
- Show students a good example of a student annotated bibliography entry as many students have never created one before. Use the example to help them understand the quality standards set by you and the instructor.
- Show students how to use an online citation management tool, such as EasyBib or NoodleTools, to help them keep track of their notes, write their annotations within an online platform, and share their projects with you and their instructor. Both of you can write comments directly in the online platform, making it easier to give students feedback in a timely manner.

NOTE

For more information about librarian feedback on annotated bibliographies in a for-credit information literacy class, see the following article:

Brandy Whitlock and Julie Nanavati, "A Systematic Approach to Performative and Authentic Assessment," *Reference Services Review* 41, no. 1 (2013): 32–48.

FAST 39: Cloze Assessments

Description: Students demonstrate their understanding of key concepts or ideas after a lesson by filling in blanks in a paragraph that summarizes the lesson's key points.

Instructor Collaboration: Low

Audience Size: Small, medium, or large

Feedback Level: Individual

Time Frame: 3+ minutes

Materials/Technology: Cloze paragraph

Standards:
  ACRL Information Literacy Standards: Any
  Standards for the 21st-Century Learner: Any

How: Before class, prepare a paragraph that summarizes the key points to be addressed in the lesson. Insert blank lines where the key terms or ideas should be written, making a "cloze" paragraph. At the end of class, ask students to complete the paragraph by filling in the blanks with the appropriate words. In small to medium classes, move around the room, look over students' answers and provide individual feedback. In larger classes, ask volunteers to share their answers with the class and facilitate a discussion to reinforce or clarify key points.

   Tip: Include enough context in a cloze paragraph to allow learners to determine the appropriate ideas but not so much that the answer is obvious.

   Ideas for Adapting: Use cloze paragraphs to gauge students' current level of understanding or during the lesson to hold them accountable for main ideas.

Example:
The following cloze paragraph is an excerpt from a worksheet created by Lycoming College librarian Melissa Correll. The cloze assessment was combined with Jigsaw Presentations (FAST 25) and used to hold non-presenting students accountable for listening well to their classmates' presentations.

> **Group 1: Credo Reference**
> Group 1 used _____, which is a collection of hundreds of reference books that are available online. The link to this resource is on the _____ part of the library homepage. Group 1 used Credo to find an _____ _____ article about backgammon. They chose an article from _____.
>
> **Group 2: Reference Resources—Reference Universe**
> Group 2 used Reference Universe to search for an encyclopedia article about backgammon. Reference Universe helps you find encyclopedia articles and other reference resources by searching for your terms in the _____ of these sources. Although Reference Universe is on the _____ section of the library website, the sources themselves are books in the _____ section on the _____ floor of the library.
>
> **Group 3: Journal Articles—Academic Search Elite database**
> Group 3 used the Academic Search Elite database to find _____ articles about math and backgammon. They used an _____ in their search to find various endings for the word math. They used _____ limiters in their search to refine their results. The article they wanted was not available in full text, so Group 3 clicked _____, and requested the article through _____ _____.

Figure 7.1. Cloze Paragraph

NOTE

Thomas Angelo and K. Patricia Cross, "Empty Outlines," in *Classroom Assessment Techniques: A Handbook for College Teachers*, 2nd ed. (San Francisco: Jossey-Bass, 1993), 138–141.

FAST 40: Conferences

Description: Students meet with the librarian to discuss their research as they work through a project for a course.

Instructor Collaboration: Medium

Audience Size: Small, medium, or large

Feedback Level: Individual

Time Frame: 10–30 minutes for each conference

Materials/Technology: None

Standards:
  ACRL Information Literacy Standards: Any
  Standards for the 21st-Century Learner: Any

How: Meet with students as they conduct research to discuss the student's progress, roadblocks, questions, and next steps as they work to complete their class assignment. This can be done in a scheduled work session with the class or in private reference consultations outside of class. Share the workload with the instructor so that half of the students meet with you while the other half meet with the instructor.

  Tip: Keep conferences informal by letting the students lead the discussions. Do not use pre-determined talking points because they prevent students from getting the help they need most from the conference.

FAST 41: Exit Slips

Description: Students complete exit slips to help the librarian quickly gauge each student's level of understanding as he or she leaves the classroom.

Instructor Collaboration: Low or medium

Audience Size: Small, medium, or large*

Feedback Level: Individual

Time Frame: 5 minutes

Materials/Technology: Note cards

Standards:
   ACRL Information Literacy Standards: Any
   Standards for the 21st-Century Learner: Any

How: At the end of class, ask students to complete some type of assessment—answer a question, write three things they learned, etc.—on note cards. Instruct students to give you the card as they leave—satisfactory completion of the exit slip is a student's ticket to leave. Ask any student with an unsatisfactory level of understanding to try again, giving him or her specific feedback for improvement. Use this method to ensure all students have met the most fundamental learning target(s).

*****Ideas for Adapting for a Large Audience:** If time is short or the group is large, simply collect exit slips as students leave the room, and then read and respond to the students' responses through e-mail, a written letter distributed to the students by the instructor, an FAQ web page, or another class with the students.

Example:

> Before you leave the classroom, please show your responses to the following two questions to the librarian.
> 1. How might your keywords differ depending on which database you are using (PsycINFO vs. ERIC)?
> 2. How will you determine if an article you found in a database is peer reviewed?

Figure 7.2. Exit Slip

NOTE

Lara Greenstein, "Part 2: Using Formative Assessment," in *What Teachers Really Need to Know about Formative Assessment* (Alexandria, VA: ASCD, 2010), 45–48.

FAST 42: Research Process Journals

Description: Students keep a written or online journal of their research experiences.

Instructor Collaboration: High

Audience Size: Small, medium, or large

Feedback Level: Individual

Time Frame: Usually completed by students and evaluated by the librarian outside of class; however, students may schedule research consultation with the librarian at a later time, which can take 10–30 minutes per student

Materials/Technology: Notebook, online blog, or online forum

Standards:
  ACRL Information Literacy Standards: Any
  Standards for the 21st-Century Learner: Any

How: Ask students to write journals as they go through the research process. In their journals, instruct students to analyze what they did well and what could be improved, list questions they have, and reflect on their thought processes. Throughout the project, collect and read journal entries, or combine this assessment with Conferences (FAST 40).

For journals to be beneficial to the students, they must receive specific, descriptive feedback from you and the instructor throughout the process. Research journals are designed to facilitate a dialog between mentors (the instructor and librarian) and apprentice researchers.

Give feedback promptly. This can be facilitated by dividing the group so that each mentor provides feedback to half of the class at each submission. Rotate the groups so that students have an opportunity to receive feedback from both you and the instructor.

Tip: Treat the journals as informal writings ignoring grammar and spelling mistakes and putting the focus on students' reflections of their information literacy skills.

Example:
Below is an of a research journal assignment, "How to Create a Research Map," designed by criminal justice professor Dr. Kerry Richmond at Lycoming College.

How to Create a Research Map

A research map is a tool to assist you with your research. It is a way for you to keep track of the steps you have taken as you review the literature. It also helps you to better focus your search, because you can see what strategies have provided you with the best results.

There are many different ways to create a research map. However, for this class, the purpose is to provide you with an opportunity to reflect upon the process you use to conduct research for a paper. This will help you to identify what strategies are most successful so that you can utilize them in the future. It will also identify what strategies you did not take so that you can fill in any gaps in your research.

You will be required to hand in your research map at the second library session on Monday, March 11th. However, it is essential that you begin to compile your research map as soon as you begin to conduct research on your paper. If you take notes as you are conducting your research, it will be less time-consuming than if you try to go back and re-create what you did at the last minute.

For your research map, please include the steps that you have taken to compile literature for your paper. In addition, after each step, take down notes on whether this step was successful in terms of finding appropriate research. Then identify the next step that you took and why. If you have to request an article via ILL or a book through EZ Borrow, please make note of that.

For example, your research map would look something like this if your paper is evaluating prison industries programs:

1. Conducted a search in Snowden Super Search using the term "prison industries."

There were 4,869 results. However, most were government documents and not specific to criminal justice. Decided to search in Criminal Justice Abstracts.

2. Conducted a search in Criminal Justice Abstracts using the term "prison industries."

There were 465 results, but nothing seemed relevant to the paper topic. The sources that came up were too broad. Perhaps narrowing the search will be more effective.

3. Conducted a search in Criminal Justice Abstracts using the terms "prison industries" AND "recidivism."

> There were 44 results. 8 of them were useful. Had to request two books via EZ Borrow (Flanagan (1988) Effect of Prison Industry Employment on Offender Behavior and Anderson (1995) Evaluation of the Impact of Participation in Ohio Penal Industries on Recidivism) and one article through ILL (Maguire, 1988).
>
> 4. In skimming through the sources that I was able to retrieve from Lycoming, I realized that only two were suitable (Saylor et al., 2001 and Moses and Smith, 2007). After reading those two, I reviewed their reference list to identify any other articles that might be useful and requested the Saylor and Gaes (1997) article via ILL.
>
> 5. Went onto Google Scholar to see if there were any articles that had cited the two articles that I had found. Found an article by Richardson (2005) that was related to my topic.
>
> This is just the initial stage of the research, but it gives you an idea of how to put together the research map. Again, it is simply a way for you to identify the steps that you took in conducting your research and whether it was effective. It better ensures that you try different ways to search the literature, rather than repeating the same steps over and over again.

Figure 7.3. "How to Create a Research Map" Assignment

NOTE

Trixie Smith, "Keeping Track: Librarians, Composition Instructors, and Student Writers Use the Research Journal," *Research Strategies* 18, no. 1 (2001): 21–28.

FAST 43: Check-In Points

Description: Students receive feedback from the librarian on their research assignment's check-in points.

Instructor Collaboration: High

Feedback Level: Individual

Audience Size: Small, medium, or large

Time Frame: Usually completed outside of class

Materials/Technology: None

Standards:
  ACRL Information Literacy Standards: Any
  Standards for the 21st-Century Learner: Any

How: Help instructors evaluate their students' research assignments by offering to give students feedback on the assignment's check-in points: thesis statement, appropriate keyword list, Annotated Bibliography (FAST 38), or Research Journal (FAST 42).

More specifically, in collaboration with instructors, provide students formative feedback in the following areas:
- appropriate scope of thesis,
- keyword evaluation,
- suitability of sources selected,
- other areas in which students say they are struggling.

Tip: Give timely feedback, ensuring its usefulness to students.

NOTE

For more information on instructor-librarian collaboration on grading in school libraries, see the following article:

Kristin Fontichiaro, "Nudging toward Inquiry: Formative Assessment," *School Library Monthly* 27, no. 6 (March 2011): n.p., http://www.schoollibrarymonthly.com/curriculum/Fontichiaro2011-v27n6p11.html.

FAST 44: One-Minute Papers

Description: Students write a very short paper at the end of the library class on what they learned and what they still want to know. The librarian responds in person or in writing.

Instructor Collaboration: Medium

Audience Size: Small, medium, or large

Feedback Level: Individual

Time Frame: 2–5 minutes, plus time outside of class to read and respond to students

Materials/Technology: None

Standards:
  ACRL Information Literacy Standards: Any
  Standards for the 21st-Century Learner: Any

How: Towards the end of a library class, ask students to write one thing they learned and one thing they would still like to know. Review the students' papers after class. Then respond to the students through e-mail, a written letter distributed to the students by the instructor, an FAQ web page, or another class with the students.

Ideas for Adapting:
- Ask students to complete this assessment about fifteen minutes before class ends, giving you time to quickly read their papers and use the last five to ten minutes of class time to respond.
- There are many possible twists to the one-minute paper—just ask students to write one thing they would still like to know, or ask them to write what they learned on one color of sticky notes and questions they still have on another color, and post them on a classroom wall for an end-of-class discussion.

Example

What is your overall opinion of the Library "Game" Tutorial? *It was not fun, but informative.* **Do you have any suggestions for improvements?** *I think it would be better to have us walk around and do things with a list.*

Figure 7.4. Student Responses

NOTES

Thomas A. Angelo and K. Patricia Cross, "Minute Paper," in *Classroom Assessment Techniques: A Handbook for College Teachers*, 2nd ed. (San Francisco: Jossey-Bass, 1993), 148–153.

Esther S. Grassian and Joan R. Kaplowitz, *Information Literacy Instruction*, 2nd ed. (New York: Neal-Schuman, 2009).

Janet McNeil Hurlbert, "The Five-Minute Paper," in *Designs for Active Learning: A Sourcebook of Classroom Strategies for Information Education*, ed. Gail Gradowski, Loanne Snavely, and Paula Dempsey (Chicago: Association of College and Research Libraries, 1998): 23–24.

FAST 45: Peer Review of Research

Description: Students give each other feedback throughout a research project and receive feedback from their instructor and the course's embedded librarian.

Instructor Collaboration: High

Audience Size: Small, medium, or large

Feedback Level: Individual

Time Frame: Duration of research project

Materials/Technology: None

Standards:

>**ACRL Information Literacy Standards:** Any
>**Standards for the 21st-Century Learner:** Any

How: The instructor primarily leads the peer review of research process with support from you, an embedded librarian. Just as instructors have students provide feedback on each other's writing, students also comment on each other's integration of research. This process is not only valuable for the feedback students receive, but also for encouraging students to think critically about their own drafts after reviewing each other's.

   Ideas for Adapting:
   - Use electronic peer review in a course management system to facilitate peer review of research paper drafts outside of the classroom.

Example:
Anthropology professor Ryan Adams of Lycoming College uses an advanced peer review system that lasts over the course of the whole semester. He forms groups of three to four students who have related topics to work together throughout the research process. Groups may change during the research process as participants' topics change.

   Group members collaborate in the creation of individual research questions then visit the library together outside of class time to collect articles related to their topic. Groups meet to discuss how their library research is going throughout the collection and organizing process. The research leads to a day of student presentations, after which each student evaluates their group members' performance in a written document. It includes recommendations on grammar, style, suggestions for data collection, and other article citations that the researcher should look at.

Students use the feedback they receive from each other, you, and the instructor to write their final drafts. Students then submit the drafts to their group members for peer feedback. They hold individual meetings with the instructor and you to discuss integration of peer feedback before turning the draft into a final paper.

The students' evaluations of each other do not go into the final paper grade, so the feedback given and received is strictly for students' development as writers and researchers.

FAST 46: Questioning

Description: Students have the opportunity to ask higher-order questions helping them learn to do it independently during the research process and allowing the librarian to have a snapshot of the depth of students understanding.

Instructor Collaboration: Low or medium

Audience Size: Small, medium, or large*

Feedback Level: Individual, small group, or whole group

Time Frame: 10+ minutes

Materials/Technology: None

Standards:
  ACRL Information Literacy Standards: Any
  Standards for the 21st-Century Learner: Any

How: Near the end of the lesson, instruct students to create questions that support a variety of levels of thinking around the learning target(s). Allow students to use question stems from Bloom's Taxonomy as they work individually or in small groups to create questions, which can then be exchanged and answered by their peers. Be sure to rotate around the classroom to support students in both question development and answering. Ask students to report to the class about the questions they wrote and the questions they answered to reflect on what they needed to understand to do each (an example of metacognitive thinking). This activity gives you a glimpse of the level of understanding students have, based on the quality and content of the questions they create. Use the last few minutes of class to address minor misunderstandings or questions, evidence of widespread confusion can be discussed with the instructor to determine how to proceed.

  *__Ideas for Adapting for Large Audiences:__ Use a technological tool that allows students to enter text (Google Forms, Twitter, TodaysMeet, Socrative, blog comments) and enables you to quickly review many student responses, giving you an overall picture of the class's understanding and a report of trends that can be addressed during the lesson.

Example:
In an introductory accounting course, students performed peer presentations in small groups about different databases. At the end of class, the librarian asked each group to create quiz prompts about their database to ask the rest of the class. Students were given verbs from Bloom's Taxonomy to create questions with increasing levels of complexity. After each group created their questions, groups traded questions and answered the questions they received. Groups then read their questions and answers aloud to the class for a whole class discussion and review.

Group 1: Hoover's Database

LEVEL	VERB	QUESTION/PROMPT
REMEMBER	NAME	**Name** a search tab the Hoover's provides.
UNDERSTAND	EXPLAIN	**Explain** the purpose of the NAICS codes.
APPLY	SHOW	**Show** how one would make a summary of the financial ratios provided by the database.
ANALYZE	COMPARE & CONTRAST	**Compare** the reports provided by Hoover's with the Marketline reports in Business Source Premier.
EVALUATE	CRITIQUE	**Critique** the data provided by Hoover's compared to other databases.
CREATE	PREDICT	**Predict** the challenges you foresee for the industry.

Figure 7.5. Verb and Question Prompts

NOTE
Thomas A. Angelo and K. Patricia Cross, "Student-Generated Test Questions," in *Classroom Assessment Techniques: A Handbook for College Teachers*, 2nd ed. (San Francisco: Jossey-Bass, 1993), 240–243.

FAST 47: Video Retellings

Description: Students retell information through making videos, helping them cement their understanding and allowing the librarian to gauge the extent to which students have met the learning target(s).

Instructor Collaboration: Low or medium

Audience Size: Small, medium, or large

Feedback Level: Small or whole group

Time Frame: 3–20 minutes

Materials/Technology: Smartphones, iPads, video recorders, or audio recorders

Standards:
    ACRL Information Literacy Standards: Any
    Standards for the 21st-Century Learner: Any

How: Ask students make short video clips that retell key points of the lesson and e-mail them to you. The clips can then be viewed by the whole group at the end of class or at a later time by you and the instructor, providing students feedback by e-mail. Another option is to ask students to post the clips online, such as to course management software like Moodle or Blackboard, and then require students to view a specified number of classmates' videos and post a critique that analyzes the extent to which each video meets the established criteria.

Tips:
- Set clear criteria for what the retelling should address.
- Set a time limit.

FAST 48: Wordle or Tagxedo

Description: Students sum up main points or express ideas by inputting terminology into a word cloud generator like Wordle or Tagxedo.

Instructor Collaboration: Low

Audience Size: Small, medium, or large

Feedback Level: Small or whole group

Time Frame: 5–20 minutes

Materials/Technology: Projector, Internet access, and **http://www.wordle.net/** or **http://www.tagxedo.com/**

Standards:
   ACRL Information Literacy Standards:
      Standard 1: The information literate student determines the nature and extent of the information needed.
   Standards for the 21st-Century Learner: Any

How: Ask students to submit any kind of free-text assessment via e-mail or Google Forms. Compile these assessments into one word cloud using Wordle, which makes most-used words larger in size. The most frequently used terms will appear largest, demonstrating what students most value. Use this quick assessment of students' free-text responses to generate a class discussion.

Or use Tagxedo to generate word clouds that form shapes. Unlike Wordle, Tagxedo enlarges words based on order of input. Ask students to use one computer where they take turns inputting terms to create a class word cloud, a useful way for sharing keywords and strategies.

Example: In an introductory marketing course, students needed to answer a question about their product (a soft drink OR an online auction website), "How can it be marketed to a new cultural group?" Students had to support their conclusions with substantial research from database articles. A major problem for students in this type of research process was determining effective keywords. Groups brainstormed possible keywords representing the larger industry factors surrounding the product. The librarian checked each group's keywords and provided feedback. Groups were instructed to put their best keywords into Tagxedo. The value of Tagxedo is that it allows students to

Formative Assessment Snapshot Techniques for After Instruction

view each other's best work. This leads to students reflecting on their own choices and additional research angles.

Below are two examples of word clouds that students created in Tagxedo for the marketing course.

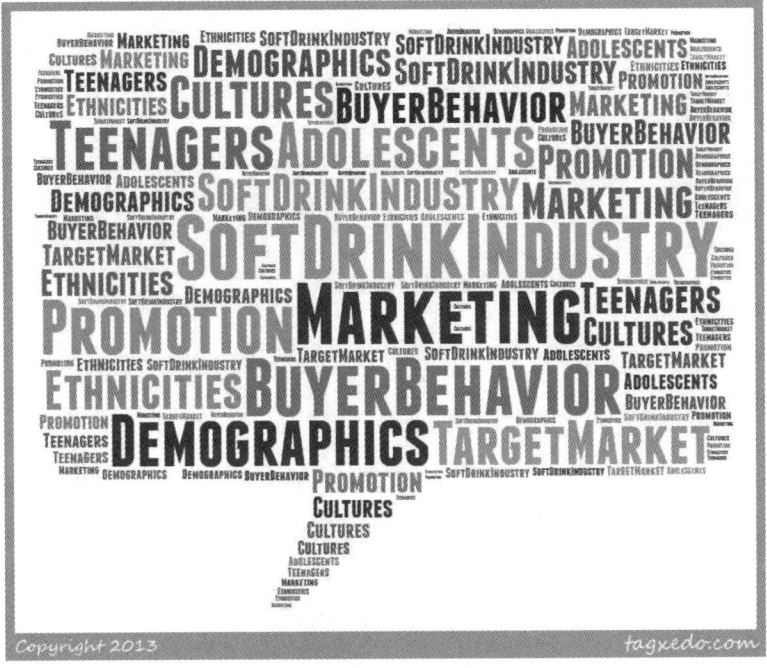

Figure 7.6. Tagxedo Wordles Created by Students

PART III
Digging Deeper into Formative Assessment

Chapter 8

The Relationship between Formative Assessment for Student Learning and for Teaching Improvement

The focus of this book has been to explore the use of formative assessment of *student* learning. Yet as we briefly explored in Chapter 2, "Are Academic Librarians Doing Assessment?," librarians often write about "formative" feedback, assessment, evaluation, or process in the context of improving their own teaching. Alabi et al., Abreeny and Hartman, Ragains, and Samson and McCrea all extensively discuss formative feedback in relation to peer observation of teaching.[1] Snavely and Dewald write, "Formative assessment of one's instruction is designed to provide feedback to instructors so that they will be able to improve their performance. It should give them clear constructive advice so that they know how they can improve. The term comes from the idea that it is given while instructors are 'forming' or developing, in this case, their teaching ability."[2] Librarians are not alone in this use of "formative feedback" for teaching improvement; Weimer uses it in her book, *Improving College Teaching: Strategies for Developing Instructional Effectiveness*.[3] We feel that this concept of "formative assessment" for the librarian's teaching improvement is worth exploring in a chapter of its own.

To start, we must be clear about the motivation behind the kind of assessment described in this chapter. Assessment of library instruction can have three different purposes. The first is for programmatic assessment, or how well the library's instruction program is meeting its goals and the mission of the institution. The second is for personnel decisions such as raises, tenure, or promotion. While formative assessment results may have a secondary benefit of assisting programmatic assessment or personnel decisions (if provided voluntarily), this chapter will focus on the third and final purpose: how assessment results can be used to help an instruction librarian improve teaching over time.

Barclay's often-cited article discusses the numerous barriers to library assessment. He discusses problems with the ethicality of control groups, the lack of quality standardized tests at the time, and the problems with multiple-choice and free-response tests.[4] Finally, he says librarians are in a "Catch-22" where they are expected to perform regular and formal assessments to obtain more resources, but they do not have the resources to do such formal assessments. He concludes by advising librarians to simply do the best they can and use a variety of assessment methods.

We feel that assessment for instructional improvement can be one of the easiest types of assessment to do. The formative assessment snapshot techniques we describe in this book are usually informal, often fun, and provide feedback not only for immediate improvement (which is the primary focus of this book) but also for improvement of a librarian's teaching skills over time. Additional summative assessments of student learning, such as surveys and knowledge tests at the end of a library session, do not have to be as rigorous as those used in preparation for publication. It does not have to be difficult, expensive, or time-consuming to collect data to inform future teaching goals.

Just as it is important to provide a safe learning environment for students when using formative assessment in the classroom, it is equally important to provide the same safe learning environment for librarians to grow. Librarians should be able to seek feedback on how they are doing without fear of harsh punishments for poor results. Such feedback is critical to grow as an educator. This is particularly important as librarians need to be able to experiment in the classroom with new teaching techniques, which may work the first time but quite often need tweaked, if not entirely revamped or thrown out, to reach their full potential. Furthermore, such "improvement initiatives should not be based on premises of remediation and deficiency with activities targeted only for those who need them."[5] No matter how good we are as instructors, there is always room for improvement. Assessment is an iterative process and developing an institutional culture that supports this is crucial for library instruction to have the largest possible impact. This culture of assessment will be discussed further in Chapter 11, "Working towards a Culture of Assessment."

While there are many ways librarians seek formative feedback to improve their instruction skills, the feedback tends to fall into five broad categories:
- informal assessments and reflection,
- diagnostic assessments,
- surveys of affective learning,
- surveys of cognitive learning,
- peer observation or coaching.

We will discuss each one in depth. Because each has strengths and weaknesses, it is critical to balance different types of assessments to get the most accurate picture of teaching performance possible.

Informal Assessment and Reflection

Assessment of teaching performance should start with informal assessment and self-reflection. Informal assessments are the appraisals educators make every second based on nonverbal behaviors demonstrated by students and the subsequent teaching adjustments. For example, if students look confused, good educators may ask students to share with their neighbors one thing they believe they understand and one thing they do not fully understand. The educator can listen in on these conversations and randomly call on a pair to share with the class what they discussed. If students look bored or like they are not paying attention, good educators may ask students to take a two minutes to write on an open-ended question, and then they collect the papers and randomly select a few to read to the class and discuss. We may realize after a class that students were not engaged by the activity we planned, so we look for another technique to use next time. These are examples of formative assessment of the affective aspects of student learning as educators are reacting to evidence of students' feelings and levels of engagement to improve teaching on the spot or over time.

For a long time, education scholars have considered reflection a critical component of good teaching. There are many types of reflections that affect our teaching. Brookfield encourages educators to reflect on their autobiographies as learners and educators.[6] He says that the strongest influence in determining what we value as educators are the memories of loved and hated teachers and "emotionally charged" memories of what worked and did not work for us when we were students. For example, if we hated group work as a student, we are less likely to assign it to our students. As many of these values are created and applied unconsciously, he challenges educators to become aware of these assumptions and evaluate their validity through reflection.

Similarly, we should reflect on our own experiences as educators. After each class, we often have a sense of how the class went. Some classes make us excited, others bring us down, and some we struggle to identify what did or did not go well. Sometimes this is informed by a brief conversation with an observing instructor as students are leaving the room. We should take time to think of what worked or did not work after each class, then use our conclusions to inform decisions made for the next class. Radcliff et al. say that this self-reflection plays two roles: It helps us "assess and reassess the effectiveness of our instruction on the spot ... [and] it can serve as a way to wrap-up or process an instructional experience."[7]

It is often helpful to bring real-life examples of students' questions or experiences from one class to another. For example, we have found students find the following introduction credible: "In the past semesters, students struggled with today's lab assignment until they discovered the *Gale Encyclopedia of Medicine*. The short and easy-to-read explanations in here will make your assignment much easier to complete." The first time this biology lab was brought to the library, there was not an adequate endorsement of the reference book, and the librarian informally observed students struggling to complete the lab questions designed by the instructor because they were relying on questionable and incomplete websites. The reference book was not only more authoritative but also simply better suited to the lab than the content they were finding on the websites. Because the librarian observed in the first class the relief students experienced once they discovered this resource halfway through the exercise, she has passed on the endorsement to future classes, which students have taken with more credibility than the librarian's original introduction. In the subsequent classes, students have always gone straight for the *Gale Encyclopedia of Medicine* instead of the Internet, and they complete their assignment in much less time. This is an example where informal observation allows us to pass on "cheats" or "short-cuts" from our past students' experiences to our future students, which they often appreciate.

Radcliff et al. point out that librarians need to be comfortable with their lessons and activities if they want to get the most out of informal observation.[8] If they are less comfortable, they will concentrate on themselves more and their students less. The more experience they have with a specific lesson, the more they will know where students have trouble, and they can make an effort to observe students more closely at those points.

Librarians have an additional challenge with becoming reflective educators in comparison to their instructor counterparts. While instructors teach the same number of hours each week over the course of the semester, our instruction load is usually "feast or famine." Because instructors tend to bring students into the library at the beginning of the research process, we may teach twelve classes in the third week of the semester and be done teaching by October or March. This means that we are often too busy to thoroughly reflect on our teaching during the first half of the semester and forget what desired actions our reflections inspired by the time the next semester comes around three to eight months later.

It is for this reason that a written record can be particularly useful to librarians. Radcliff et al. suggest scheduling five to twenty minutes after each class for reflection.[9] They also suggest keeping an informal assessment record with

- title of class,
- date,
- goals and objectives,
- observations,
- any thoughts or questions as a result of the observations,
- conclusions or actions.

They provide an example of what such a record would look like. Brookfield suggests a teaching log consisting of weekly records of memorable impressions.[10] "Events that excite or enrage us often do so because they confirm or contradict our assumptions. Events that engage our emotions are those that tell us most about ourselves."[11] Further information on journaling the library teaching experience can be found in Tompkins's useful article, "A Reflective Teaching Journal: An Instructional Improvement Tool for Academic Librarians."[12] She kept a teaching journal of her experiences teaching fifteen classes within the freshman learning community program. Her journal included planning, recording correspondences with the instructors, and reflection on how the class went. In the following semester, she used the journal to guide her instructional design and successfully improved engagement by moving away from the PowerPoint presentations that seem to bore students and providing additional support for ESL students who struggled with spelling in the databases.

Reflections of teaching can come in several other forms as well as Brookfield shows us.[13] A survival memo requires writers to pretend it is their last day on the job and have them write letters to their imaginary successors on what would help them succeed in the position. He also discusses the power of watching a video recording of oneself in front of a classroom, which can help us see how others see us. Such videos can help us recognize verbal and nonverbal tics that students may find annoying, actions that are encouraging or discouraging, or defensiveness, to name a few examples. In addition to the benefits Brookfield mentions, watching such a video can also help us analyze the types of questions we ask, how engaged the students are, how we prompt students to work towards the learning targets, and how we resolve students' misunderstandings. Brookfield warns that such videos are limited, though, because they do not necessarily help us know what to *do* once we have identified aspects we want to change.

At the end of the semester's teaching schedule, the librarian can review the individual class reflections and draw big-picture conclusions. These reflections, combined with more structured assessments, can help the librarian set personal goals for the upcoming semester. Brookfield suggests performing a periodic "Teacher Learning Audit" either once a semester or once a year.[14] This activity encourages educators to look at their recent experience and the knowledge and insights they have developed as a result. He provides example prompts to facilitate this type of reflection such as "Compared with this time last term/year, how do I know that … ?"[15]

Informal assessments as described here and reflections are not often thought of as "assessment," but they should be. We strongly believe that by viewing them as legitimate assessment, we can make the most of the information gathered. That is not to say they should be the only method of assessment. As Brookfield points out that through self-reflection, "we can never completely avoid the risks of denial and distortion."[16] However, it is an invaluable starting point. Data gathered through these informal observations can and should often be the root of decisions on what to assess with other, more formal evaluation methods.

Diagnostic Assessments

General diagnostic assessments are sent to large portions of our student body to understand more about their general backgrounds and views, usually through surveys and invitations to participate in focus groups. These assessments are not library satisfaction surveys like LibQual or tests of information literacy knowledge gains. They are more similar to the pre-assessment techniques suggested in Chapter 5, "Formative Assessment Snapshot Techniques for Before Instruction," but broader in scope and not focused on a specific class. These types of assessments help us more accurately understand the state in which students arrive to the library classroom. As this type of assessment is meant to measure the state of students' knowledge, attitudes, and habits *before* instruction, this type of assessment is *only* useful for the purpose of improving library services and not for accountability or personnel decisions. A number of authors who have conducted baseline surveys say that librarians do not do this enough.[17]

Standardized surveys that *can* be used to assess the baseline knowledge in incoming students include HEDS, Project SAILS, Information Literacy Test (ILT), and iSkills.[18] All of these are multiple-choice tests that can be used in many ways, including as a benchmarking tool. Because information issues are broader than research and information literacy, related campus departments may be implementing standardized surveys that are relevant to teaching information literacy. EDUCAUSE's ECAR survey looks at what technologies students use in their academic work and how they feel about their professors' use of various instructional technologies.[19] As many libraries deliver information literacy instruction online in various ways as well as provide common technologies to support learning in general, such survey results are indeed useful for librarians to be familiar with.

Standardized surveys have a number of benefits. They save librarians time—they're ready to use, and many are tested for reliability and validity. They also usually provide comparative data. This means that librarians receive the value of knowing how their own students feel, think, and behave in relation to other schools or based against a national average. This can be very useful as each student body has its own personality, and many librarians tend to be aware of national trends but less aware of how their students relate to those trends at a local level.

However, there are a number of reasons a library would want to create its own surveys. First, many of the standardized surveys are expensive, and many libraries do not have the budget to perform these on a regular basis. Above all, information found through scholarly library literature and informal observations may cause a library to want to target an information issue that is not covered by a standardized survey. Self-designed surveys are infinitely more flexible. For example, librarians at Robert Morris University surveyed freshmen about attitudes towards library research.[20] The results led to a commitment among the instruction librarians to place greater emphasis on the affective skills involved in the research process.

Helmke and Matthies describe an effort at Butler University where they realized they needed to assess incoming freshmen's skills and attitudes in preparation for designing a library tutorial and because of anecdotal reports of negative attitudes.[21] They found that a significant majority of students already had fundamental library skills learned from school and public libraries, and that experiences at those libraries were satisfactory. Therefore, the anecdotal evidence of negative attitudes towards libraries was not representative of students' actual attitudes, and the librarians designed their tutorial so that it would help transition freshmen to an academic library, building on the skills they learned at other types of libraries.

At our institution, we have done several homegrown diagnostic surveys. In 2009, we surveyed incoming freshmen about their background knowledge of plagiarism and how much plagiarism education they had previously received.[22] While the overall results were surprisingly favorable, partially due to the self-selection of participants, the survey still showed students' knowledge of how to avoid plagiarism varied greatly. This information was shared with professors and incorporated into an online educational game and annual freshmen workshops.[23]

In 2011, we surveyed students and instructors about their use of social media for academic work. The primary goal was to understand our students better in order to inform our collections and instruction, although we also published the results.[24] It is useful for us to understand our students' use of and contribution to such sites as *Wikipedia* and YouTube for research. While not a surprise, one of our biggest findings is that students are very confident in their evaluation skills while instructors remain frustrated with students' lack of evaluation competence. This has helped us form partnerships with instructors in teaching sound evaluation skills—the librarians contribute expertise on information sources and broad evaluation skills while the instructors help students apply those skills into specific academic disciplines.

In addition, we do regular focus groups on topics, such as educational games, Twitter, and Facebook, plus informal surveys and discussions in class. Some of these have confirmed what we suspected based on anecdotal evidence, national trends, or outright assumptions. Others have yielded very useful advice or insights into how students think, feel, and behave. At the very least, these relatively informal assessment results help the librarians build credibility in students' eyes by avoiding outdated references to their MySpace pages or assumptions that they contribute to *Wikipedia* just because they consume it.

Finally, it is important to consult your local Institutional Review Board (IRB) to see if your assessment, whether standardized or locally made, requires approval. The IRB was established to protect research participants from abuse and therefore fits into our professional values of ethical research. Even if the subject of a library assessment is not sensitive and the results are not intended for publication, most formal surveys, tests, or focus groups require at least expedited IRB approval, but the process at most institutions is relatively painless. Assessments that take place as part of the learning experience, such as the formative assessment snapshot techniques discussed elsewhere in this book, are exempt from the IRB approval process. Consult your local IRB contact for more detailed information.

Surveys of Affective Learning

Surveys of affective learning ask students, and sometimes instructors, if they felt they learned from the session and how effective the instruction librarian was. They can also ask students to self-assess their library skills. These surveys are concerned with students' feelings and confidence and are the most common type of assessment in library instruction.[25] This includes surveys asking "Would you recommend this class to a friend?" as well as One-Minute Papers (FAST 44); the first is a question of satisfaction and the second is a student's self-report of what was learned and what is still needed.

There are a number of articles that criticize this group of assessment methods.[26] Colburn and Cordell write, "This type of assessment has not, in most cases, been particularly useful. At most, it provides information about how the student perceives the librarian's presentation and how he or she feels about the library and/or the librarian."[27] Gustavson argues that such assessments are not useful because they only show what students *think* they have learned and not what they have *actually* learned.[28] Ragains even says affective assessments could be potentially harmful as they can cause educators to become unnecessarily defensive and lose confidence.[29] We strongly disagree with these statements because we feel that it is very important to know how students perceive our instruction sessions as fostering students' positive emotions and confidence are critical parts of being effective educators. While limited, such evaluations have an important role to play in a library's overall assessment program.

Building on Mellon's theory of "library anxiety," Vidmar makes a convincing case for the importance of the affective learning domain in library instruction.[30] For most students, the very idea of going to the library and doing research leads to negative feelings such as fear, shame, helplessness, frustration, and inadequacy. Even those freshmen who have experience with libraries (which is by far not all, as we learned in a local implementation of the HEDS survey), their past experiences are likely to be at small schools and public libraries. These places are very different from academic libraries, which tend to be larger, more scholarly, and use the Library of Congress shelving system. Because students often have previous experiences with other libraries before arriving to *our* libraries, these feelings are the "first contact points with the library, librarians, and the process of finding information."[31]

Library instruction, as it has developed, tends to be tool-based and focused on the cognitive and behavioral domains. We seem to theoretically value building good relationships with students, but we seem to think it just happens on its own because we are nice people with good intentions. Perhaps our frustrations in this area are because we do not pay enough attention to the feelings of our students. Motivation falls squarely in the affective domain and is based on confidence, value, and interest. Many librarians struggle with engagement in the library classroom, and we cannot entirely blame the students for their apathy when we have not given them a good reason to care about what we have to share with them. Finding the root of their apathy or even hostility through assessment of the affective domain can help us reach those students and turn them into confident and self-reliant researchers.

Library instruction is one of the biggest factors in relieving library anxiety. Van Scoyoc used Bostick's Library Anxiety Scale to compare a control group (no library instruction) to a group of students who received in-person instruction and a third group of students who received library instruction through an online tutorial.[32] They found that while both types of instruction improved affective barriers overall, only the group that received in-person instruction had a significant reduction in library anxiety. This is because the largest of the five subscales of this survey are barriers with staff, and it was concluded that an opportunity to begin building a relationship with a librarian through an instruction session was the determining factor.

Librarians should involve satisfaction surveys into the library's overall assessment plan and, more specifically, into the assessment of certain library classes. "Seeing ourselves through students' eyes is one of the most consistently surprising elements in any teacher's career."[33] Students can misinterpret our efforts to be polite and respectful, or their feedback from such surveys can reveal our own disruptive behaviors of which we have been unaware. It is our job to encourage students' positive attitudes towards research as well as imparting knowledge about the skills and behaviors involved. This starts with fostering attitudes of well-being and confidence in the library classroom.

Measurements of Cognitive Learning

While we do not agree with the outright dismissal of the affective aspect of the classroom interaction between students and librarians, we do agree there should be a high level of importance placed on effectiveness when assessing library instruction. It is true that surveys assessing student satisfaction and self-reported learning do not provide evidence that students actually learned anything. Therefore, measures of actual learning play a crucial role in an instruction program's overall assessment plan. If students are not learning much from the instruction, improvements must be made.

Of the cognitive learning assessments in library classes, many, if not most, are multiple-choice quizzes. This type of assessment has the advantage of being familiar to students and easy to grade. However, multiple-choice tests have several important disadvantages as well. The first is that separate time must usually be set aside for them, which is problematic when librarians only have about an hour of contact time. The more significant drawback is that multiple-choice tests are most effective for evaluating memorization of facts, which is not an accurate reflection of the behaviors, skills, and critical thinking students need to perform adequate library research.

Assessment of actual learning can happen in many ways. Most often, librarians simply want to know if the learning objectives were met by the end of the class or assignment. In other cases, librarians want to isolate and measure the learning that happens *during* an information literacy session. The first is easier but librarians must recognize that they cannot entirely take credit for student learning if they are unaware of the skills students had before they came into the library classroom. It is therefore sometimes useful to take the time to assess how much learning happens within the contact time librarians have with students.

There are two ways to isolate the learning that happens *during* the session that are helpful for librarians' teaching improvement. The first way is the pretest/posttest method. We advocate pretests elsewhere in this book to match the librarian's learning objectives with students' needs. However, they can also serve as a benchmark in which to compare post-instruction test scores to isolate how much learning happened while in the library classroom. A librarian at our institution was able to partner with a criminal justice professor to do a pretest several weeks before the students came to the library classroom. The information collected from this pretest was used to design the session. As the instructor did her own posttest at the end of semester, she included the same library questions as in the pretest, which provided the instructor and the librarian evidence of students' learning gains from the research assignment as a whole.

There are a vast number of pre- and posttests reported in the literature, though the authors' level of diligence to ensure scientific results is unnecessary when being used strictly for teaching improvement. Librarians at SUNY Geneseo used a pre- and posttest to evaluate the overarching goals of the library's part of the freshman writing and critical thinking course.[34] After several semesters' worth of assessment results, the librarians found that students came into the program with competence in certain areas, such as catalog searching, and never developed other skills by the time they completed the semester. The librarians eliminated instruction on skills the assessments showed students already had to allow for more time to be spent on skills they continued to struggle with. Assessment results showed improvement, though the authors planned to continue refining this program.

The second way is to compare a control group and an experimental group. In this type of assessment, several groups of students are compared. Between the groups, there is a single aspect of the instruction that is different so that the assessor can see which group performs better after instruction. This is often done with a summative assessment at the end of the class in order to have recorded data to compare. This is particularly useful for testing new instruction methodologies. However, this can be controversial as it means withholding something potentially valuable from a group of students for the benefit of being scientific.[35] It may also be difficult at small institutions or when there is only one section of a particular class, making comparison impossible. Furthermore, as each class has its own personality and differing levels of previous knowledge, results with small sample sizes are only indications, not proof, of the validity of conclusions. However, for the purpose of improving teaching, librarians can use past classes as a control group to compare new teaching strategies with current students, particularly if they have previously administered summative assessments at the end of instruction.

Meaningful, non-multiple-choice assessments of cognitive learning may sound like a daunting task, but it does not have to be. Oakleaf describes an implementation of the Information Literacy Instruction Assessment Cycle (ILIAC) at North Carolina State University.[36] ILIAC is a systematic cycle to assess and improve information literacy instruction that involves seven stages: (1) review learning goals, (2) identify learning outcomes, (3) create learning activities, (4) enact learning activities, (5) gather data to check learning, (6) interpret data, and (7) enact decisions. In the case study, they assessed an interactive online tutorial that all English 101 students are required to take. The tutorial already has built-in questions that check for student understanding such as asking them to explain why the authorship of a website indicates it is a credible source. Librarians then used a rubric to grade students' responses and inform the librarians' ideas for the tutorial's improvement.

There is a movement in the recent library instruction assessment literature towards "authentic" measures. The exact definition of what this means varies from one source to the next, but the general idea is that students are given an activity that simulates a part of the research process. Authentic assessments of student learning include using a rubric to evaluate evidence of research skills in portfolios, research papers, and annotated bibliographies. These examples are summative evaluations of student learning, but they also provide very useful feedback to librarians for improvement of teaching. There are numerous additional examples of authentic assessment in the library literature. Whitlock and Nanavati describe their authentic assessment for a for-credit information literacy class as helping to grade students' research logs where students were required to record the steps they took and the thought processes that led to their decisions throughout the research process.[37] Brown and Kingsley-Wilson describe a library treasure hunt activity with journalism students that evolved over time into a departmental assessment.[38] In this assessment, students provided answers and citations to six questions carefully designed with subject instructors to mimic the research process of professional journalists. Scharf et al. describe a project where student writing portfolios were analyzed for competence in citation, evidence of independent research, appropriateness, integration, and overall information literacy.[39] Knight evaluated freshman annotated bibliographies, finding they were strong in some areas and not in others.[40]

While many of the articles on authentic assessment grade the students' completed course assignments and happen outside of the one-shot, authentic assessments can happen during a library class. Many active learning techniques recommended in this book are examples of authentic formative assessments of student learning. They also provide useful formative feedback for the librarian. Examples include students working together to sort popular and scholarly periodicals (FAST 28: Periodical Sorting), selecting and refining keyword searches (FAST 26: Keyword Sorting Exercise), and locating a particular book using a call number (FAST 31: Scavenger Hunt). Whitlock and Nanavati describe an in-class assignment where they required students to conduct a search for a simulated research project, then turn in a printout of their search history from the database, and then choose the three most relevant resources in the list of results.[41] This helps the librarian and instructor see into students' thought processes as they attempt to answer an academic research question similar to what they will undertake after the library class. All of these are simulations of small parts of the research process and can easily be performed and assessed in a short period of time.

Assessing cognitive learning outcomes is crucial to any instruction program, but it does not have to be difficult as many active learning techniques can also serve as assessments. The level of formality varies greatly in this type of assessment and should be considered carefully. Many authentic assessments allow the instructor to know if students understand concepts addressed but do not necessarily provide recorded evidence for later analysis. Even written work, such as Guided Practice Templates (FAST 22), usually go home with students as an educational reminder rather than remain with the librarian for assessment evidence. Yet the types of assessments that do not provide recorded evidence often fit more naturally into the flow of a library class and align more closely with learning objectives. Authentic assessments of annotated bibliographies or final papers are difficult to grade and require more collaboration with instructors. They are impossible to do in every course, but selecting key courses may provide important insights that are not obtained through other methods. Consider carefully the level of formality of results needed when selecting assessment methods for cognitive learning.

Peer Review

Perhaps one of the most important tools for becoming a better educator is through peer review. In this method, instruction librarians, and even instructors, observe library classes and give the instruction librarian feedback on what works and suggestions for improvement. This method of evaluation is relatively easy to implement and not only provides suggestions for improvement but also confirms what is going well. This builds confidence, which in itself improves teaching.

The literature on peer observation (also known as peer coaching) stresses the importance of a *peer* group rather than a *mentoring* process. Status, seniority, and reporting chains should be taken into account when establishing a peer-coaching group. Another option is to create a group of people rather than just a pair. The instruction librarian who wishes to be observed can then choose which individual in the group is best suited for a particular class or a particular issue on which he or she wishes to obtain feedback. In addition, participation in such a program should be voluntary and the results should be confidential. These suggestions can help maintain an emphasis on *formative* assessment for improvement rather than professional, summative evaluation.

There are several useful articles on establishing formal peer review of teaching (PROT) programs in academic libraries. Samson and McCrea describe a program's implementation at the University of Montana with eleven participants while Alabi et al. established a similar program for seven pre-tenure librarians at Indiana University-Purdue University Indianapolis.[42] Both articles recommend a three-step process to obtain the most benefit from the experience:

Pre-observation: The observer and observee meet to discuss learning objectives and what the observee wishes to be observed. Participants also discuss whether the observer will be introduced and if he or she will participate in the class.

Observation: The observer attends a class and takes notes. Samson and McCrea suggest looking at class content, interaction, presentation, and instructional materials.[43]

Post-observation: The two participants meet to discuss what went well and suggestions for improvement. This meeting should take place within a few days of the observation while it is still fresh in both participants' minds. This sometimes is followed by a written letter or report as documentation for the instruction librarian's personal teaching file.

All participants in both of these PROT programs found the experience incredibly useful with the only drawback being the time involved and the inconvenience of scheduling a mutually available time for the observation. However, all participants reported that these drawbacks were minor when compared to the benefits.

In the literature on peer review among students, Li, Liu, and Steckelberg have concluded that it is actually the process of critiquing others that leads to performance improvement, perhaps even more than feedback the observers receive on their own instruction.[44] This is confirmed in the context of peer review in library instruction programs by Samson and McCrea's and Alabi et al.'s studies.[45] Observation of others teaching naturally causes one to reflect on his or her own classroom experiences and draw new conclusions and ideas. Observers reported finding renewed energy or creativity, possible solutions to problems they themselves struggled with, and confirmation of what they were doing well.[46]

These programs also report a number of additional benefits. Formal PROT or peer coaching programs encourage open conversations about teaching between pairs of instructors and observers and among the larger group of PROT program participants. There is a greater sense of community and a reduction in the feelings of isolation as participants gain confidence in what they do well in addition to realizing others share their struggles. This confidence allows educators to focus more on the learning objectives and evidence that students are meeting them than on the mechanics of teaching. Finally, the act of explicitly sharing learning objectives with a peer helps librarians articulate these learning objectives to the students, which is highly encouraged by many instruction librarians as a way to get students to care more about the library class and library research.[47]

Conclusion

A library instruction program dedicated to assessment includes most if not all of these types of assessment. None of these methods can be dismissed as ineffective. They each have their strengths and weaknesses, and they each complement each other to build the most accurate possible picture of us as educators. Informal observations and reflections are the most accessible form of assessment and must be the basis of our decisions on what to assess using other methods. Having a good idea of what skills and attitudes our students broadly have when they come to the library classroom is useful in forming safe assumptions on which to base our learning targets, activities, and lectures. Cognitive learning is at the center of what needs to be assessed, though balanced with the positive attitudes, relationships, and satisfaction that enable such learning to happen. Peer educators have the educational background and experience to provide valuable feedback on how to improve teaching, however, they do not think like students. Therefore, balancing peer feedback and student feedback is critical as well.

Regardless of the combination of assessment methods one chooses to use to inform his or her personal development as an instructor, the process will begin and end with reflection. As previously stated earlier in this chapter, many ideas for assessment come from reflection upon anecdotal experiences that may challenge or reveal our long-held assumptions. Once the assessment is completed, the results must be analyzed and reflected upon. Surveys and tests that yield numerical data must be interpreted into something meaningful, and unsatisfactory results should turn into an action plan.

While most of the suggestions in this chapter can contribute towards assessment of a program or for personnel evaluation purposes, the primary purpose is to inform efforts to improve as instructors. In each example provided, librarians used assessment results to inform new teaching strategies. Librarians have also used assessment results to negotiate more time with instructors or additional resources from library or institution administration. Using negative assessment results may help librarians show the need for more time with students while later evidence of improvement may help request more contact time with other instructors.

Due to the growing overall emphasis on assessment in libraries, we believe that libraries will begin adopting assessment management systems (AMSs). Oakleaf, Belanger, and Graham have compared a number of competing AMSs and found some to be more suitable for formative assessment than others.[48] Including formative assessments in an AMS can greatly facilitate a library's ability to draw big conclusions from multiple bite-sized assessments to demonstrate the value-added from the library instruction program.

At our institution, while we do not have an AMS, we perform annual reflections for the library director and periodic comprehensive portfolios for the institutional instructor-review process. Just as instructors include evidence of being effective educators, we too include various assessment results to show positive performance. Part of these results involves summative peer observations by instructors, some whom we work with on library instruction and some whom we do not. However, we can also choose to include the kind of formative assessment evidence that we describe in this chapter. We have a campus-wide emphasis on demonstrating effectiveness and improvement in teaching over time, and the evidence we select to put in the portfolio to show this is a personal choice. Under these conditions, assessment results that are originally intended for formative, personal development as instructors may be used in the personnel evaluation system. However, such inclusions must be strictly voluntary, or the motivation to assess becomes threatening, which is extremely harmful to the original intent.

The underlying idea of this chapter is that as educators, we are always evolving. Because teaching is an art, we will never reach our full potential. While this may sound discouraging, it is far from it. A continual quest for improvement keeps teaching interesting and fresh. Many librarians and instructors went into the field of education because they like to learn. Formative assessment from an educator's perspective allows us to learn about ourselves as teachers, establish effective relationships with students, and both get and give the best we can in the library classroom.

NOTES

1. Jaena Alabi, Rhonda Huisman, Meagan Lacy, Willie Miller, Eric Snajdr, Jessica Trinoskey, and William H. Weare, "By and for Us: The Development of a Program for Peer Review of Teaching by and for Pre-Tenure Librarians," *Collaborative Librarianship* 4, no. 4 (October 2012): 165–74; Pam Arbeeny and Chris Hartman, "Empowering Librarians to Be Better Teachers: The Value of Peer Coaching to Library Instruction," *Colorado Libraries* 34, no. 4 (October 2008): 39–45; Patrick Ragains, "Evaluation of Academic Librarians' Instructional Performance: Report of a National Survey," *Research Strategies* 15, no. 3 (January 1997): 159–75; Sue Samson and Donna E. McCrea, "Using Peer Review to Foster Good Teaching," *Reference Services Review* 36, no. 1 (2008): 61–70, doi:10.1108/00907320810852032.
2. Loanne Snavely and Nancy Dewald, "Developing and Implementing

Peer Review of Academic Librarians' Teaching: An Overview and Case Report," *Journal of Academic Librarianship* 37, no. 4 (2011): 343.
3. Maryellen Weimer, *Improving College Teaching: Strategies for Developing Instructional Effectiveness* (San Francisco: Jossey-Bass, 1990).
4. Donald Barclay, "Evaluating Library Instruction: Doing the Best You Can with What You Have," *RQ* 33 (1993): 195–202.
5. Maryellen Weimer, *Inspired College Teaching: A Career-Long Resource for Professional Growth* (San Francisco: Jossey-Bass, 2010), 22.
6. Stephen D. Brookfield, *Becoming a Critically Reflective Teacher* (San Francisco: Jossey-Bass, 1995).
7. Carolyn J. Radcliff, Mary Lee Jensen, Joseph A. Salem, Jr., Kenneth J. Burhanna, and Julie A. Gedeon, *A Practical Guide to Information Literacy Assessment for Academic Librarians* (Westport, CT: Libraries Unlimited, 2007), 29.
8. Ibid.
9. Ibid., 29–30
10. Brookfield, *Becoming a Critically Reflective Teacher*.
11. Ibid, 72.
12. Elizabeth K. Tompkins, "A Reflective Teaching Journal: An Instructional Improvement Tool for Academic Librarians," *College & Undergraduate Libraries* 16, no. 4 (2009): 221–38.
13. Brookfield, *Becoming a Critically Reflective Teacher*.
14. Ibid.
15. Ibid, 75.
16. Ibid, 33.
17. Jacqueline Courtney Klentzin, "The Borderland of Value: Examining Student Attitudes towards Secondary Research," *Reference Services Review* 38, no. 4 (2010): 557–70, doi:10.1108/00907321011090728.
18. "HEDS Surveys," HEDS Consortium, accessed January 8, 2014, http://www.hedsconsortium.org/heds-surveys/#RPS; "About Our Information Literacy Test," Project SAILS, accessed January 8, 2014, https://www.projectsails.org/AboutTest; "Information Literacy Test," Madison Assessment, accessed February 11, 2014, http://www.madisonassessment.com/assessment-testing/information-literacy-test/; "The iSkills Assessment," ETS, accessed February 11, 2014, https://www.ets.org/iskills/about.
19. EDUCAUSE Center for Applied Research, *ECAR Study of Undergraduate Students and Information Technology, 2012*, accessed January 8, 2014, http://net.educause.edu/ir/library/pdf/ERS1208/ERS1208.pdf.
20. Klentzin, "The Borderland of Value."
21. Jonathan Helmke and Brad S. Matthies, "Assessing Freshman Library Skills and Attitudes Before Program Development: One Library's Experience," *College & Undergraduate Libraries* 11, no. 2 (December 2004): 29–50.

22. Mary J. Snyder Broussard and Jessica Urick Oberlin, "Using Online Games to Fight Plagiarism: A Spoonful of Sugar Helps the Medicine Go Down," *Indiana Libraries* 30, no. 1 (2011): 20–21.
23. "Plagiarism Game: Goblin Threat," Lycoming College, accessed January 8, 2014, http://www.lycoming.edu/library/instruction/tutorials/plagiarismGame.aspx.
24. Mary J. Snyder Broussard, Rebecca A. Wilson, Janet McNeil Hurlbert, and Alison S. Gregory, "Faculty and Undergraduate Perceptions of Expertise within Social Media," in *Social Software and the Evolution of User Expertise*, ed. Tatjana Takseva (Hershey, PA: Information Science Reference, 2013), 227–46
25. Ragains, "Evaluation of Academic Librarians' Instructional Performance."
26. Amy Gustavson, "Using ILIAC to Systematically Plan and Implement a Library Information Literacy Assessment Program for Freshman Classes," *Public Services Quarterly* 8, no. 2 (2012): 97–113; Nancy W. Colborn and Rosanne M. Cordell, "Moving from Subjective to Objective Assessments of Your Instruction Program," *Reference Services Review* 26, no. 3-4 (1998): 125–38; Ragains, "Evaluation of Academic Librarians' Instructional Performance."
27. Colborn and Cordell, "Moving from Subjective to Objective Assessments."
28. Gustavson, "Using ILIAC."
29. Ragains, "Evaluation of Academic Librarians' Instructional Performance."
30. Constance A. Mellon, "Library Anxiety: A Grounded Theory and Its Development," *College Research Libraries* 47, no. 2 (March 1986): 160–165; Dale J. Vidmar, "Affective Change: Integrating Pre-Sessions in the Students' Classroom Prior to Library Instruction," *Reference Services Review* 26, no. 3-4 (September 1998): 75–95.
31. Vidmar, "Affective Change," 75.
32. Anna M. Van Scoyoc, "Reducing Library Anxiety in First-Year Students," *Reference & User Services Quarterly* 42, no. 4 (2003): 329.
33. Brookfield, *Becoming a Critically Reflective Teacher*, 33.
34. Bonnie J. M. Swoger, "Closing the Assessment Loop using Pre- and Post-Assessment," *Reference Services Review* 39, no. 2 (2011): 244–59, doi: 10.1108/00907321111135475.
35. Barclay, "Evaluating Library Instruction."
36. Megan Oakleaf, "The Information Literacy Instruction Assessment Cycle: A Guide for Increasing Student Learning and Improving Librarian Instructional Skills," *Journal of Documentation* 65, no. 4 (2009): 539–60.
37. Brandy Whitlock and Julie Nanavati, "A Systematic Approach to Performative and Authentic Assessment," *Reference Services Review* 41, no. 1

(2013): 32–48.
38. Carol Perruso Brown and Barbara Kingsley-Wilson, "Assessing Organically: Turning an Assignment into an Assessment," *Reference Services Review* 38, no. 4 (2010): 536–54.
39. Davida Scharf, Norbert Elliot, Heather A. Huey, Vladimir Briller, and Kamal Joshi, "Direct Assessment of Information Literacy Using Writing Portfolios," *The Journal of Academic Librarianship* 33, no. 4 (2007): 462–77, doi:10.1016/j.acalib.2007.03.005.
40. Lorrie A. Knight, "Using Rubrics to Assess Information Literacy," *Reference Services Review* 34, no. 1 (February 2006): 43–55, doi:101108/00907320510631571.
41. Whitlock and Nanavati, "A Systematic Approach."
42. Samson and McCrea, "Using Peer Review to Foster Good Teaching"; Alabi et al., "By and for Us."
43. Samson and McCrea, "Using Peer Review to Foster Good Teaching."
44. Lan Li, Xiongyi Liu, and Allen L. Steckelberg, "Assessor or Assessee: How Student Learning Improves by Giving and Receiving Peer Feedback," *British Journal of Educational Technology* 41, no. 3 (2009): 525–36, doi:10.1111/j.1467-8535.2009.00968.x.
45. Samson and McCrea, "Using Peer Review to Foster Good Teaching"; Alabi et al., "By and for Us."
46. Alabi et al., "By and for Us."
47. Vidmar, "Affective Change"; Alabi et al., "By and for Us"; Debra Gilchrist and Anne Zald, "Instruction and Program Design through Assessment," in *Information Literacy Instruction Handbook*, ed. Christopher N. Cox and Elizabeth Blakesley Lindsay (Chicago: Association of College and Research Libraries, 2008), 164–92; Whitlock and Nanavati, "A Systematic Approach."
48. Megan Oakleaf, Jackie Belanger, and Carlie Graham, "Choosing and Using Assessment Management Systems: What Librarians Need to Know" (paper presented at the Association of College and Research Libraries Conference, Indianapolis, IN, April 2013), http://www.ala.org/acrl/sites/ala.org.acrl/files/content/conferences/confsandpreconfs/2013/papers/OakleafBelangerGraham_Choosing.pdf.

Chapter 9

Technology and Formative Assessment in Student Learning

Though we have already described a number of assessments that involve technology in Chapters 5–7, we feel that the relationship between technology and formative assessment deserves special attention and merits its own chapter. While those chapters focused on the *assessments*, this chapter will focus on the *tools* that can facilitate formative assessment. This chapter may be of particular use to librarians teaching information literacy in an online environment, though none of the authors of this book have experience teaching in a strictly online setting.

Information and technology are inherently related in today's world. Due to the ubiquity of the Internet, our students are bombarded with information in many forms. Yet they do not necessarily know what to do with so much information or have the required tools to deal with the information overload they are subjected to on a daily basis. Because of the increase in use of information technologies in our everyday lives, it makes sense to include appropriate technology in our teaching of information literacy skills. Using emerging technologies to help students learn critical information skills can help them manage information and technology better and prepare them to be lifelong learners, which is perhaps the most important goal of higher education, particularly in the liberal arts.

We must begin this chapter with two warnings. The first is that we do not condone adopting technology for the sake of technology. As educators, we must always carefully choose the right technology for the job and be comfortable with it before we offer it to students. This is particularly important for technology-based assessments because we conduct them to find out what the students know, which requires an authentic assessment environment. If we pick an assessment technology that we are not comfortable with or that does not work well for its purpose, students' responses will be affected by the incompatibility, leaving us with an inaccurate picture of their learning.

The second warning is that we name and describe specific web-based services in this chapter that our readers may not have access to. We share them because there are many tools that perform the similar functions. Furthermore, we recognize that these technologies will evolve. New ones will replace these, and some of these examples may be obsolete by the time this book is published. However, they are still worth discussing in this level of specificity because the underlying qualities and usefulness for formative assessment will be the same or perhaps better in the new tools of the future.

If we carefully pick the right tools for the job, technology can greatly improve many formative assessment techniques. Many of the low-tech ideas mentioned in Chapters 5–7 can be enhanced with technology, particularly for instruction librarians. Technology can help us make the most of our extremely limited face time with students in two ways: by speeding up the collection, delivery, and processing of student assessment data and by extending our relationship with students beyond our time together. Speed of assessment and extension of contact time will be discussed together as they are so closely related that they are difficult to separate.

Computer-Based vs. Computer-Assisted Assessments

When discussing technology-based assessments, it is important to distinguish between two kinds. The first is computer-*based* assessment, where the assessment is not only delivered by a computer but also graded by it. The other is computer-*assisted* assessment, which facilitates the collection of assessment data, but the computer does not perform the actual evaluation.[1] Both facilitate time-efficient communication between educators and learners, though the two assessment types often differ in the kind of learner data they can handle and when the educator invests his or her time in the assessment process. We will explore each type in this chapter, and then look at specific technologies that are examples of each.

Computer-*based* assessments can help provide accurate and time-efficient assessments when a high student-to-faculty ratio prohibits meaningful individual feedback in a low-tech environment. While the technology exists to allow computers to grade students' short answers and even essays, this technology is not yet freely available. Most computer-based assessments are limited to multiple-choice questions, which often provide the user written feedback after he or she has chosen a particular answer. While several articles in the broader higher education literature discuss this in relation to large, first-year classes with several hundred students, this means something different for librarians.[2] While it is quite obvious that a single professor cannot provide individual feedback for 400 students at regular intervals over the course of a semester, librarians cannot do this even for twenty-five students when limited to the typical one-shot library session. Technologies such as computer-based assessment can help collect evidence of student learning and provide feedback to students in a very short period of time.

Additionally, students come to college with varying degrees of preparation for college-level research. Computer-based assessments can assist with adaptive testing: efficiently sorting individual learners based on abilities and connecting each one to the best-suited resources. In such a system, students in the same class would be provided different instruction based on their individual starting points. Some would be directed towards remedial resources while others continue on to develop advanced skills. SurveyMonkey, Qualtrics, and Moodle allow survey designers the option to place respondents on different tracks based on their answers in order to obtain the most useful information possible. Google Forms also allows survey designers to send the user to a designated URL based on the specific answer he or she chose.

While such adaptive systems have not yet been applied to library instruction as far as we know, it would not be difficult to incorporate them into an online tutorial. This could allow librarians to individually tailor learning experiences within a library one-shot so some students can receive the remedial work they need while other students can move on to the higher-order information literacy skills that librarians never seem to have time to address. The pretest diagnostic activity would directly lead each student to the most appropriate activity, and perhaps this would alleviate students' common complaint that library instruction is repetitive. Because such online systems would need to be sophisticated, it would be useful for a company to develop such a platform that could be individually customized and sell it to libraries at a reasonable price, rather than individual libraries investing in their own proprietary systems.

It is important to consider that while computer-based assessments usually provide immediate feedback, they are not necessarily less time-consuming for the instructor. JISC warns that while computer-based instruction saves the instructor time in grading, it does take more time before class to develop.[3] Creating good multiple-choice questions is difficult, particularly because we no longer think like students. Questions must be clear, and the wrong choices need to be plausible so that students are less likely to guess the right answer because it is the only logical choice. Furthermore, such questions need to be entered into a tool such as Google Forms or a course management system, which takes time. It takes a great deal more time if a tutorial is being programed from scratch. However, these computer-based assessments often pay off when they can be re-used in multiple sections or over several semesters, providing a higher return on investment.

The biggest drawback of computer-based assessments is a dependence on quantitative student input, which often emphasizes multiple-choice assessments as this is the easiest type of assessment for computers to evaluate. However, multiple-choice questions are known to not be the most effective method of evaluation.[4] They tend to focus on definitions and factual recall, rarely inspiring critical thinking or true understanding of the material. Even worse, "it is now accepted wisdom that assessment measures tend to influence what is learned as well as the way in which it is learned."[5] Multiple-choice assessments tend to isolate bits of information, so that students may do well on each piece but do not understand how the content of each question relates to each other, preventing real communication about the content. This leads to learners who come to know the content in "small 'bites' of knowledge" without knowing how to put it together or use it in a meaningful way.[6]

Finally, a multiple-choice quiz "reinforces the idea that someone else already knows the answer to the question so original interpretations are not expected."[7] Yet we are helping students become novice researchers, and research is all about original interpretations. While such foundational and tool-based questions have their place, we cannot limit library assessments to questions such as "What database can you use to find newspaper articles?" Training is needed for writing effective multiple-choice assessments, and when designing such assessments, librarians need to focus on higher-order thinking skills to encourage students' development of the necessary problem-solving skills required for research.

In one of the seminal articles in the literature on formative assessment, Sadler wrote that because formative assessment has such an emphasis on qualitative assessment, it can never be automated by a computer.[8] While technological advances since he wrote that in 1989 have somewhat proved him wrong, computers remain limited in what they can assess, and our access to many sophisticated emerging technologies is limited. However, computer-*assisted* assessment facilitates the transfer of qualitative (word-based and subjective) data. These tools foster direct communication between the instructor and learner. This communication, in the form of feedback, is at the heart of formative assessment. Computer-assisted assessments are also important to libraries because research is a complex skill, and its assessment should often be more qualitative than computer-*based* assessments often allow. While we may be able to program quizzes about the *tools* we teach, information literacy is too complex to be wholly limited to clear-answer assessments. Even the most experienced professional researchers often struggle with library research, and there are always difficult choices to make in the research process as well as complex patterns to identify and an abundance of information to critically evaluate and organize. We need rich communication tools that help us mentor novice researchers through this complex process.

Communication tools are one of the most quickly growing areas of technology, and many can be used for computer-assisted formative assessments. Traditional models of education involve of the teacher lecturing at the front of the room with the students communicating to the teacher only on the test, when it is too late to improve learning, but there is a rapidly increasing emphasis on active learning. Similarly, television, movies, radio and books used to be one-way communication, with the consumer having little to no options for interaction beyond programs' popularity ratings. Yet most of our students today interact with various forms of media daily, and they do not remember a time when they could not contribute through social networks and other social media applications. Television companies are superimposing viewers' tweets onto shows. Social media provides shows with free publicity through word-of-mouth marketing, which, if favorable, is the most coveted kind of publicity. In a similar manner, students are independently choosing to use social media to communicate with classmates, collect survey data for projects, take collaborative notes, and snap digital pictures of class materials. The integration of information tools into their personal and academic lives will only grow with the increasing pervasiveness of smart phones and tablets.

For instruction librarians, technology has a lot of potential to improve communication with students and extend our limited contact time with students through asynchronous tools. Social media allow us to share additional content (instructor-to-student communication) but also provide ways for the students to respond, contribute, and create their own original content to share with the instructor and their fellow classmates. While educators may not be using such tools the way their developers intended, the ability for students to participate is already built into these tools. Additionally, we can make use of the advanced features in learning management systems such as Moodle or advanced subscription services marketed specifically to libraries or more generally to educators. All of these extend our ability to communicate with students outside of the library classroom's walls, through a formal flipped classroom experience or in "bite-sized" pieces. And any tool that facilitates and encourages student participation can be used for formative assessment.

Sample Technologies for Formative Assessment:

Now that we have explored computer-based and computer-assisted assessments, it is time to look at individual tools that can be used as one or the other of these. Many of them blur the line between computer-based and computer-assisted assessments as many can change when combined with another technology, or they can aggregate some results for easy interpretation by the educator but do not actually *grade* student entries. Most of the nine tools we will discuss can be combined with discussion or other educational techniques to get the most value out of them as formative assessment tools.

1. Classroom Response Systems

Clickers (FAST 16) and other classroom response systems are examples of computer-graded assessment where the assessment results are immediate. Timely feedback is important to formative assessment, and immediate feedback is ideal, and, moreover, students *like* immediate feedback.[9] Clicker questions are usually multiple-choice, though some brands can allow for short answer. With clickers, the educator asks a question that is usually projected onto a screen at the front of the room. Students have a short amount of time to submit their answer. When all responses have been submitted, the educator can display the results, usually in the form of a bar graph or pie chart. Because the results are provided in a visual form, the instructor can immediately gauge the class's understanding. Because the correct answer, if there is one, is immediately given, students can immediately gauge their own understanding. Both parties then have the opportunity to adapt their teaching or learning strategies.

There is no shortage of scholarly articles on clickers in libraries. The authors of these articles are decisively divided in their conclusions on clickers' effectiveness as learning tools. One of the most cited articles on clickers in library literature is Dill who did not feel clickers improved student learning.[10] To her credit, she is clear about the limitations of her study; in an effort to isolate clickers as the only variable in the study, both the experimental and control groups had the same classroom experience besides the use of clickers. This eliminated any possibility for formative assessment, which inherently makes each class different. Dill is not the only one who is skeptical of clickers. Moniz et al. found they were not any more effective than raising hands.[11] Chan and Knight, even providing evidence of using clickers for formative assessment, found clickers had little effect on student learning, although they improved affective aspects of the classroom.[12]

Yet others who clearly are using clickers as part of formative assessment are very pleased with them.[13] A number of these articles specifically mention adjusting teaching based on the student data collected.[14] Collins, Tedford, and Womack write, "The benefit of asking for the answers through clicker responses is that the instructor gets immediate feedback on problem areas and can revisit content in response to incorrect answers."[15] As this quote demonstrates, one of the most common and easiest ways to use clickers for formative assessment is to ask students questions on the fundamental facts they need to know to complete the assignment, which serves as a test of what they already know. These questions may be more meaningful if phrased in the form of scenarios, asking what should be done in a simulated research situation. If a majority of the class gets the question right, the class can move on. If the students' answers are divided or mostly incorrect, the librarian can lead a discussion on that topic.

The main advantage clickers have over low-tech class response systems, such as hand raising and response cards, is that clickers allow students to participate anonymously. It is in both the literature and our personal experience that the ease and anonymity of participation with clickers leads to nearly every student participating.[16] Having such high levels of participation provides the librarian with more accurate results of the class's understanding as a whole. Furthermore, this ability to gather information about students' understanding is not any more difficult for a librarian teaching fifteen students than a librarian teaching fifty.

As clickers do not inherently incorporate formative assessment, we believe that it would be useful to provide some advice on ensuring that they are used most effectively. Briggs and Keyek-Franssen write that the benefit of clickers is that they facilitate the ability to "monitor student learning and to immediately respond to students' needs for clarification or additional practice."[17] Clicker questions should be designed to inspire discussion on the results. They have found clicker results to lead to increased classroom engagement in the discussions following each question. No two classes using the same set of clicker questions will have the exact same class because the librarian is adapting to each group's unique educational needs. Students benefit immediately from this flexibility.

There are several other alternatives to class response systems that still use technology. Zdravkovska et al. gave students laser pointers to use to vote by directing their beams on the projected choices at the front of the room.[18] The laser pointers had the advantage of being less expensive and more portable than clickers so that librarians could use them in any room on campus. Poll Everywhere allows students to use their cell phones' texting feature so that no special hardware or software is required. This is also less expensive for the library and more portable than clickers. Socrative, a free online tool, allows students to use any Internet-connected device to respond to the educator. It allows for richer and more spontaneous communication between the educator and students than most clicker software as it supports short-answer texts and even allows students to vote on the best of the student-supplied answers to the previous question.

2. Google Forms

Forms in Google Drive, commonly called Google Forms, are a free and easy way of collecting survey information. When creating a new form, there are many question types for educators to choose from, including multiple-choice, drop-down, check-box, short text, scale, and more. Survey designers can allow aggregate results to be viewed just after one participant submits a response or viewed after all surveys have been collected. The results are showed in visually appealing and easy-to-interpret graphs.

I defined keywords or synonyms	I used Britannica Online to do a general search on my topic	I formed a thesis statement gained from initial searches	I completed a works cited in MLA format
56/74 (76%)	45/74 (61%)	56/74 (76%)	67/74 (91%)
I paraphrased my notes instead of copying word-for-word	I wrote the paper in my own words and did not plagiarize	I handed in a completed essay	I included in-text citations that referred to my works cited list.
68/74 (92%)	73/74 (98%)	65/74 (88%)	68/74 (92%)

Figure 9.1. A Google form used to show students' responses to a Checklist (FAST 14) designed to help them self-assess whether they effectively completed each step of the research process.

Google Forms can facilitate formative assessment in several ways. A Google form can be used to deliver a pretest as homework before the librarian meets with students or as a mid-instruction assessment using the computers in the information literacy classroom. It can be used in a one-shot class to bring many students' responses or opinions into one central place. In each of these cases, the results of a survey can be displayed and discussed in class, giving instructors a way to adapt to a class's unique learning needs. In the following example, students were directed to use a Google form to complete a Checklist (FAST 14) to self-assess whether they *effectively* completed each step of the research process.

Because Google Forms was used rather than administering the survey through paper, the results were immediately available to show the class in an easy-to-understand format. This format allows the librarian to lead a class discussion on why students made the choices they did.

Other free online services can enhance the functionality of Google Forms and improve its utility in facilitating formative assessment. Because Google Forms was simply designed to collect data, not serve as an educational tool, it does not provide educators the ability to grade students' submissions or provide feedback. However, it can be combined with another free online tool called Flubaroo to do just this. Flubaroo can evaluate multiple-choice questions submitted through Google Forms and then e-mail students with their results, turning Google Forms from a computer-assisted assessment tool to a computer-based one. Google Forms can also collect longer textual responses, which cannot always be easily processed by the instructor within class. However, such responses from students can be turned into visual feedback by copying and pasting the text into Wordle or Tagxedo (FAST 48). Wordle will make the most common words in the assessment larger than others, which can allow the librarian and instructor to draw some quick conclusions during the class and facilitate a responsive class discussion. This is a powerful way to quickly assess large amounts of student writing without sophisticated or expensive software.

3. Learning Management Systems

Online learning management systems, such as Blackboard and Moodle, are intended to augment in-person instruction through links to assignment descriptions and drop boxes, readings, websites, online tools, and quiz features. They serve as a digital portal that facilitates student learning outside of the classroom. Several of the common course management tools can be useful for librarians to increase their time with students and assess their learning.

Using online learning management systems to create quizzes is mildly time-consuming but relatively intuitive with many options to suit various assessment needs. Questions can be stored in a quiz bank and re-used for other classes. Students are able to get immediate feedback after answers are submitted, not just in the form of a grade but also a textual response to each answer chosen. Individual students' results are displayed instantaneously to the instructor.

Course management programs offer more advanced features such as Moodle's "lesson," which allows educators to create interactive online tutorials. Librarians can use a Moodle lesson to create a flipped classroom where students can watch an embedded screen capture video, then answer a few short comprehension questions. Students can repeat this lecture-assessment cycle to cover all of the desired content within Moodle, and then be ready for hands-on activities when the librarian and students meet for information literacy instruction. The assessment here serves two purposes. The first is to ensure that students complete the homework; the second is to check that students comprehend the main points of each mini-lesson. These Moodle lessons do take time for the educator to set up, but once they are complete, they can be transferred and tweaked for other classes.

Moodle's "workshop" module facilitates electronic peer review, which has been shown to be an effective teaching method for improving student writing, providing an invaluable tool for helping students develop the complex skills necessary for integrating library research into their papers. While articles on peer review focus primarily on writing skills, students can also be instructed to look at each other's integration of research, in-text citation placement, and appropriateness of sources in the bibliography. Li, Liu, and Steckelberg have shown it is effective to not only receive peer feedback but also for students to provide formative feedback on each other's writing.[19] The experience of examining a classmate's writing causes students to reevaluate their own. Yet peer review is time-consuming and cannot happen in a single library one-shot class. Electronic peer review can allow the process to take place outside of the classroom and allow the librarian to be involved without sacrificing additional class time.

In all of these activities, Moodle offers advanced settings to maximize the potential for formative assessment. For example, students can be given multiple opportunities to complete each assignment, with either the mean or the highest score as the one that goes to the grade book. All computer-graded activities provide places for the educator to provide textual feedback customized to the answers the student chose, meaning the educator can provide mini-tutorials when a student selects a wrong answer, which helps the student learn on subsequent assessment attempts.

Finally, learning management systems, such as Moodle, offer options for adaptive testing in two ways. First, there is the option to limit access to a lesson until a competency level is reached on a previous lesson. Second, with each page or assessment question, students can be directed towards the tools they need most to advance in the class. For example, if a student answers a question incorrectly, he or she can be sent back to the tutorial page or a special remedial page that is only seen if he or she shows a lack of understanding on that topic. Setting up any of these advanced options in Moodle can be a little time consuming, but this is because the program has so many powerful options.

4. Citation Software

While well-established programs like EndNote and RefWorks were initially designed for graduate students and are strictly personal citation management programs, emerging online citation programs such as subscription editions of EasyBib and NoodleTools are being developed as educational tools for developing researchers as well as citation managers. These new citation programs are more intuitive and have features that lend themselves to more steps of the research process than just the bibliography. While their citation-creating features are not yet as sophisticated as the other more established programs, EasyBib and NoodleTools require students to be responsible for their citation formats while providing mini-tutorials and tips to enable them to do so. These programs are also designed for notes management. In EasyBib, students can easily create annotations for each book or article and use the notebook feature to create virtual note cards for individual pieces of information. These virtual note cards are further broken down into separate boxes for quotes, paraphrases, and comments, encouraging students to think about such distinctions in the note-taking stage of their research. Furthermore, research organization is facilitated by the ease in which note cards can be connected to a source in the student's bibliography, and the note cards can be used to create an outline.

EasyBib and NoodleTools can be used for formative assessment by requiring students to collect and annotate their sources from any computer, then "share" it with their instructor and librarian (FAST 38: Annotated Bibliography). The instructor and librarian can also use the program to keep track of student progress at any time, discouraging student procrastination. Instructors can look at the projects' subject content while librarians can look for the appropriateness of the sources chosen, and the two can share responsibility for evaluating the critical thinking displayed in the students' annotations. EasyBib even contains a comment feature so that the educators can provide feedback directly within the program.

5. Online Tutorials

Another powerful tool for computer-based formative assessment is interactive online tutorials. Such tutorials require students to work through content, and students are held accountable for the content through quizzes and activities. These tutorials are most effective if at least some of the activities require students to use real digital library resources, encouraging critical thinking by solving a puzzle or figuring out how to use the tools themselves.

The Association for College and Research Libraries (ACRL) maintains a database of peer-reviewed online tutorials called PRIMO.[20] Many technologies have been used to develop the tutorials included in PRIMO, including, but not limited to, Captivate, Camtasia, Adobe Flash, and LibGuides. Many, if not most, of these tutorials are interactive and have periodic or summative information checks. Some allow multiple attempts at each question until the right answer is selected. However, the textual feedback to tutorial users is disappointing, mostly limited to some form of correct or incorrect message, if any feedback is given at all. Librarians who design these online tutorials are missing out on potential student learning opportunities by skipping feedback. When designing a tutorial for formative assessment, librarians need to include a good amount of specific feedback after each question or activity.

For libraries who do not have the resources to create their own tutorials, there are several companies that can make customized tutorials for a fee. Some of these are pre-packaged tutorials with room for customization, such as Imagine Easy's ResearchReady, or are custom-made to specifications like those offered through the Credo Literati service.[21] ResearchReady is a new product that has a lot of potential for formative assessment. The platform has prepared content, mostly focusing on the big-picture information literacy skills that we often do not have time to teach. The content and questions were designed by trained librarians, and the developers have sought feedback from customers throughout the design process. In addition to the prepared content, the program allows customization, including adding images, videos, and several types of questions.

ResearchReady was designed to *complement* rather than replace in-person instruction, and it is an excellent technological platform for a flipped library classroom. It can easily be used to host interactive tutorials or pretests, with options for computer-graded assessments and textual feedback from students. While much of the functionality of ResearchReady can be done in learning management systems, such as Moodle, this subscription service offers three advantages:

The prepared content and assessment questions save a great deal of time for the librarian. In Moodle, for example, because there are so many options, setting up a "lesson" with a lot of content is very time consuming. Personalizing small parts of the prepared content is much easier than starting from scratch.

The prepared content focuses on big-picture skills. All student data is presented in a way that can be easily reviewed by educators as individual students or class aggregates. Library instruction has, due to time constraints, evolved to focus on tools rather than these big-picture skills. Having already created content and assessment questions, which are not tool-focused as ResearchReady is marketing this to a wide range of library types, can help instruction librarians break out of the tool-based mode and get to the topics we want to cover but do not have time for or have forgotten how to teach.

The assessment data can be arranged in a variety of visual ways, allowing for quick analysis. Assessment results can be arranged by question so that the librarian can perform a pretest before or at the beginning of class, and the resulting graphs immediately show which areas are the most problematic for a particular group of students, allowing the librarian to adjust on the spot as needed.

ResearchReady may also be a great platform for following up after a one-shot assessment; librarians can create tutorials about content in which students were insecure, and then add a brief assessment to check for understanding one final time.

6. Feedback Facilitation Tools

There are many communication tools that can facilitate communication between educators and students. Hatzipanagos and Warburton compared blogs and wikis' usefulness for formative assessment with four "first-generation technologies:" electronic quizzes, e-mail, discussion lists, and discussion forums.[22] They concluded that the social software technologies were more conducive to formative assessment and learning in several ways. The informal nature of writing in blogs and wikis encourages reflection, open conversations, and self-regulated learning. The most useful feedback for learning is not when the instructor simply tells students what to do to improve but when the instructor and students engage in dialog on the various ways students can improve their work. Social media tools have been built to enable and encourage this dialog between participants. Finally, these tools encourage timeliness, which is emphasized as a key quality of effective feedback.

In library instruction literature, Click and Petit used blogs in a for-credit information literacy class.[23] Students were required to explore various library tools and practice new research skills, and then write their reflections as blog entries on WordPress. The librarians found that the quality of students' reflections greatly improved because they were making their work public and reading each other's entries; student feedback on the experience was positive. In an article describing students' contributions to *Wikipedia* as part of a college history course, Chandler and Gregory describe how technology improved feedback throughout the research and writing process.[24] Within *Wikipedia*, the instructor and librarian could monitor students' work by looking at each page's history, where changes are recorded and attributed to the login name of the group responsible for the change. Additionally, students and the two educators used the forum of the class's Moodle site to discuss technical and research issues and provide timely troubleshooting and support.

Twitter (FAST 34) is an increasingly common tool for audience members to interact with speakers at large conference sessions. Just as announcing a common hashtag at the beginning of a conference session can help audience members connect with the speaker and each other, an educator announcing a hashtag at the beginning of a class can enhance student learning and be used as formative assessment. Having students summarize their understanding into a very short sentence can be a very powerful opportunity for formative assessment. Students must think critically about the content to pull out the main point. Because tweets are so short, the educator can read and evaluate these summaries on the spot. For this reason, the 140-character limit in Twitter fits in nicely with formative assessment. Librarian Julie Kent uses Twitter as a classroom response system, a platform for students to ask her questions, and a way for students to discuss and share information with each other.[25] These exchanges on Twitter promote communication between the librarian and students as well as among students, much of which would have otherwise never happened.

One of the drawbacks with using social media applications to solicit student feedback in a library one-shot is that students need to create an account on the chosen platform. These accounts can be difficult to set up during the limited class time, and requiring students to set up accounts before class creates additional difficulties. There are several options for using social media without requiring students to have individual accounts. Because many students may not have a Twitter account, or may not want to use their personal account for class, educators may consider TodaysMeet. Like Twitter, TodaysMeet allows for 140-character entries, but educators create a room where students can meet and interact without requiring participants to have individual accounts. As this was designed for conference presentations, another form of a one-shot, this tool may be quite suitable for information literacy instruction. Additionally, entries can be opened to any user, regardless of whether they are signed in with an account on that platform. Abate, Gomes, and Linton used blog comments to facilitate small group contributions to class discussions in very large classes.[26] Students could post answers to a scenario question or URLs of example websites, which then led to discussions as a whole class.

There are other tools that are not considered social media that can facilitate formative communication. The iAnnotate PDF app for the iPad provides a number of multimedia options to annotate many types of documents. Not only can the user highlight, draw, or add virtual sticky notes to a document, but he or she can also attach pictures or audio clips. When the annotation process is done, the document is turned into a PDF and can be sent by e-mail to be viewed on any computer. Librarians can use this program to give rich feedback on students' drafts, worksheets, or research logs, looking at source quality, appropriateness, and citation while the instructor focuses on subject content. Together, the educators can link to other articles, websites, or even past models of student work, pointing out particular parts the student may want to look at as a model for improvement. The resulting PDFs can then be e-mailed to the students outside of class. Additionally, if in a class small groups of students each had an iPad, they can be asked to make a PDF of a particular website for evaluation (FAST 32: Source Evaluation), annotating what is credible and not credible and linking to websites that are more reputable on the same topic. Students can also annotate a catalog or database entry, highlighting the controlled vocabulary and various pieces of information required to create a citation. There are many possibilities for this app.

An education professor at Otterbein College was challenged by being physically unable supervise all of her students' field assignments.[27] She uses Digication ePortfolios, which allows for not only text but also audio and video clips of reflections or actual evidence of what is going on in their classrooms. Twice a week, students have an entry due by 5:00 pm, and they are promised feedback by midnight from either herself or the field supervisor. Over the semester, the students' entries became more like a dialog, and she was able to pull out real-world example experiences to troubleshoot or discuss as a class, which greatly enriched the class content. This could be adapted to library research by requiring students to create multimedia research journals. Students may be more likely to reflect critically in such a log if other students will see it and they are promised timely feedback from their instructor and librarian, who can take turns providing feedback to half the class on each check-in day.

7. Plagiarism Detection or Prevention Tools

While Turnitin is commonly known as the leading plagiarism detection service, it markets itself as an education tool for writing improvement. In other words, it can be a formative assessment tool. Students submit their papers (drafts or final products) to the service, or instructors can submit student papers, and the program highlights any part of the student paper that matches its database of articles, websites, or previously submitted student papers. The ensuing document is called an "originality report." Educators must recognize the limitations of Turnitin. The system only detects word-for-word matches; it cannot detect whether pieces of information have an appropriate accompanying in-text citation or if citations are formatted correctly. While this report gives a raw percentage of how much of the student's paper matches other sources, most of Turnitin's reports still need to be manually interpreted by the instructor.

Turnitin's default settings do not allow students to view their own originality reports. This encourages many instructors to use the program solely for summative plagiarism detection. However, this catch-and-punish approach to plagiarism does not help improve student understanding of the underlying information literacy issues. Turnitin has options for being used as a teaching or learning tool by allowing students to view their own originality reports on drafts with the intention that students will revise poor results. Instructors who do this must help students understand the originality reports and provide additional paraphrasing and citation instruction as necessary.

The literature is just starting to explore the use of Turnitin for formative assessment, and so far the results are mixed. Rolfe explored its use with first-year university students. She found Turnitin's use was not entirely beneficial, and instructors and students were unaware of Turnitin's limitations.[28] Davis and Carroll similarly explored its use with international master's degree students.[29] The originality report was gone over with each student by a tutor, and they found a reduced amount of plagiarism as a result of using Turnitin for drafts. Clearly, the details of how such an assignment is implemented are important to its success, but those helpful guidelines are not yet fully established. Davis and Carroll's findings suggest best practice may involve combining Turnitin's originality reports with conferencing. We strongly feel that if Turnitin is going to continue to be used to provide evidence for punishing offenders, it needs to first be used as a learning tool, and librarians should be leading the way to discover and share best practices for getting the most out of this important tool.

8. Technology-Assisted Jigsaw Presentations

Jigsaw Presentations (FAST 25) are a well documented way to teach information literacy skills.[30] In this teaching method, the instructor divides the class into small groups and then assigns each group a topic. Each group must investigate their assigned topic (often with a worksheet to guide them) and present what they learned to the whole class. Students tend to investigate a tool or skill more completely when they have to teach it to the class, and they tend to pay attention to each other more than they do to the librarian. The presentations serve as evidence of each group's understanding of their topic, and there is an opportunity for the librarian to provide feedback if students missed or misunderstood a key piece.

However, the jigsaw method is very time-consuming, and it can be difficult to comfortably rely on this method of instruction in a single hour. Easy screen capturing software, such as Jing, and easy access to digital video cameras enables librarians to assign students a topic and require them to create a video demonstrating competency in their assigned area. The creation of this video may happen inside the classroom or as homework. Also, student presentations can be easily recorded. Such videos can be posted to YouTube or a blog or wiki, and students in other groups can post comments and questions as well as look for feedback from the librarian and/or the course instructor. Recorded presentations have the additional advantage of being available after the class if students need a reminder when they are conducting their actual research.

Finally, wikis can be used in a constructivist classroom to turn the jigsaw method into an online course guide. The librarian sets up the wiki's homepage, possibly in a course management system so that students do not need to set up new accounts. Each group of students explores their assigned skill or tool and creates a page, which is then linked to the wiki's homepage. Students then review each other's pages and leave comments and questions for each group to be responsible for. The librarian coordinates and intervenes only as necessary, and the wiki takes the place of a traditional class handout.

9. Location-Based Assessments

At our institution, we have designed a number of location-based assignments. Much of the research process involves *finding* something, whether it is a book in the stacks or a relevant article. Clearly, *finding* should be a frequent learning target. In Scavenger Hunt (FAST 31), we discuss various scavenger hunt techniques. There are a number of ways to assess whether students have found a particular location. One is to simply ask the students to find assigned book titles using the Library of Congress call numbers found in the catalog. This activity can be enhanced when each student group has access to an iPad. The librarian gives students a list of locations to find in the library, and students prove they have found those locations by taking a picture of them with the iPad. This can be further enhanced with an app such as iAnnotate, where students are given a map of the library with important locations marked. Students then take the pictures of those locations and attach it to its appropriate place on the map. When they are finished, they send their maps as a PDF to the librarian, who can quickly review the maps as they arrive in his or her e-mail inbox.

QR codes can also enhance location-based assessments. In the context of a campus history game, the learning target was for students to find current and past buildings. Students were given campus maps that showed each location to be "captured," and each team was given a unique cardboard "avatar" on a popsicle stick. When students arrived at each location, they found a poster containing three things: a picture of the building, a label with the location name, and a QR code. Students took pictures of their teams' cardboard avatars in front of the poster, and then used the QR code to upload the image as an e-mail attachment to send to a specific Picasa album, using the poster's location label as the subject line. The various avatars allowed the game managers to identify which team took the picture and how successful that team was finding each location.

Figure 9.2. For a location-based assessment, students took pictures of their teams' cardboard avatars in front of each location's designated poster and then used a QR code to upload the image as an e-mail attachment to send to a specific Picasa album, using the poster's location label as the subject line.

While this was done to encourage exploring the campus's physical history, it could just as easily be done for any other location-based learning target. This assessment could be adapted for a library orientation where the learning target is to visit a certain number of key locations. It could also be used in a class where one assessment technique is to prove they could locate a book title in the catalog, then read call numbers, and find the book. When students retrieve the book, it could contain the QR code, and they could take a picture and e-mail it to the Picasa account. These indoor adaptations have the advantage of enabling students to use the wireless connection rather than having to use their data plans for the activity and may open up additional options for using institution-owned mobile devices like iPod touches or iPads.

Technology and Special-Needs Students

While adaptive technologies are generally outside of the scope if this book, there is a certain mindset of consideration that should be adopted with classroom technologies in general. Flash tutorials *can* be made compatible with screen-reading software for students with a visual impairment, but this is often forgotten. Poll Everywhere is not accessible to those same students. English language learners may be at an equal disadvantage if class content is delivered using overly oral technology while students with dyslexia may be at a similar disadvantage if everything is textual. Students who are colorblind may struggle with content delivered through technology if the colors are poorly chosen or directions are dependent on color vision such as "Click on the Thesaurus button in the *green* bar."

Taking disabilities and related special needs into consideration need not be overwhelming. When a class is being scheduled or collaboration discussed, librarians can ask instructors if there are any students with special needs in the class. If there are not, then content developed specifically for that class does not require accommodations. If there are, the instructor is likely to be a good source of information for any necessary adjustments, often having received information from the institution on what accommodations the student is entitled to or would facilitate his or her learning. For general tutorials posted on the library website and other educational materials that will be used in multiple classes over time, general accommodations should be made. Most campuses have support services for students with various special needs and are excellent resources in making important information literacy learning objects accessible to as many students as possible.

Conclusion

It is important to reiterate the need to carefully match each technological tool with the right learning target. There may be other considerations such as the availability of wireless Internet access or devices. Also, many of these tools are unfamiliar to students, or students might be asked to use familiar social tools used in unfamiliar educational ways. Devices such as laser pointers may require a surprising amount of time to introduce so that students can use them to provide accurate data of their learning. Be sure to take this into consideration when designing a formative assessment using technology.

The most challenging part of adapting well-established formative assessment practices to the library classroom is the limited amount of face time we have with students. Even when instructors are willing to collaborate with librarians outside of the one-shot, there are still barriers to involving time and place. This chapter touches on nine examples of tools that can facilitate and enhance our ability to collect student evidence of understanding as well as provide them with feedback on that evidence. While technology is certainly not a requirement for formative assessment, it can give librarians a much-needed boost to make the most of the short time we have with students, extend our communication with students outside of the classroom, and provide judgment-free places to practice new knowledge.

NOTES

1. Joint Information Systems Committee (JISC), *"Effective Practice with E-Assessment: An Overview of Technologies, Policies and Practice in Further and Higher Education,"* accessed January 8, 2014, http://www.jisc.ac.uk/media/documents/themes/elearning/effpraceassess.pdf.
2. Tess Miller, "Formative Computer-Based Assessment in Higher Education: The Effectiveness of Feedback in Supporting Student Learning," *Assessment & Evaluation in Higher Education* 34, no. 2 (2009): 181–92; Moragh Paxton, "A Linguistic Perspective on Multiple-Choice Questioning," *Assessment & Evaluation in Higher Education* 25, no. 2 (2000): 109–19.
3. JISC, "Effective Practice with E-Assessment."
4. Paxton, "A Linguistic Perspective"; Caroline V. Gipps, "What Is the Role for ICT-based Assessment in Universities?" *Studies in Higher Education* 30, no. 2 (April 2005): 171–80, doi:10.1080/03075070500043176.
5. Paxton, "A Linguistic Perspective," 109.
6. Ibid., 113.
7. Ibid., 115.
8. D. Royce Sadler, "Formative Assessment and the Design of Instructional Systems," *Instructional Science* 18, no. 2 (1989): 119–44.
9. Teague Orblych and Michelle Dunaway, "Formative Assessment: Transforming Education in the Library" (poster presented at Library Orientation Exchange [LOEX] Annual Conference, Fort Worth, TX, May 6, 2011), http://www.loexconference.org/2011/program/presentation_files/FormativeAssessment.pdf; Patricia Keogh and Zhonghong Wang, "Clickers in Instruction: One Campus, Multiple Perspectives," *Library Hi Tech* 28, no. 1 (2010): 8–21.
10. Emily Dill, "Do Clickers Improve Library Instruction? Lock in Your Answers Now," *Journal of Academic Librarianship* 34, no. 6 (2008): 527–29.

11. Richard J. Moniz, Joe Eshleman, David Jewell, Brian Mooney, and Christine Tran, "The Impact of Information Literacy-Related Instruction in the Science Classroom: Clickers Versus Nonclickers," *College & Undergraduate Libraries* 17, no. 4 (2010): 349–64.
12. Emily K. Chan and Lorrie A. Knight, "Clicking with Your Audience," *Communications in Information Literacy* 4, no. 2 (2010): 192–201.
13. Laura E. Abate, Alexandra Gomes, and Anne Linton, "Engaging Students in Active Learning: Use of a Blog and Audience Response System," *Medical Reference Services Quarterly* 30, no. 1 (2011): 12–18; Bobbie L. Collins, Rosalind Tedford, and H. David Womack, "'Debating' the Merits of Clickers in an Academic Library," *North Carolina Libraries* 66, no. 1-2 (2008): 20–24; Christina Hoffman and Susan Goodwin, "A Clicker for Your Thoughts: Technology for Active Learning," *New Library World* 107, no. 9-10 (2006): 422–33; Keogh and Wang, "Clickers in Instruction"; Michelle Kathleen Dunaway and Michael Teague Orblych, "Formative Assessment: Transforming Information Literacy Instruction," *Reference Services Review* 39, no. 1 (2011): 24–41.
14. Collins, Tedford, and Womack, "'Debating' the Merits of Clickers." Dunaway and Orblych, "Formative Assessment"; Anne C. Osterman, "Student Response Systems: Keeping the Students Engaged," *College & Undergraduate Libraries* 14, no. 4 (2007): 49–57.
15. Collins, Tedford, and Womack, "'Debating' the Merits of Clickers," 22.
16. Osterman, "Student Response Systems."
17. Charlotte L. Briggs and Deborah Keyek-Franssen, "Clickers and CATs: Using Learner Response Systems for Formative Assessments in the Classroom," *EDUCAUSE Quarterly* 33, no. 4 (2010), http://www.educause.edu/ero/article/clickers-and-cats-using-learner-response-systems-formative-assessments-classroom.
18. Nevenka Zdravkovska, Maureen Cech, Pinar Beygo, and Bob Kackley, "Laser Pointers: Low-Cost, Low-Tech Innovative, Interactive Instruction Tool," *Journal of Academic Librarianship* 36, no. 5 (2010): 440–44.
19. Lan Li, Xiongyi Liu, and Allen L. Steckelberg, "Assessor or Assessee: How Student Learning Improves by Giving and Receiving Peer Feedback," *British Journal of Educational Technology* 41, no. 3 (2009): 525–36, doi:10.1111/j.1467-8535.2009.00968.x.
20. "PRIMO; Peer-Reviewed Instructional Materials Online," Association of College and Research Libraries, accessed January 8, 2014, http://www.ala.org/acrl/aboutacrl/directoryofleadership/sections/is/iswebsite/projpubs/primo.
21. "Teach Effective and Ethical Research Methods to Students," ResearchReady, accessed January 8, 2014, http://www.researchready.com/; "Literati Academic," CREDO, accessed January 8, 2014, http://corp.credoreference.com/solutions/literati-academic.html.
22. Stylianos Hatzipanagos and Steven Warburton, "Feedback as Dialogue:

Exploring the Links between Formative Assessment and Social Software in Distance Learning," *Learning, Media and Technology* 34, no. 1 (2009): 51.

23. Amanda Click and Joan Petit, "Social Networking and Web 2.0 in Information Literacy," *The International Information and Library Review* 42, no. 2 (June 2010): 137–42.
24. Cullen J. Chandler and Alison S. Gregory, "Sleeping with the Enemy: Wikipedia in the College Classroom," *History Teacher* 43, no. 2 (2010): 247–57.
25. Julie Kent, "Library Instruction with Twitter," *Transliteracy Librarian* (blog), March 6, 2012, http://transliteracylibrarian.wordpress.com/2012/03/06/library-instruction-with-twitter/.
26. Abate, Gomes, and Linton, "Engaging Students in Active Learning."
27. Jean Kelly, Jeffery Smith, and Carrie Scheckelhoff, "Digital Formative Assessment: Apprenticeship in Thinking, Seeing, and Talking" (presentation, Lilly Conference, Bethesda, MD, May 30–June 2, 2013).
28. Vivien Rolfe, "Can Turnitin Be Used to Provide Instant Formative Feedback?" *British Journal of Educational Technology* 42, no. 4 (July 2011): 701–10, doi:10.1111/j.1467-8535.2010.01091.x.
29. Mary Davis and Jude Carroll, "Formative Feedback within Plagiarism Education: Is There a Role for Text-Matching Software?" *International Journal for Educational Integrity* 5, no. 2 (October 2009): 58–70.
30. Patrick Ragains, "Four Variations on Drueke's Active Learning Paradigm," *Research Strategies* 13, no. 1 (1995): 40–50.

Chapter 10

Formative Assessment in School Libraries and Media Centers

While this book in its entirety can be adapted for any instruction librarian, we felt it necessary to include a chapter exclusively for school librarians. Much of the theory and teaching strategies addressed earlier transfer easily from the academic library to the K–12 library; however, there are conditions and situations that are unique to school librarians. In any case, it is beneficial for school librarians to implement formative assessments. Harada and Yoshina state in their book, *Assessing for Learning: Librarians and Teachers as Partners*, that "for library media specialists to be true instructional partners, they must be actively engaged in assessment with students," which allows opportunity for students to reflect on their learning not only in their regular classrooms but in library instruction as well.[1] While Harada and Yoshina provide one of the main texts on assessment for school librarians, their fairly comprehensive book only touches on formative assessment. Our book, particularly this chapter, can provide even more assistance to school librarians in implementing formative assessments.

School librarians, unlike academic librarians, are first and foremost educators whose primary responsibility is teaching. This training is understandable as school librarians are often required to complete a distinct certification process to instruct in K–12 schools. Formative assessment techniques, or assessment techniques in general, were most likely introduced in librarian certification programs, and many school librarians continue to develop these skills with on-going professional development activities that focus on assessment itself. Fontichiaro also says school librarians simply have a natural skill for formative assessment in classroom situations such as circling a computer lab and commenting on student search strategies or responding with a quick mini-lesson when students ask the same recurring question.[2] With this knowledge and skill, school librarians have the opportunities and capabilities to incorporate formative assessments into their instruction.

However, while school librarians have the background and growing knowledge of assessment implementation, evidence suggests that this is not being taken advantage of to the extent that it can affect student learning, or it is not utilized at all. Lindauer offers several ideas on why librarians may avoid assessment.[3] First, she attributes some hesitation to an assumption that assessment requires expertise in assessment methodologies and data analysis or that it is too complex of a task in general.[4] Most pressing, however, is that it may take too much time to do extensive assessments.

In addition to Lindauer's reasons for assessment avoidance, the school librarian is sometimes viewed by fellow educators, administrators, and students as the person who simply checks out books or babysits the occasional study hall class. As Alexander, Smith, and Carey show, principals often perceive school librarians as simply a resource for students who need help with print materials. In their five-point scale on principal's ratings of the importance of the school librarian's roles, learning and teaching fall as fourth, which is highly different from their view of the classroom teacher's role where teaching is first.[5] School librarians developing assessments may not be seen as beneficial by schools or school districts, and eventually, school librarians may feel that assessment has no meaning for their role in the K–12 structure. Even if a librarian has opportunities to teach lessons, assessments may not be a top priority for the librarian or the cooperating teacher. School librarians know that they have the skills and training to be effective teachers but getting this idea across to others can be difficult.

Although the school librarian may have hesitations in implementing formative assessment, making the decision to do so will contribute greatly to his or her value within the school district. In actuality, formative assessment techniques can solve many of the issues Lindauer mentions. Also, because the school librarian acquired his or her position by demonstrating the ability and expertise to instruct, stereotypes and inaccurate views of the school librarian's position are deterred when using formative assessment. In Zmuda's "Six Steps to Saving Your School Library Program," she lists formative assessment as one of the main strategies that will provide value for the school librarian's position.[6] When school districts are losing budget monies to keep full-time, certified school librarians, it is essential for librarians to show their essential role and their significant impact on student learning.

Zmuda says to "take responsibility for student learning by coming up with a formative assessment model and encourage colleagues and supervisors to evaluate you."[7] When school librarians utilize formative assessments, their roles and positions within the school system change for the better, improving students' learning as well.

Implementing formative assessment for school librarians can be simpler and more flexible than for the academic librarians. It can also be more difficult because of certain challenges affecting school libraries today. As stated in Chapter 3, "Embedding Formative Assessment in Library Instruction," academic librarians have challenges dealing with time constraints, getting to know the audience, and providing a nonthreatening environment when implementing formative assessment. Not all of these challenges are experienced by school librarians. Instead, school librarians have different challenges and advantages—standard-based lessons and curriculums, time concerns and assignment design, collaboration, standardized testing and grades, and feedback. This chapter will help school librarians apply the concepts of this book to increase students' understanding and application of information literacy and show the important role librarians play in schools' ability to improve standardized test scores.

Standard-Based Lessons and Curriculums

Lessons incorporating formative assessment should start with an end goal in mind formulated from a set of standards. Most branches of education have content standards, for example, the Association of College and Research Libraries' Information Literacy Competency Standards for Higher Education for academic librarians and the American Association of School Librarians' Standards for the 21st-Century Learner for school librarians. Although standards are meant to guide educators in determining age-appropriate content and understanding the depth of knowledge within their fields, they, in a way, dictate how one teaches and should also dictate how one performs formative assessments.

A trend seen in education during the past decade is to use content standards as learning objectives. However, this does not work for teaching information literacy. Content standards are broad and designed to be taught and learned over several days or even weeks; they are not specific enough to be utilized as learning objectives. School librarians may be able to use standards to create learning objectives, as discussed in Chapter 1, "Introduction to Formative Assessment." This allows them to plan and implement formative assessments designed to help students meet specific learning targets based on learning objectives. Students benefit from knowing what learning targets—small, bite-sized chunks of understanding—they need to master. Learning targets help them to focus on the specific task at hand and motivate them to make progress. For example, school librarians can use Research Journals (FAST 42) to track how each learner evolves along the pre-determined learning progression. Each entry in the journal can be linked to specific learning targets that build on one another to assist the learner in accomplishing the end goal, which is proficiency with the standard. Not only does the journal provide formative assessment data during the learning process, it also creates a story of these bite-sized assessments for a more summative use of the FAST at the conclusion of a lengthy unit.

Along with the Standards for the 21st-Century Learner, school librarians can look towards a newer set of standards: the Common Core State Standards (CCSS). The majority of the states in the U.S., along with the District of Columbia and four territories, have adopted these standards, and most will have fully implemented them by the 2015–2016 school year.[8] It is essential for school librarians to design their assessments to connect with CCSS, staying relevant to changing school curriculums. The New York Library Association's Section of School Librarians made t-shirts saying, "Your Library IS the Common Core," claiming the skills at the center of these standards is what librarians teach every day.[9] In light of these new standards, the American Association of School Librarians devised a "crosswalk" to show how the Standards for the 21st-Century Learner and CCSS can combine.[10] In these charts, each standard is aligned to current CCSS standards within certain content areas. Librarians can use this crosswalk to make new connections to their assessments within their lessons. Assessments must be conducted to support these claims of the librarian's impact and their important connection to CCSS.

CCSS has placed an emphasis on higher-level thinking; information literacy skills and the library support higher-level thinking within lessons. On the downside, CCSS has yet to develop a special section dedicated to information literacy. This does not mean, though, that school librarians should ignore the CCSS but rather create connections through their own lesson goals and that of the CCSS. In one librarian's example of incorporating CCSS, teachers claimed that the best part of the librarian's lessons were the formative assessments through Graphic Organizers (FAST 20), which were clearly embedded with the CCSS.[11] Fontichiaro states that the nearly universal adoption of the Common Core Standards is bringing formative assessment to the forefront saying it is crucial for responsive teaching and reflective learning.[12]

The public education system focuses on standardized tests based on content standards, giving school librarians a case for using formative assessment in all of their lessons. Although information literacy is not specifically tested in these state tests, many studies, such as those by Keith Curry Lance, show the positive impact school librarians have on test scores.[13] Loertscher points out that assessment is here to stay, and the door is wide open to school librarians wanting to help their schools improve test scores, enabling them to showcase their expertise in teaching and learning.[14] To do this, Loertscher says the librarian cannot simply state that they taught students something; they must show results. When librarians can show how an assessment measures and supports a student's progression toward grade-level standards, their value to student learning and their school's goals becomes more prominent. Along with Loertscher, Farmer and Henri say that for assessment to have meaning for a school district's mission, data has to be compared to something such as a desired standard.[15] Beginning with these end goals in mind can guide librarians to successful formative assessments. The standards by which school districts base their curriculum offer a beneficial building block for librarians' curriculum and assessments.

In using set standards, school librarians should work with their curriculum directors to design a program that builds on both the content standards and the Standards for the 21st-Century Learner. A school district's libraries should collectively base the K–12 curriculum to ensure a path that leads to all students being efficient and skilled in these standards. Breaking these standards down into learning objectives and ultimately learning targets will prove that the library is essential to student learning.

In a curriculum designed at Warrior Run School District, Turbotville, PA, school librarians, Jessica Oberlin, an author of this book, and Kathryn Makatche, developed formative assessments for each phase of the research process.[16] They felt the need to develop their own interpretation of standards for their school population's needs. Their research process design was entitled "P.L.U.S.S. + A Positive Way to Research," meaning "Plan, Locate, Use, Show, Self-Reflect." In each phase the research process, students performed an assessment of their research skill. For example, in the plan phase, students' goals were to create a set of searchable keywords, gain general knowledge of their topic, devise a thesis statement, and develop a plan of action for their research. During this process, students sifted out keyword choices, read for general knowledge on a topic, and questioned ideas, forming their own direction for research. The process, a high level of thinking, allowed the librarians to conduct formative assessments by breaking down ideas into smaller chunks of learning. Graphic Organizers (FAST 20), a simple formative technique, were used to assess the plan stage. Along with Graphic Organizers, other FASTs can be utilized for keyword formulation such as the Keyword Sorting Exercise (FAST 26). After students formed keywords and found appropriate reference resources, they then read through the nonfiction pieces to comprehend basic knowledge on their topics. Oberlin and Makatche asked students to practice their paraphrasing skills (FAST 27: Paraphrasing Practice) while reading these texts to assess how well they read and grasped concepts within library materials.[17] At the conclusion of the plan stage, students devised a thesis statement, determined which resources would be used, and evaluated their information by completing a brainstorming assessment (FAST 4: Brainstorming). The seemingly simple task of planning a research strategy involved four FASTs, which engaged students, helped them assess their own learning and provided evidence of students' learning to the librarians.

In previous lessons for this assignment given solely by the classroom instructors with no information literacy instruction, students produced low-level research results and thesis statements. With the inclusion of the librarians' assessments and lessons, students were able to form clear thesis statements and complete learning targets successfully. Evidence was shown of students attaining goals set by the standards at the end of each research step. With a set curriculum for library instruction, the library became an essential partner in the school's district goals and collaborations with classroom teachers.

Another helpful example of an end product for curriculum design for libraries is student portfolios. Harada and Yoshina describe the development of portfolios by attaching assessments and activities to each Standard for the 21st-Century Learner.[18] This process is a beneficial way to gather student work and documents at different phases of the learning process. Similar to Oberlin and Makatche's P.L.U.S.S. model, the portfolio product ends with students reflecting on their learning, which is a formative assessment in itself. Although these curriculum examples are lengthier than the academic librarian's one-shot lesson, they include short formative assessments that feed into a bigger picture of what students ultimately gain from library instruction. Monitoring the progress of these portfolios can also be done with formative assessments such as Admit Slips (FAST 1) for each class or Conferences (FAST 40) scheduled with the librarian. School librarians have the benefit of creating a curriculum and larger scale units unlike academic librarians in most cases. Implementing formative assessments embedded into the curriculum design enhances instruction and learning and is fairly simple for the school librarian.

With so many standards leading the way for instruction in school libraries, librarians are wise to implement these standards with formative assessments to show student advancement. Through all of these set standards, school librarians have a strong argument and base to incorporate formative assessments into daily lessons and curriculums.

Time and Assignment Design

Obviously, aligning standards with assessments and creating curriculums take time. Academic librarians typically refer to their lesson designs as one-shot sessions. While the school librarians can teach in this way, they can also work with a class for a lengthier time, such as a week, to complete research requirements. The examples of bite-sized assessments in Chapters 5–7 are helpful and can be adapted if the librarian has the liberty of spending more instructional time with students. The "after" assessments may be especially helpful for the school librarian who has more scheduled time with classes. In this sense, the school librarian may have an easier time performing the lengthier, more complicated assessments than the academic librarian.

There may be situations where time is no issue for school librarians, but this may not be typical. Dawn Frazier captures a possible barrier for librarians and classroom teachers alike when she states, "Teachers often have little planning time embedded in their day. Some may perceive a collaborative effort with the school librarian as an intrusion on the few precious minutes they do have."[19] If the school librarian needs the cooperation from the classroom teacher to embed formative assessments into the lesson, the issue of time constraints can impede this. Again, some assessments described in Chapters 5–7 need little time for preparing and collaborating, but when more collaboration is needed, the school librarian may hit a roadblock.

To overcome time constraints and roadblocks, school librarians have several options. The easiest and quickest idea would be to have a set of prescribed formative assessments that are adaptable to any class such as Exit Slips (FAST 41) or a KWL Chart (FAST 6). These activities take little planning time and can be used repetitively in various subject areas. Sending an e-mail with an example of an exit slip or a KWL chart in your lesson plan to a classroom teacher would perhaps make collaboration easier.

Although we can implement quick assessments that do not require much planning, a more in-depth collaboration is beneficial. To overcome time constraints in these situations, the school librarian, with cooperation from administration, can become part of each subject's department or grade level teachers' group. Taking a few minutes during department or group meetings, a time set aside for them to work together, to show possibilities for formative assessments in library instruction will increase chances of collaboration. Depending on the dynamic of the school district, there may be other opportunities for librarians to share their lesson ideas and specifically show formative assessment examples and their positive effect on student learning.

FASTs that deal with website evaluation or citations are a great place to start collaborating with subject-specific teachers. Often, teachers express frustration when their students use unreliable websites, create incorrect citations, or have no citations at all, resulting in plagiarism. One FAST a librarian can share with teachers is how to assess students' ability to evaluate web sources (FAST 32: Source Evaluation). In addition, showing classroom teachers Citation on Walls (FAST 15) can also offer a quick, easy assessment that remedies citation issues in student work. Having a few minutes present at a teachers' group meeting can have a large impact on their perceptions of library instruction and can demonstrate how easily and quickly these research skills assessments can be implemented.

The flipped classroom, discussed in Chapter 3, "Embedding Formative Assessment into Library Instruction," may also be a beneficial solution to time crunches for school librarians as well. The literature for flipped classrooms presents itself more so for school librarians and school educators than for academic librarians. One essential resource to help implement this type of classroom in a school setting is Valenza's *NeverEnding Search* blog entry, "The Flipping Librarian," where she claims librarians are already "flipped."[20] In the end, depending on the atmosphere for each school librarian, time can be an asset or a barrier in implementing assessments; however, in either situation, various formative assessments can be implemented to adapt lessons and improve student learning.

An effective assignment design process can also help solve the issue of time. In most instances, the school librarian begins his or her position being embedded in the school's curriculum with the various subjects and courses that utilize the library's instruction possibilities. First, in assignment design, is the school library's print and media collection, which should already be in place and mostly developed to support the school's curriculum and classes. In developing assignments with this collection, the school librarian can get an idea of what the students need as far as completing their assignments, which saves time in planning assessments. Working with a classroom teacher who has a somewhat prescribed curriculum based on the library collection is another advantage the librarian has. In this light, the school librarian may already have a better venue for performing formative assessments compared to the academic librarian.

In designing assignments, school librarians deal with the same collaborative challenges as the academic librarian: limited collaboration with a last-minute request or one-shot sessions with not much time. Depending on the task given to students for each class, school librarians can use FASTs from Chapters 5–7 and incorporate them into the methods in which they use to teach the class. As we will discuss in Chapter 11, "Working towards a Culture of Assessment," starting to implement formative assessments into lessons may not always be straightforward and easy, but once implemented, vast improvements in student's learning and the librarian's teaching quality are seen.

Collaboration

To avoid time constraints and develop successful assignments that have embedded formative assessments, collaboration is essential for the school librarian. Collaboration in the K–12 arena is discussed here as both a benefit and a possible challenge for school librarians. Much of what the school librarian will be working with is based on past practice of how the district views its libraries and librarians. Administrators and their experiences and views of libraries influence their outlook of the library whether it is positive, negative, or not even acknowledged at all.

In a positive light, some school librarians have excellent collaboration with classroom teachers and administrators, which makes implementation of formative assessments smoother. They are doing innovative practices with technology in the classroom, helping students dive into reading nonfiction for research, or simply providing a reading time that many students do not receive at home. Pietsch describes how librarians in the Omaha Public School were part of the district action plan to incorporate formative assessment strategies into their teaching practices.[21] Not only did librarians participate in creating formative assessments, they documented the results as well to show their impact on student learning. The results of this action plan will be reviewed in fall of 2013.

We, as librarians, constantly see the benefit of our programs and integration into the curriculum, but we must collaborate with classroom teachers to allow others to see this valuable impact too. Formative assessments with concrete results can help in this collaboration and improve the sometimes-skewed view of school librarians. Harada and Yoshina point out many benefits of collaboration in terms of using formative assessment, saying that it creates map for planning lessons that facilitate this collaboration.[22] Lindauer also points out that one of the best opportunities where assessment can be explored is when classroom instructors and the librarian discuss learning outcomes or develop assignments together. Lindauer gives some examples of assessment that are brief evaluations during or after classroom presentations such as the one-minute paper or the one-sentence summary.[23] In the end, formative assessments can enhance already established collaborations or initiate new connections with classroom teachers.

School librarians and the atmosphere they create allow them to have more personal and collaborative relationships with students than most academic librarians, improving their chances of successful implementation of formative assessments. Since school librarians interact with students in other library activities other than instruction, including choosing fiction reads and being involved with clubs, they do not need to develop a relationship with students as much as the one-shot academic librarian may need to. Also, after instructional sessions with the librarian, students are more willing to ask questions and consult the reference desk. Students also get to know a librarian after seeing them over the course of several years.

With formative assessments proving that librarians impact student learning, more collaboration with classroom teachers will follow. Buzzeo, librarian, trainer, speaker, and author of *The Collaboration Handbook*, says that "data-driven collaboration carries all of the same rewards as collaboration does with the added advantage of fully addressing the school's instructional goals, which inevitably are built around the need to move students forward in deficient areas."[24] School librarians can show their role in collaboration with teachers and support for the school district's goals with evidence from formative assessments to show their impact on student learning. Loertscher says that everyone should understand that when librarians and teachers collaborate, learners win: "Those classroom teachers who ignore us do so at their learner's peril."[25] To show how librarians affect learning, collaboration is essential in implementing formative assessments.

Standardized Testing and Grades

When collaboration time is bogged down, the most likely culprit is state tests and essential units within the approved curriculum for subject-specific teachers. Time with the librarian may seem unessential to the classroom teacher. However, study after study, such as the Keith Curry Lance studies previously mentioned, shows that librarians positively affect state tests and essential units.[26] With the reality that state testing is here to stay, the value of libraries seems to diminish in the eye of administrators, teachers, community members, and students. Although not all ignore this value, the pressure of state testing decreases the time spent in the library for instruction.

Along with state testing requirements, another area in which school librarians have little control is grading. Often, the research done and library resources used do not affect students' grades. Students, at times, view library sessions as a time that does not count, so why pay attention? Unfortunately, for the librarian who is attempting to complete formative assessment techniques, these situations make it quite difficult to get accurate feedback.

State testing and grades are most likely never going to lose their importance, so solutions are needed to include formative assessments in a way that the librarian, students, teachers, and school administrators see library sessions as valuable to student learning. One possible solution, as discussed earlier, is collaboration with classroom instructors. Once the librarian establishes these collaborations, he or she should ask if part of what the students are doing in the library sessions can count as part of the assignment's grade and offer to complete the grading themselves. On a larger scale, library curriculum and assessments can be embedded into the curriculum where a visible "information literacy" score is included. This not only puts a numeric value on a report card but also shows value of the library curriculum's impact on state tests as well.

In Warrior Run's library curriculum mentioned earlier, an initial unit for all incoming freshmen in the high school provided an opportunity for graded assessments. In collaboration with English teachers, the librarian created a four-day unit introducing students to resources and ways in which they can utilize the library throughout their high school years. Each day ended with a bite-sized assessment. For example, on the second day, a Scavenger Hunt (FAST 31) based on students' background knowledge of locations in the library, which they had learned the previous day, assessed students' ability to utilize the library's locations. On the fourth and final day, all of the assessments were collected and graded by the school librarian and counted as part of their English course grade. This unit fed into later collaborative research projects with the English and the history departments. Starting with this unit, students saw that library lessons were an important part of their grade and success in their classes.

Simultaneously, formative assessments can be used to test information literacy skills while students complete graded classroom assignments in library instruction. By focusing on these skills and using FASTs from Chapters 5–7, formative assessments can be an exploration of skills rather than the usual mundane library tasks. Carl Harvey of North Elementary in Noblesville, Indiana is quoted in Fontichiaro's article saying that he always assessed journals at the end of a project—until one day he realized that it would be more helpful if he looked at them during the project to see if students were on track.[27] From this realization, he implemented exit slips to gradually get feedback as the unit was taking place. Using this immediate feedback, he adjusted his teaching to the students' needs. By taking a small part of the already graded assignment and breaking it down into bite-size formative assessments, like exit slips, Harvey was able to adjust lessons based on the feedback he received, which contributed even more meaning to his graded assignment. Margaret Buck, librarian at Annapolis Middle School, is quoted stating that, "Formatives don't need to be grades! Propose other options like exit slips or checks for understanding."[28] Whether librarians are already showing their impact on state tests or incorporating grading into their instruction, formative assessments can be used in either situation. Ultimately, having feedback from any assessment situation is beneficial to the librarian's unique teaching situation.

Feedback

All of these areas of difficulty or success in implementing formative assessments rest on the shoulders of how feedback is used by the librarian and students. Schools, no doubt, are more data driven than ever. This means that the school librarian should take part as well in applying this data to his or her teaching situations. With such data, the librarian can assess students before they enter the library for a lesson, giving him or her more power for impact on student learning.

School librarian Justin Ashworth claims, "If you had asked me five years ago to define my role as a school librarian, taking a leadership role working with student assessment data wouldn't have been part of the conversation."[29] Ashworth goes onto explain his participation in Partners in Achievement: Library and Students (PALS). Ashworth's participation in this program shows how data defines students' needs and gears instruction towards those needs, which is the idea behind formative assessments as well.[30] From Ashworth's work, he was able to collaborate with a classroom teacher to define gaps in students' learning as well as devise an action plan and units to address these gaps. Ultimately, the greatest success from this participation in looking at feedback was that the "data-driven dialogue between the school librarian and grade level teachers has resulted in collaborative, informed instruction that is targeted at the identified achievement gaps" and the impact on student learning.[31] Although many school librarians may not have the support or time to carry out a focused two-year plan based on state tests scores as Ashworth has, using smaller formative assessments to collaborate and gather feedback is an effective tool for school librarians in establishing their credibility as teachers and their positive impact on student learning.

More specifically than Ashworth's example, Bates, McClure, and Spinks address formative assessments directly in describing data-driven library programs: "Most importantly, a library media specialist can use data about his or her own library media program to guide decision-making and spur *immediate* improvements.... If a library media specialist uses a formative assessment tool to discover that a particular lesson was not effective, he can re-teach the concepts using a different instructional strategy."[32] Bates, McClure, and Spinks also believe that this type of data showing that a librarian's assessments "directly led to student learning" improves the librarian's overall role in the school as a collaborative partner in learning.[33] With examples of students' pre- and post-assessments, the librarian has direct evidence of student achievements. Some examples of assessments that can help spur immediate improvements are Anticipation Guide (FAST 2), Pre-Assessment (FAST 9), Quick Write (FAST 29), Response Card (FAST 30), or Cloze Assessment (FAST 39).

In the academic arena, the librarian may see a student's performance in an entry-level history class but may not see him or her again until his or her graduating capstone course, having minimal assessment feedback or memory of how this student performed earlier. How can the academic librarian know if he or she made an impact over this approximately four-year span? The school librarian's situation is different: seeing students fairly regularly over the course of a few years adds a benefit to using assessment feedback. The ideal goal is to have an assessment at each grade level measuring each student's information literacy skills. In the librarian's curriculum, a modified capstone Checklist (FAST 14) can be used to create a numeric value that represents each student's level of understanding of information literacy and research skills as he or she potentially head into higher education. From Bates, McClure, and Spinks's examples, we can see that the feedback from formative assessments in school library instruction is a benefit to the school librarian. Not only can it show the librarian's impact on student learning, but it can also make the case for the value school librarians provide to their school's goals.

Conclusion

Even though the school librarian has the teaching background and knowledge to implement formative assessments, there may be some hesitation to actually incorporate these into their lessons. There are multiple reasons why this hesitation may be; however, in the end, formative assessments will enhance librarians' teaching, improve students' learning, and make librarians invaluable leaders within their schools and school districts.

State curriculum standards and the emphasis on standardized test scores make implementing formative assessments in the library classroom easier. With this text in its entirety, along with the acknowledgement of certain challenges and possible solutions, school librarians can successfully implement formative assessments into their lessons by collaborating with administrators and teachers.

NOTES

1. Violet H. Harada and Joan M. Yoshina, *Assessing for Learning: Librarians and Teachers as Partners* (Santa Barbara, CA: Libraries Unlimited, 2010).
2. Kristin Fontichiaro, "Nudging Toward Inquiry: Formative Assessment," *School Library Monthly* 27, no. 6 (March 2011), http://www.schoollibrarymonthly.com/curriculum/Fontichiaro2011-v27n6p11.html.
3. Bonnie Gratch Lindauer, "The Three Arenas of Information Literacy Assessment," *Reference & User Services Quarterly* 44, no. 2 (Winter 2004): 122–29.
4. Ibid.
5. Linda B. Alexander, Robert C. Smith, and James O. Carey, "Education Reform and the School Library Media Specialist," *Knowledge Quest* 32, no. 2 (November/December 2003): 10–13.
6. Allison Zmuda, "Six Steps to Saving Your School Library Program," *School Library Monthly* 27, no. 5 (February 2011): 45–49.
7. Ibid, 46.
8. "Common Core: Standards Initiative—In the States," National Governors Association and Council of Chief State School Officers, accessed January 8, 2014, http://www.corestandards.org/in-the-states.
9. Ana Canino-Fluit, "Flying High with the Information Fluency Continuum," *Knowledge Quest* 41, no. 5 (May/June 2013): 46–50.
10. "AASL Learning Standards & Common Core State Standards Crosswalk," American Association of School Librarians, accessed January 8, 2014, http://www.ala.org/aasl/standards-guidelines/crosswalk.
11. Ibid.
12. Fontichiaro, "Nudging toward Inquiry."
13. "School Library Impact Studies," Keith Curry Lance, accessed January 8, 2014, http://keithcurrylance.com/school-library-impact-studies/.
14. David Loertscher, "Curriculum, the Library/Learning Commons, and Teacher-Librarians: Myths and Realities in the Second Decade," *Teacher Librarian* 37, no. 3 (February 2010): 8–13.
15. Lesley S.J. Farmer and James Henri, *Information Literacy Assessment in K–12 Settings* (Lanham, MD: Scarecrow Press, 2007).
16. Jessica Urick Oberlin and Kathryn Makatche, "H.S. Information Literacy Map" (unpublished lesson plan, Warrior Run School District, Turbotville, PA, 2012), Microsoft Word file.
17. Ibid.
18. Harada and Yoshina, *Assessing for Learning*.
19. Dawn Frazier, "School Library Media Collaborations: Benefits and Bar-

riers," *Library Media Connection* (November/December 2010): 34–36.
20. Joyce Valenza, "The Flipping Librarian," *NeverEnding Search* (blog), August 14, 2012, http://blogs.slj.com/neverendingsearch/2012/08/14/the-flipping-librarian/.
21. Laura Pietsch, "A Step-by-Step Study of Formative Assessment," *School Library Monthly* 29, no. 5 (February 2013): 5–7.
22. Harada and Yoshina, *Assessing for Learning*.
23. Lindauer, "The Three Arenas."
24. Toni Buzzeo, "Make the Move from Collaboration to Data-Driven Collaboration," *Library Media Connection* (November/December 2008): 28–31.
25. Loertscher, "Curriculum."
26. "School Library Impact Studies."
27. Kristin Fontichiaro, "Formative Assessment Using Feedback," *School Library Monthly* 28, no. 7 (April 2012): 51–52.
28. Ibid.
29. Judith Dzikowksi, Mary Tiedemann, and Justin Ashworth, "The Data-Driven Library Program," *Library Media Connection* (August/September 2010): 10-12.
30. Ibid.
31. Ibid, 11.
32. Joanne Bates, Janelle McClure, and Andy Spinks, "Making the Case for Evidence-Based Practice," *Library Media Connection* (August/September 2010): 24–27.
33. Ibid, 25.

Chapter 11

Working towards a Culture of Assessment

External regulating agencies continue to place more and more emphasis on assessment and accountability for institutions of higher education, K–12 school systems, and public libraries. Just as administrators and instructors must incorporate more evaluation into their programming and curriculum, instruction librarians must become more focused on gathering and using evidence to support their instructional decisions. Much of the current literature surrounding assessment in library classrooms has focused on evidence solicited by administrators to prove program effectiveness or for the instruction librarian to improve in the future. Often times, this requires setting aside valuable instructional time to conduct evaluations that may not directly benefit those current students.

As we have seen throughout this book, formative assessment can provide librarians with valuable assessment data that helps immediately improve student learning while not costing precious face time with students. Because instruction librarian's face time with students is so limited, formative assessment allows an efficient and productive use of time for all involved parties. These frequent, often informal assessments are fully integrated into the learning process. In fact, most formative assessments are active learning exercises with an emphasis of using the resulting evidence of student learning to guide instruction. Students are learning while the librarian is simultaneously assessing them, and this assessment enhances learning rather than take time away from it.

Above all, the education literature has provided convincing evidence that formative assessment is a crucial part of effective teaching. Marzano describes formative assessments as being the most powerful educative assessments teachers can use.[1] Black and Wiliam concluded after a literature review of several hundred articles that it is the most effective way to improve student learning.[2] Brookhart, Moss, and Long found students' standardized test scores improved greatly over two years when their school began emphasizing formative assessment.[3] Furthermore, the use of formative assessment allows for students to receive feedback that is applicable to future learning experiences and helps them to take ownership of their learning.[4] Formative assessment has the power to assist us in quickly understanding our audience and allowing our thoughtful and creative lessons to have the most impact.

Information literacy is critical to our information society, and we are given very little contact time with students to achieve very abstract and complex learning goals. If formative assessment is as powerful as these authors claim from their research, it can be a critical tool not only for collecting evidence of student learning but also for making the most of the time we have with students. While many librarians are already incorporating techniques that could serve as formative assessment, we believe there is a widespread lack of intentionality—we can improve.

Getting Started

While we have stressed how easy certain individual formative assessment techniques can be to implement in the classroom, a thorough, effective utilization of the process can be a challenge initially. For most instruction librarians, formative assessment will be entirely new, or, at least, the intentionality we are advocating for will be new. Formative assessment requires educators to change their way of thinking in the classroom with its emphasis on observation of evidence. It takes time to learn the most efficient techniques for your curriculum, your teaching style, and your students.

For librarians interested in formative assessment, there are only a few articles in the library literature that emphasize formative assessment, and none elaborate on how to implement more than one or two formative assessment techniques. Even knowing all of the benefits that come with utilizing these bite-sized assessment practices, it is still overwhelming at times to find ways to adapt them to the one-shot library session. Not only is our face time with students limited, there are barriers, such as the lack of time or place or collective effort from all parties, to the amount of collaboration we are able to have with instructors to even design appropriate and effective instruction. Librarians working with the one-shot format will need to be yet more organized, efficient, and intentional than their instructor counterparts.

Furthermore, the literature describing successful, highly developed examples of formative assessment is intimidating. Some of the techniques suggested in this book require advanced collaboration with faculty or unfamiliar technologies. In response to this common fear, Popham writes, "Don't let pursuit of the instructionally perfect prevent you from reaping the rewards of the instructionally possible."[5] This quote captures our view on implementing formative assessment practices: To improve in anything, you have to start somewhere. We are certainly on this journey towards improvement along with our readers.

We urge librarians to avoid starting with elaborate and time-consuming activities, which are too often not sustainable. Instead, we recommend starting and maintaining simplicity in your formative assessment practices. If your students are going to benefit, you need to implement small steps that are easily accomplished by your students and by you. Angelo and Cross stress adopting their classroom assessment techniques (CATs) gradually and provide some guidance on how to do so, which are of varying degrees of usefulness as we adapt them to library instruction.[6] They suggest five activities that are easy to plan and implement for instructors who are new to CATs: "Minute Paper," "Muddiest Point," "One-Sentence Summary," "Directed Paraphrasing," and "Applications Cards." However, as you will see below, we feel a new list is needed for librarians as the amount of time it takes to process the data collected and provide feedback from these assessments is too great for the library one-shot.

Angelo and Cross selected all of their CATs because the assessments were structured activities, yet flexible enough to fit into many academic disciplines. In Chapters 5–7, we selected techniques that are well suited for information literacy instruction with varying degrees of collaboration with faculty. Our intention was to select many that could be performed within the library one-shot as a starting place. Unlike Angelo and Cross, some of our techniques are very specific and can only be used for a particular lesson, and some of these are the easiest to implement. In fact, many of our readers may already be doing them, and our suggestion to them would be to focus on the evidence of student learning that these techniques produce. Because many of the basic lessons of library instruction transfer from one academic discipline to another, we feel that it is acceptable to suggest specific techniques for the library classroom. They are

- Periodical Sorting (FAST 28),
- Think-Pair-Share (FAST 33),
- When to Cite Paragraph (FAST 35),

- Boolean Operators Shading (FAST 13),
- Exit Slips (FAST 41).

These five techniques are the easiest to implement, with little planning or preparation required. They can also be interpreted on the spot and combined with discussion to dynamically react to the evidence of student learning.

In addition to the five starter CATs, which must be adjusted for library instruction, Angelo and Cross provide five additional suggestions to help instructors get started with structured formative assessment:

1. If a classroom assessment technique does not appeal to your intuition and professional judgment as a teacher, don't use it.
2. Don't make classroom assessment into a self-inflicted chore or burden.
3. Don't ask your students to use any classroom assessment technique you haven't previously tried yourself.
4. Allow for more time than you think you will need to carry out and respond to the assessment.
5. Make sure to "close the loop." Let students know what you learned from their feedback and how you and they can use that information to improve learning.[7]

We whole-heartedly agree with their advice, and these suggestions are completely applicable to librarians looking to adopt formative assessment. Teachers must be comfortable with the assessment activities assigned and their abilities to interpret and react to results. Students will sense when the teacher is uncomfortable. Particularly when technologies are used for formative assessment, educators' insecurities about the assessments can skew the results, defeating the purpose of the assessment in the first place. We recommend anticipating what students will be comfortable with and what will challenge them and then plan possible instructional responses. This will assist you in thinking and adjusting on the spot. While you may not respond "perfectly," you will have the opportunity to reflect and determine how to proceed in future circumstances.

You Are Not in This Alone: Developing a Formative Assessment Support Group

The idea of adopting formative assessment into your library classes may be daunting or even outright terrifying. There are many books on improving one's teaching ability, which often start with the barriers to improvement. In many places, teaching seems to be such an isolated activity, and it is indeed difficult to become a better teacher when operating in isolation. However, finding or even creating opportunities for dialogue about teaching will support your desire to develop these techniques and your intentionality. You may find it helpful to begin a professional learning community with other librarians in your institution. It may also help to start such a group with librarians from neighboring institutions or an online community that focuses on effective implementation strategies. Such groups serve as professional support groups where participants share useful pieces of literature, discuss plans, and, perhaps, perform peer observation for teaching improvement.

Brookfield lists colleagues' experiences as one of the four lenses for becoming a critically reflective teacher.[8] He writes, "Although critical reflection often begins with autobiographical analysis, its full realization occurs only when others are involved."[9] Learning is a social process, and we become learners when we dedicate ourselves to becoming better teachers. Talking with others about our efforts and our experiences invites new perspectives and solutions that we would never have conjured up on our own. Starting such a group may at first feel unnatural, but it has many benefits. Many educators feel they are independently operating in the classroom. We are not encouraged to share experiences, which leads to feelings of isolation and inadequacy. "Peer conversation also helps to break down the isolation many teachers feel," helping participants realize that other people share the same struggles, or that their own teaching is better than they had previously thought.[10] Of course, it also leads to creative, collaborative problem solving, and such group work has the potential to add up to more than the sum of its parts.

While such a support group does not have to include peer observation, many of the case studies on peer observation in the library literature provide positive examples and helpful suggestions on starting a teaching support group.[11] Finley et al. talk about "peer planning" where pairs or groups of librarians design classes together and may team teach but do not have a structured observation program.[12] These groups have different structures and levels of formality, some include training and some simply set aside time for informal conversations. However, even the more structured programs tend to value the flexibility needed to make the group as useful to participants' changing needs as possible. Common traits include an emphasis on constructive feedback, non-threatening environments, community building, and confidentiality. Participants should be able to share successes, problems, and failures, all with the sole purpose of becoming better teachers. While many of these groups initially focused on a peer review of teaching program, they found an equal amount of value in the community and group conversations about teaching.

When developing a teaching support group, it is important to consider hierarchical relationships. The groups we highlight here stress the emphasis on *peer* groups. Alabi et al. write, "The peer-to-peer approach enabled us to teach each other and to learn from each other at the same time."[13] The group dynamic will change significantly if participants have an equal relationship and directions are chosen by consensus as opposed to participation being driven by administration. The latter will lead to a more classroom-like dynamic, with the expert and the novices. We already know how difficult it is to get students to share their experiences in such an environment compared to student-driven collaborative learning opportunities. In a peer support group, the feeling of trust will be easier to develop among participants because it will be self-evident that anything shared will only be used for formative improvement and not for personnel decisions like tenure and promotion.

In many cases, it may be useful to also *temporarily* mentor new librarians or new members of the group to acclimate them to the group's values. New instruction librarians, who have probably not been trained as teachers, can benefit from observing formative assessment in action and being guided by a more experienced instruction librarian. However, the mentor and the group should recognize even new librarians have contributions to make, and the goal of the mentoring should be to facilitate his or her ability to quickly become a peer participant.

Some groups can function quite well naturally while others may need some intervention. Brookfield lists a number of problems he has witnessed with some groups, such as the potential to fall into groupthink, extension of external power issues, lack of participation, and judgmental exchanges.[14] He stresses the need for healthy and safe environments that encourage all to participate as peers. However, he also provides some advice on laying the foundations of healthy group dynamics. He suggests several sets of questions based on "Critical Incidents" to get groups started or lay ground rules. To encourage everyone to take turns participating, he advocates role-playing. Participants can take turns playing three roles:

- Storyteller—"the teacher who is willing to make herself the focus of critical conversation by first describing some part of her practice."[15]
- Detectives "help her come to a more fully informed understanding of the assumptions and actions that frame her teaching."[16]
- Umpire—"the teacher who has agreed to monitor conversation with a view to pointing out when people are talking to each other in a judgmental way."[17]

Professional support groups do not have to be limited to librarians. Instructors can benefit from learning about bite-sized formative assessment as a way to begin adopting formative assessment in their own classrooms. Additionally, as librarians share responsibility for teaching the research process, instructors can benefit from our research-focused activities. Such librarian-instructor interactions can lead to stronger collaboration and assignment design that is more effective for teaching research and information literacy.

Creating a Culture of Assessment

There is growing talk about "cultures of assessment" in the library literature. Schroeder and Mashek define organizational culture as "a shared mental model that members of an organization hold."[18] Organizational cultures involve the "overt and covert rules, values, and principles an organization owns that are influenced by history, customs, and practices. These enduring tenets and norms form the basis of a social system and allow its members to attribute value and meaning to the external and internal events they experience."[19] Because so much of what creates an organizational culture is that which participants take for granted, the deep-rooted assumptions that drive everyday actions and decisions are very difficult to change.

A culture of assessment is a particular type of organizational culture in which the whole staff is so dedicated to assessment and evidence-based decision making that the assessment cycle becomes self-sustaining. Participants in such a culture are customer-service driven—they find out what their patrons want and use that information to improve services. In a culture of assessment, participants *like* assessment and feel empowered to develop their own assessment measures.[20]

A culture of assessment requires "leadership from above and support from below."[21] Administration must support it through re-writing policies and job descriptions, hiring the right people, providing the resources, and, above all, leading by example by making evidence-based decisions. Resources may include money, but most importantly, a culture of assessment requires time for training and the actual assessment. The assessment cycle (data collection, reflection, and implementation) is a time-consuming process, so other tasks may need to be reduced in priority if assessment is to be raised. In a survey of over 672 academic libraries, Farkas, Hinchliffe, and Houk found that the features most often associated with the presence of a culture of assessment (as self-reported by respondents) was administration making assessment a priority, providing clear understanding of the expectations, and leading by example.[22]

Nevertheless, because a true culture of assessment must be self-sustaining, it requires staff buy-in as well. While the library administration can initiate the culture change and support a culture to develop it, the main drive must come from all staff. They must see the inherent value of assessment, evidence-based decision making, and planning for assessment in all new programs and classes. In other words, the staff must be intrinsically rather than extrinsically motivated.

More specific to library instruction, all instruction librarians in a culture of assessment are dedicated to becoming better teachers and improving student learning. There is a dedication to collecting assessment data to improve learning. Furthermore, such data can be used with faculty and college administration to increase and improve the instruction program.[23] Schroeder and Mashek describe a program at Wartburg College in which they were able to use assessment data to institute an Information Literacy Across the Curriculum (ILAC) program.[24] All students' information literacy skills are assessed at the beginning of their freshman and sophomore years, library one-shots are integrated more systematically into academic programs, and the assessment data is openly shared with other members of the community. Because of their culture of assessment, the institution has placed a much greater emphasis on all students graduating with developed information literacy skills.

The traits of a culture of assessment as it applies to an instruction program are surprisingly similar to the traits of formative assessment. Both are focused on continuous improvement first, with accountability as a secondary goal. They are both learner/customer-focused. Both emphasize creating an environment of trust, where participants feel safe to experiment; being flexible and able to adapt based on evidence; and valuing intrinsic rather than extrinsic motivation among all participants. For library instruction in a culture of assessment, assessment is a natural part of the instructional design process.

Whether a culture of assessment exists at the institutional or even at the library level, a truly strong information literacy instruction program must develop a culture of assessment. This includes many types of assessment to meet various needs and purposes. Formative assessment is not meant to replace the summative assessments happening in libraries; rather it is to be added to it. Of the many types of assessment, none can be dismissed as ineffective; they each have strengths and weaknesses that complement each other.

So how do instruction programs develop a culture of assessment? Farkas theoretically applies Kotter's eight-step change model to developing a culture of assessment in libraries.[25] These eight steps include (1) establish a sense of urgency, (2) form a guiding coalition, (3) create a vision, (4) communicate the vision, (5) empower others to act on the vision, (6) plan for and create short-term wins, (7) consolidate improvements to create more change, and (8) institutionalize new approaches. It is arguable whether these must occur in this exact order, but Farkas describes how each step plays an important role in the likelihood of a change process to succeed. The main advantage to Kotter's model is an emphasis on changing behavior first and then changing culture later.

Such change could be initiated by a grassroots effort. We suggest starting voluntary teaching communities among librarians who are dedicated to teaching improvement through formative assessment. This would be a small step towards big changes and would allow all participants to help create the vision of the role assessment can play in improving student learning. Successful implementation of such a voluntary community, combined with administrative support, can spark the development of a culture of assessment within an instruction program.

The value added to student learning as a result of formative assessment techniques is, of course, crucial. However, we must keep in mind the power formative assessment has to help us as reflective librarians to recognize needed adjustments in our instruction. Formative assessment is an ongoing process, and one that is dependent on a variety of variables. Students' skills and needs, instructors' characteristics and goals, and available resources and technology are just a few of the variables in this ongoing reflection process, and all impact how we modify our instruction for future learning experiences. Furthermore, the information collected from assessments can be used to advocate for our positions, our role in the college experience, and our need for additional resources or allocation of funds.

Conclusion

There are two critical goals of information literacy instruction. The first is to facilitate students' research assignments, giving them the tool-based skills to efficiently and effectively complete the impending assignment given to them by the instructor. There is also the bigger, more important yet infinitely more complex and elusive goal of facilitating students' ability to become lifelong learners and handle the information overload that has become a part of the modern world. Students must learn to evaluate, organize, and synthesize information to be responsible members of our society. We share the ultimate responsibility to develop these skills in our students with classroom instructors, and we need evidence to help us know *how* to do this.

Through familiarity with what makes a good reference transaction, which most academic librarians come to know in their graduate programs, librarians already know how to adapt on the spot to evidence of a patron's understanding. Now is the time to take this skill and transfer it from the reference desk to the library classroom. Just as we ask questions and are sensitive to what is said and unsaid at the reference desk to inform us on how to proceed with a reference transaction, we can use formative assessments to gather information at the individual, small group, and class level, then immediately adapt to best meet the needs of the students who sit in front of us.

In this book, we have explored the theoretical and evidence-based research on formative assessment in the education literature and how it can be adapted to the unique conditions in which librarians teach critical information literacy skills. Formative assessment helps us penetrate the invisible happenings in our students' heads. We currently allow too many assumptions to inform our instructional design, whether they are our own assumptions or ones inherited from instructors. Formative assessment techniques, such as those suggested in this book, coupled with a dedication on the part of the librarian to look for and respond to evidence of student learning, have the potential to shatter these assumptions and give us the snapshots of reality we desperately need to be effective teachers.

Formative assessment shows an enormous amount of promise in alleviating many of the frustrations we have as educators. Because we do not usually see students' final products, we often feel ignorant of our impact on students. We know that the library one-shot session is an ineffective model of teaching information literacy, working for only some assignments. When the one-shot session is truly ineffective to meet the librarian's or the instructor's learning targets for students, formative assessment provides us the necessary evidence to expand collaborations with faculty. Perhaps it can even lead to a greater integration of information literacy into departments' curriculums or the institution as a whole.

This book is meant to support you as you further explore the use of formative assessment in your classroom. It is a reflection of where we are and where we want to be. It is our hope that this book will be the avenue for designing and implementing practical, effective formative assessment techniques that are accessible to a variety of library instruction scenarios.

NOTES

1. Robert Marzano, *Classroom Assessment and Grading That Work* (Alexandria, VA: ASCD, 2006).
2. Paul Black and Dylan Wiliam, "Inside the Black Box: Raising Standards through Classroom Assessment," *Phi Delta Kappan* 80, no. 2 (1998): 139–48.
3. Susan Brookhart, Connie Moss, and Beverly Long, "Formative Assessment That Empowers," *Educational Leadership* 66, no. 3 (2008): 52–57.
4. Harry Torrance, "Formative Assessment at the Crossroads: Conformative, Deformative and Transformative Assessment," *Oxford Review of Education* 38, no. 3 (2012): 323–42.
5. W. James Popham, *Transformative Assessment* (Alexandria, VA: ASCD, 2008), ix.
6. Thomas A. Angelo and K. Patricia Cross, *Classroom Assessment Techniques: A Handbook for College Teachers* (San Francisco: Jossey-Bass, 1993).
7. Ibid, 31.
8. Stephen Brookfield, *Becoming a Critically Reflective Teacher* (San Francisco: Jossey-Bass, 1995).
9. Ibid, 140.
10. Brookfield, *Become a Critically Reflective Teacher,* 141; Jaena Alabi, Rhonda Huisman, Meagan Lacy, Willie Miller, Eric Snajdr, Jessica Trinoskey, and William H. Weare, "By and for Us: The Development of

a Program for Peer Review of Teaching by and for Pre-Tenure Librarians," *Collaborative Librarianship* 4, no. 4 (October 2012): 165–74.
11. Alabi et al., "By and for Us"; Pam Arbeeny and Chris Hartman, "Empowering Librarians to Be Better Teachers: The Value of Peer Coaching to Library Instruction," *Colorado Libraries* 34, no. 4 (October 2008): 39–45; Lee-Allison Levene and Polly Frank, "Peer Coaching: Professional Growth and Development for Instruction Librarians," *Reference Services Review* 21, no. 3 (January 1993): 35–42.
12. Priscilla Finley, Susie Skarl, Jennifer Cox, and Diane VanderPol, "Enhancing Library Instruction with Peer Planning," *Reference Services Review* 33, no. 1 (February 2005): 112–22, doi:10.1108/00907320510581423.
13. Alabi et al., "By and for Us," 167.
14. Stephen Brookfield, "Holding Critical Conversations about Teaching," in *Becoming a Critically Reflective Teacher* (San Francisco: Jossey-Bass, 1995), 140–159.
15. Ibid, 155.
16. Ibid.
17. Ibid.
18. Randall Schroeder and Kimberly Babcock Mashek, "Building a Case for the Teaching Library: Using a Culture of Assessment to Reassure Converted Campus Partners while Persuading the Reluctant," *Public Services Quarterly* 3, no. 1-2 (2007): 84.
19. Amos Lakos and Shelley E. Phipps, "Creating a Culture of Assessment: A Catalyst for Organizational Change," *Portal: Libraries and the Academy* 4, no. 3 (July 2004): 348.
20. Meredith Gorran Farkas, "Building and Sustaining a Culture of Assessment: Best Practices for Change Leadership," *Reference Services Review* 41, no. 1 (February 2013): 13–31, doi:10.1108/00907321311300857.
21. Meredith Gorran Farkas, Lisa Janicke Hinchliffe, and Amy Harris Houk, "Creating a Culture of Assessment: Determinants of Success" (presentation given at the Association of College and Research Libraries [ACRL] 2013 Conference, Indianapolis, IN, April 10–13, 2013), http://www.learningtimes.net/acrl/2013/creating-a-culture-of-assessment-determinants-of-success/.
22. Ibid.
23. Ibid.
24. Schroeder and Mashek, "Building a Case for the Teaching Library."
25. Farkas, "Building and Sustaining a Culture of Assessment"; John P. Kotter, "Leading Change: Why Transformation Efforts Fail," *Harvard Business Review* 73, no. 2 (March 1995): 59–67.

Appendix

Formative Assessment Guided Implementation Template

Learning Target(s): Identify the learning target(s) and how you will share them with your students.	
ACRL Standard(s): Identify the ACRL Standard(s) your lesson will be addressing.	
Formative Assessment Snapshot Technique(s): Name, page number, and description of specific use for learning target(s) and library instruction format (one-shot or multiple session).	
What do I anticipate they will master easily? How will I encourage them to go beyond this?	
What do I anticipate they will be challenged by? How will I provide additional support?	
Plan to use formative assessment results: How are you going to use the results to continue with the next step in your lesson? This must be flexible.	
How will the learners reflect on the process? What structure or support will you provide so they are able to answer the following: "Where am I going? Where am I now? If there is a gap, how can I close the gap?"	
Notes for next use: What will you keep the same? What will you do differently? This can be determined from your personal reflection and from student input.	

3m

OCT 13 2014

FLORIDA STATE COLLEGE AT JACKSONVILLE LIBRARY
3 3801 01278520 2

REC
9/14